The Unconscious without Freud

Dialog-on-Freud Series
Series Editor: M. Andrew Holowchak

The Dialog-on-Freud series invites authors to explore the history and practice of analytic therapies through critical analysis of and expatiation on the seminal work of Freud. It seeks books that critically scrutinize the numerous facets of Freud's work over the course of his life, that investigate how or to what extent Freud's thinking causally gave rise to the various sorts of therapies that currently exist, and that examine the relevance of Freud's thinking today for those therapies.

Titles in the Series

The Unconscious without Freud, by Rosemarie Sponner Sand

The Unconscious without Freud

Rosemarie Sponner Sand

ROWMAN & LITTLEFIELD
Lanham • Boulder • New York • Toronto • Plymouth, UK

Published by Rowman & Littlefield
4501 Forbes Boulevard, Suite 200, Lanham, Maryland 20706
www.rowman.com

10 Thornbury Road, Plymouth PL6 7PP, United Kingdom

British Library Cataloguing in Publication Information Available

Library of Congress Cataloging-in-Publication Data

Sand, Rosemarie, author.
The unconscious without Freud / Rosemarie Sand.
p. ; cm. -- (Dialog-on-Freud series)
Includes bibliographical references and index.
ISBN 978-1-4422-3173-3 (cloth : alk. paper) -- ISBN 978-1-4422-3174-0 (electronic)
I. Title. II. Series: Dialog-on-Freud series.
[DNLM: 1. Unconscious (Psychology) 2. Freudian Theory. 3. Psychoanalytic Theory. BF 315]
BF173.F85
150.19'52--dc23
2013043265

™ The paper used in this publication meets the minimum requirements of American National Standard for Information Sciences Permanence of Paper for Printed Library Materials, ANSI/NISO Z39.48-1992.

Printed in the United States of America

For my beloved husband, Donn Sand, who made it all possible

Contents

Acknowledgements

I owe thanks to three companions in Freud studies whose thoughts, merged with my own, went into the shaping of this book.

Philosopher of science Adolf Grűnbaum, whom I met when he left the external world of physics to investigate the internal world of psychoanalysis. The finding that we were of like mind was followed by decades of conversations and unbroken friendship.

Present in spirit was psychoanalyst Emanuel ("Manny") Peterfreund, skeptic, ready to challenge any dogma, whose untimely death prevented the completion of what promised to be an important work on the nature of psychological evidence.

In vivid memory, my father, Dr. Robert Sponner, who graduated from the Imperial-Royal School of Medicine in Vienna in 1904. As an eye witness, he told me about the reception of Freud in that city; thus, I learned about the ensuing controversy at an early age.

Preface

What would psychology be like today if Freud had remained a neurologist? If Freud had been granted what, at one time, he wanted most, a research position at the University of Vienna, would we have had a theory of unconscious mind—and what would it have been like?

Reading a century's old journals, I discovered that Freud's German and Austrian contemporaries unanimously credited the fundamental formulation of the concept of unconscious mind to Gottfried Wilhelm Leibniz (1646–1716)—a mathematician physicist, and psychologist, who, according to philosopher Bertrand Russell, was "one of the supreme intellects of all time" (Russell, 1946, 605). In France, the preeminent psychological researcher, Pierre Janet, agreed on the role then being played by Leibniz. Previously the mind had been equated with consciousness, but "today, all of the physical and psychological sciences seem to be taking us back to Leibniz in whose profound philosophy we find an entirely different concept of consciousness" (Janet, 1930, 36). This was the theory Freud inherited, the one which he used during the first decade of his career in psychology before he created his own. I suggest that the venerable theory he replaced was better than the one that replaced it. It covered a wider field, was simpler and more plausible and less likely to have provoked an interminable, progress- impeding controversy such as the "Freud war."

The first chapter of my book is devoted to Leibniz's stunning contribution to psychology; the second to his psychodynamics. The following four chapters, covering the development and dissemination of Leibnizian theory, are based entirely on previously untranslated eighteenth-century German publications. The first of these describes the popularizing efforts of Leibniz's follower, Christian Wolff, and his creation of a "Leibniz-Wolffian" psychology. This is followed by a Leibnizian's (Johann Georg Sulzer's) detailed description of the personal unconscious which reveals the period's deep understanding of the influence that thoughts, feelings and motives outside of awareness can exert on the conscious mind. The succeeding chapter tells of a Leibnizian physician's (Ernst Platner's) construction of a model of the brain accommodating conscious and unconscious functioning. The last of these chapters gives a Leibnizian's (Ludwig Heinrich Jakob's) set of rules for bringing unconscious mental contents to light, that is, free association.

The seventh chapter introduces concepts about unconscious mental functioning which are surprising because they were offered by René Descartes and John Locke, both of whom famously insisted that all thought was conscious. Apparently closely related, these views constitute a theory, totally independent of the Leibnizian, but coexisting with it; although limited, they would nevertheless have been useful.

My initial aim had been to focus solely on the "unconscious without Freud," but I found that, practically speaking, this goal had to be modified because certain concepts are so powerfully identified with Freud that mentioning them without him would puzzle readers. This is true, for instance, of the theory of repression. Aspects of Freudian theory are introduced to show how thoughts of the past survived in his work.

Chapter 8, devoted to showing the ubiquity of notions like repression, resistance and the return of the repressed, begins with Plato and carries the subject through Augustine down to modern times. In the following chapter on the Romantic era (chapter 9), we see the concept of the personal unconscious being overshadowed by metaphysical "unconscious" cosmic forces. It also played a role in the dubious "speculative medicine" of the time. Schopenhauer, in the next chapter, was also "Romantic." However, he fully understood the personal unconscious, and when, after years of neglect, his work became popular in the middle of the nineteenth century, it provided the generations that followed with a lively sense of the power of mental states outside of awareness. In Eduard von Hartmann's internationally popular work, *The Philosophy of the Unconscious* and the topic of chapter 11, the concept approached a nadir, swamped by metaphysical conceits; the book probably did the concept more harm than good by alienating the scientifically inclined.

The last three chapters, chapters 12 through 14, based on untranslated German sources, deal with what was in Freud's youth, the dominant theory of psychology in his native Austria, the psychology of Johann Friedrich Herbart. Freud's high school study of this psychology, in which all mental activity is produced by the conflict of ideas treated as forces, made a deep impression on the teenage student. Later, it shaped his theory to such an extent that no twentieth-century psychoanalytic patient escaped the influence of Herbart. What had happened was that, lodged in Freud's mind, a "pre-Freudian" theory took over and determined the shape of a hypothesis that

Freud must have assumed was purely his own. Whether Herbart's completely mechanical theory would have had a future without Freud, it is impossible to say.

Chapter One

Leibniz and the Unconscious

How far back in time must we travel to come upon the blossoming of the concept of unconscious mental functioning in the Western world? We must return to the early modern era, to the decades before and after 1700. In France, the Great "Sun King," Louis XIV, presided over the most powerful and glamorous court in the world. In England, the dour, German-speaking George I ruled reluctantly, angry at having had to leave his beloved Hanover. In the New World, Western civilization had achieved a bare toehold. New Amsterdam, with a population of around 3,000, had been forced to change its name to honor the Duke of York but it was still a Dutch town, with red-tiled, gabled roofs and windmills, huddled behind a wall.

In those years, the views of three great philosophers—one French, one English and another German—differed on a question that was fundamentally psychological: was thinking continuous? Was the mind engaged in uninterrupted conscious cogitation or was this activity sometimes suspended, for instance, during sleep? René Descartes believed that thought was continuous and conscious; John Locke insisted that it was conscious but discontinuous; Gottfried Wilhelm Leibniz suggested that it was continuous and *unconscious*.

Descartes (1596–1650) had assumed that all thinking must be conscious. Having asked himself whether there was anything at all of which he could be absolutely sure, anything which he could not doubt, he had decided that he could not doubt that he was thinking and, since he was thinking, he must necessarily exist: "I think, therefore I am" (Descartes, 1911, Vol. I, 101). *Conscious* thinking was essential to the soul.

This formula created a problem, for if the soul is defined as a thing that thinks, what happens to it when it stops thinking, for instance, when it loses consciousness during sleep? If its very being consists of thinking, must we then not suppose that it will cease to *be* when thinking stops? In that case we would have to imagine the soul as winking into and out of existence as we wake or sleep. Clearly this would not do.

Descartes was challenged on this point. He was asked how he could think during a deep, dreamless sleep or, for that matter, how the embryo in the womb could think? The embryo was assumed to be a soul, consequently, it must also be presumed to be engaged in continuous thought (Descartes, 1911, Vol. II, 141).

Descartes could have avoided at least the problem of thought during sleep if he had assumed that we dream continuously because dreaming is a form of consciousness. However, this option was not open to him because it was generally assumed that dreaming was not continuous. Therefore the question remained: does the soul think *between* dreams? Descartes' answer was ingenious: the soul always thinks but it does not *remember* what it thinks. Thought is continuous; it goes on even in a stupor, and in the embryo, but no memory traces of this thinking are "impressed on the brain" (1911, Vol. II, 211).

Descartes separated thought from the memory of thought. If you awaken and cannot remember what you were thinking a moment ago, this does not mean that you were not thinking a moment ago. You cannot remember what you were thinking last week either, but this does not signify that you were not thinking last week. Descartes pointed out that we do not remember most of the thoughts we have had, even those we entertained when we were grown up, in good health and awake (Descartes, 1911, Vol. II, 210).

England's John Locke (1632–1704) took a dim view of the proposition "that the soul thinks even in the soundest sleep, but the *memory* retains it not." He protested "That the soul in a sleeping man should be this moment busy a thinking, and the next moment in a waking man not remember nor be able to recollect one jot of all those thoughts, is very hard to be conceived" (1959, Vol. I, 132). He inveighed against the notion of unconscious thinking: Ideas "cease to be anything when there is no perception of them" but "the mind has a power . . . to revive perceptions." In the interim, although "our ideas are said to be in our memories . . . they are actually nowhere" (194). An idea that could not be perceived did not exist.

What did exist, according to Locke, were mental operations of which we were conscious: "*perception, thinking, doubting, believing, reasoning, knowing, willing.*" These were acts which we could observe in ourselves (123). He noted that it is "hard to conceive that anything should think and not be conscious of it" (130). He pointed out an apparently insurmountable problem connected with the notion: if we assume that a person can think without being conscious of it, then we must suppose also that he or she can feel pleasure or pain, without being conscious of it, or be happy or miserable, without being conscious of it. This struck him as absurd and he remarked that being "happy or miserable without being conscious of it, seems to me utterly inconsistent and impossible" (130). With regard to thought occurring in sleep he asserted that "I do not say that there is no *soul* in a man, because he is not sensible of it in his sleep; but I do say, he cannot *think* at any time, waking or sleeping, without being sensible of it. Our being sensible of it is not necessary to anything but to our thoughts; and to them it is; and to them it always will be necessary, till we can think without being conscious of it" (129).

"Till we can think without being conscious of it"—Locke found it difficult to imagine such a thing. If the psychological "Copernican revolution" can be said to have had a beginning at any particular moment, then it occurred when Leibniz (1646–1716) framed his answer to Locke on this point, for he replied that "thought need not stop just because one is not aware of it" (1981, 113) and "there are hundreds of indications leading us to conclude that at every moment there is in us an infinity of perceptions, unaccompanied by awareness or reflections; that is, of alterations in the soul itself, of which we are unaware" (53). The soul is always thinking, according to Leibniz, and not thinking only, but also desiring and willing, even when we are asleep but this activity is going on outside of consciousness (192).

Leibniz's rejoinder to Locke did not consist of a mere assertion; he offered a scientific hypothesis, a theory supportable by evidence. Although the existence within us of thoughts "unaccompanied by awareness" could not be proven by observation, their presence could be inferred thanks to "hundreds of indications" (1981, 113) In the years to come, the postulate that the reality of unobservable mental states could be established by appropriate evidence would be a hallmark of Leibnizian psychological theory.

Appropriate evidence was available because unconscious thoughts could have effects; they could act as causes. To make this point, Leibniz turned to a dream whose unconscious source, a forgotten memory, could be identified with certainty. The dream was that of Julius Scaliger, an Italian savant of the previous century.

Scaliger had written a poem praising the eminent men of Verona. Afterward he dreamed that he was approached by a man who, identifying himself as "Brugnolus," complained that he had been unjustly left out of the eulogy, since he had been eminent and had lived in Verona. Awake, Scaliger could remember no "Brugnolus" but, on the authority of the dream, wrote an elegy in his honor nevertheless. At a later date, Scaliger's son, traveling in Italy, learned that not only had a person named "Brugnolus" really existed, but as he had claimed in the dream, he had been an eminent Veronese and ought indeed to have been included among the worthies who were lauded in the poem.

The Scaliger story refuted Locke's premise that ideas that were not conscious were "nowhere." Consciously, Scaliger had not remembered Brugnolus; he could not recall him, even after the dream reminder. Yet, obviously, an unconscious memory of Brugnolus had been lodged in Scaliger's mind and had been responsible for his appearance in the dream.

What makes Leibniz's evidence for the existence of an unconscious dream source so compelling? Clearly, it is the indubitable relationship between the historical Brugnolus and the Brugnolus who appeared in the dream. An unconscious memory of Brugnolus *must* have been responsible for the production of the Brugnolus dream image. It appears therefore, that in some circumstances, the existence of a specific unconscious mental content can be established with certainty.

Leibniz commented that "it is very likely that Julius Scaliger had had some knowledge of Brugnol [*sic*] and no longer remembered it, and that his dream had in part consisted in reviving a former idea—although there had not occurred that 'remembering,' strictly so-called, which makes us know that we have had that same idea before. He commented "I think that dreams often revive former thoughts for us in this way" (106–7).

Another piece of evidence that Leibniz offered for the continued efficacy of unconscious memories was the case of a person who had written verses which he believed were original but which, it was discovered later, he had actually read "word for word, long before, in some ancient poet" (106). He had assumed that he was creating something new but, without being aware of it, he had been guided by a recollection.

Leibniz proposed that not only memories, but mental contents of all kinds—thoughts, emotions and desires—could continue to exert power outside of consciousness.

More than 200 years later, Freud described this hypothesis as an achievement of psychoanalysis. Depicting the philosophers of his day as tethered to the Lockean view, he maintained that they regarded an unconscious idea as "latent," and held that "so long as the idea was in a state of latency it was not anything psychical at all." Psychoanalysis, however, had been forced to recognize that ideas could be unconscious and yet could "produce all the effects" of conscious ideas (*S.E.*, XIX: 14).

Trusting in Freud, his followers believed that he had introduced a momentous concept: the active unconscious. Following his lead, they accepted that, before Freud, the unconscious had been regarded as purely inert, as *static.* The psychoanalytic dictionary, *The Language of Psycho-Analysis*, by J. Laplanche and J.B. Pontalis, useful when it comes to exegesis of Freud's concepts, but routinely failing to take proper note of history, proclaimed simply that "psychoanalysis replaces a conception of the unconscious described as static with one which is dynamic" (126). Thus the unsuspecting reader is introduced to a fundamental untruth.

Because Leibniz had to work with concepts for which no generally accepted expressions existed, he invented his own terminology. Some of his language was quickly dropped by his followers; some of it lasted until the twentieth century. Most of it will seem strange to a modern reader. However, acquaintance with a few of his expressions will enable the reader to understand and appreciate Leibniz's magnificent contribution to psychology.

Writing in French, then the language of intellectual discourse, Leibniz called the things in the soul of which we are unaware "perceptions," meaning by this mental states of all kinds, not merely the mental acts that we call "perception" today. Sometimes he used the word "representation." For the coming-to-consciousness of perceptions, he coined the word "apperception," from the French "apercevoir" or "to become aware of." Later, the terminology having taken root, "perceived" and "apperceived" were used routinely by many philosophers and psychologists in place of the words "unconscious" and "conscious." So, for instance, in the *Studies on Hysteria,* Freud's co-author, Josef Breuer, remarked that "sensory stimuli are perhaps perceived . . . but they are not apperceived, i.e. do not become conscious perceptions" (*S.E.*, II: 192–193).

Leibniz sometimes emphasized the unconscious quality of perceptions by referring to them as "insensible," "imperceptible" or "not noticeable." His best-known expression, however, is "minute perception," often untranslated and used in the original French: *petite perception.* Conscious perceptions were accordingly called "great" or "large" (Leibniz, 1951, 554). Describing perceptions as "minute" did not signify that they were weak. In the *New Essays on Human Understanding,* Leibniz had in mind the atomic theory of the time, according to which matter was composed of exceedingly small particles. These, like his minute perceptions were invisible, but they were not negligible on that account.[1]

Philosophy was only one of Leibniz's interests. He was a multifaceted genius who seems to have pioneered in every field that he entered. "One of the supreme intellects of all time," according to Bertrand Russell, he was far in advance of his century in his exploration of mathematical logic (Russell, 604). He discovered the infinitesimal calculus independently of Newton and designed a computing machine. Participating in the creation of modern science of physics, he was the major contributor to what are now known as the concepts of kinetic and potential energies.

His curiosity was indefatigable; he examined the mysteries of the Rosicrucians and delved into alchemy to discover whether there was anything in it. (He decided there was not.) His imagination carried him far into the future; he foresaw interplanetary travel and playfully speculated about the arrival of extraterrestrials on earth.

He marveled at the mind's unconscious creative power as manifested in dreams—"the formation of visions by a spontaneous organization carried out in a moment—a formation more elegant than any which we can attain by much thought while awake. To the sleeper there often occur visions of great buildings which he has never seen, while it would be difficult for me, while awake, to form an idea of even the smallest house different from those I have seen, without a great amount of thought. I wish I could remember what marvelous discourses, what books and letters, what poems beautiful beyond all doubt, but never previously read, I have read in dreams without my shaping them at all, just as if they had just been composed and offered to my sight. . . . I do not believe that there is a mortal man who would not confess to me that there have often occurred to him while he dreamed, spontaneously and as if made in a moment, elegant visions and skillfully fashioned songs, verses, books, melodies, houses, gardens, depending upon his interests—visions which he could not have formed without effort while awake. Even such unnatural things as flying men and innumerable other monstrosities can be pictured more skillfully than a waking person can do, except with much thought. They are sought by the waker; they offer themselves to the sleeper" (Leibniz, 1956, 177).

Leibniz's bread-and-butter profession, meanwhile, was diplomacy. In the service of the Duke of Brunswick he traveled through Europe. His conciliatory personality sustained him in his attempts to bring harmony between the states. Doubtless it was his fundamental optimism that induced him to attempt to bring about the reconciliation of the Catholic and Protestant churches. Unfortunately, from the point of view of posterity, the Duke put him to work writing a history of Brunswick, thus diverting him from his own interests. Torn between his diplomatic and historical enterprises and his scientific and philosophical concerns, he wrote "it is incredible how scattered and divided are my occupations. . . . I have so much that is new in mathematics, so many thoughts in philosophy, so many literary observations which I cannot get into shape . . . . I should like to give a description of my calculating machine, but time fails. Above all else I desire to complete my Dynamics . . . but all these works, the historical excepted, have to be done at odd moments" (Dewey, 1888, 263).

As a result of these pressures, much of what he wrote was in response to some specific occasion. We owe his *New Essays on Human Understanding* to the interest Leibniz took in John Locke's 1690 *Essay on Human Understanding* which he had attempted to read in English before a translation became available in 1700. He decided to write a response in the form of a dialogue between himself and Locke. Thus his own volume which echoes Locke's title came into being. It contained, in addition to his argument that the mind had to be assumed to be endowed with innate capacities, his stunning contribution to psychology, the hypothesis of unconscious mental activity. The book was finished in 1704 but when Locke died, Leibniz did not want to publish an argument against him. Therefore the book did not see the light of day until 1765. Followers who promulgated the theory of unconscious mind in the interim did so on the basis of Leibniz's earlier, less complete formulations of his thought.

As a physicist, Leibniz was naturally interested in the new "corpuscular theory" introduced at that time by the English chemist, Robert Boyle. Boyle was hypothesizing that matter consisted of tiny invisible corpuscles. Leibniz, who admired Boyle, and had visited him and had observed his experiments, suggested that the mind might similarly be composed of elements that could not be seen.

Physics at that time had progressed from a reliance on the observation of visible phenomena to an acceptance of the need for theories dealing with entities and activities that could not be observed. A historian has commented on the difficulty of this shift: "There is one particular form of induction that causes special distress to the empiricist: where one moves from particular instances which are observable to instances which are *in principle* unobservable. If the only legitimate ground of knowledge is sense experience, how can one justify a claim which cannot, *in principle,* be tested directly against experience? Yet the most striking feature of seventeenth-century science was its move into the 'invisible realm'" (McMullin, 15).

Leibniz moved much of psychology into the "invisible realm" when he introduced two concepts—the principle of unobservable mental contents and the principle of unobservable mental activity. He elucidated both of these premises by comparing them with contemporary physical theories.

The atomic theory proposed in ancient times by the Greek philosopher Democritus had been revived in the seventeenth century. Democritus had maintained that all matter was composed of innumerable tiny particles which, combined, formed the visible material world. According to Boyle's far more sophisticated "corpuscular theory," matter was made of up "corpuscles" whose differing attributes were responsible for the qualities of different substances. Of this hypothesis, it has been said that it "foreshadowed to a remarkable extent the physics and chemistry of our own day" (Pilkington, 159).

Leibniz compared his invisible perceptions with Boyles' invisible corpuscles and insisted on the reality of both; it would be a mistake to assume "that things of which we are unaware exist neither in the soul nor in the body" (Leibniz, 1981, 57). Leibniz likened the role of minute perceptions in psychology to the part played by invisible corpuscles in physical science: "insensible perceptions are as necessary to pneumatology [theory of the soul] as insensible corpuscles are to natural science, and it is just as unreasonable to reject the one as the other on the pretext that they are beyond the reach of our senses" (56). The mind was never devoid of content. "I believe that we are never without ideas, never without thoughts and never without sensations either" (119).[2]

Minute perceptions resembled corpuscles in another way; both were conceptualized as being in constant, unobservable motion. Boyle was suggesting that some of the properties of bodies could best be explained on the hypothesis that they were made up of moving particles. He supposed that matter was never inert, that "absolute rest" was to be found nowhere. Even in substances as hard as diamonds, there was invisible internal movement.

Leibniz suggested that the mind was as ceaselessly active as matter: "there is never a body without movement; experience is already on my side, and to be convinced one need only consult the distinguished Mr. Boyle's book attacking absolute rest." It was reasonable to conclude that "since the body is never without movement, the soul which corresponds to it will never be without perception either" (Leibniz, 1981, 112). Moreover, just as the endless invisible movements of corpuscles explained the nature of physical substances, so did the ceaseless flow of imperceptible perceptions account for the phenomena of consciousness; "it is in the insensible perceptions that the reason is found for what occurs in us; as the reason for what takes place in sensible bodies consists in insensible movements" (Leibniz, 1951, 554).

"The soul always thinks and feels," Leibniz insisted, but most of this mental activity was imperceptible; consciousness was intermittent: consciousness is not given "to any soul all the time" (Leibniz, 1956, 1036).

The emphasis on the activity of the mind would remain a hallmark of the Leibnizian orientation, one that distinguished it from the tradition that began with Locke. In British empiricism, the mind tended to be regarded as passive, as a receptor rather than an agent. The American psychologist, Gordon Allport, commented on these contrasting characteristics: "virtually all modern psychological theories seem oriented toward one of two polar conceptions"—the Lockean and the Leibnizian traditions. The Lockean point of view, that was said to "predominate in Anglo-American psychology" views man's mind as "passive." The Leibnizian, "predominant in Continental European psychology, conceives of its nature as essentially active" (Allport, quoted in Misiak and Sexton, 28).

Locke set the stage for inactivity by comparing the mind to a blank sheet of paper upon which experience engraved impressions: "Let us then suppose the mind to be, as we say, white paper, void of all characters, without any ideas:—How comes it to be furnished?" (1959, 121) Answering his own question, he suggested that ideas were acquired by "observation." The senses delivered data of the external world; an analogous "internal sense" provided information about the inner realm (123).

In Locke's scheme, the acquisition of an idea can be pictured as a one-step operation: a sensation gives rise to a conscious idea. Leibniz's theory, with its distinction between the unconscious and the conscious, demanded two. The first step was the formation of a perception; all of the contents of the mind were unconscious to begin with. Then apperception took place; this was regarded as a process in which the conscious element of the mind recognized, accepted and assimilated unconscious contents. Leibniz said of it that "noticeable [conscious] perceptions arise by degrees from ones which are too minute to be noticed" (Leibniz, 1981, 57). If this second step was not taken, the perception remained unconscious: "the soul itself does not know the things which it perceives until it has perceptions which are distinct and heightened" (Leibniz, 1952, 1040).

"Perception . . . must be distinguished from apperception or from consciousness," Leibniz insisted (1956, *Monadology*, 1046). "We are never without perceptions, but necessarily we are often without awareness" (Leibniz, 1981, 162) "It is for lack of this distinction that the Cartesians have made the mistake of disregarding perceptions which are not themselves perceived, just as people commonly disregard imperceptible bodies" (Leibniz, 1956, 1036). It is important to distinguish between "thoughts in general" and the small subset of these, the "noticeable thoughts" (Leibniz, 1981, 118). By the end of the nineteenth century, Leibniz's "minute perceptions" would be called "unconscious mental states," "unconscious representations" or "unconscious ideas" (*unbewusste Vorstellungen*).

At that time, a noted philosopher, Wilhelm Windelband, explaining that "in the language of today the *petites perceptions* would be *unconscious mental states,*" asserted that Leibniz's recognition "that the life of the soul transcends all that is clear and distinctly conscious" is "an insight of the highest value" (Windelband, 1958, 424 and 464). Leibniz "introduced an extremely significant conception into psychology and epistemology. He distinguished between the states in which the soul merely *has* ideas, and those in which it is *conscious* of them. The former he designated as perceptions, the latter as *apperception*. By apperception, therefore, he understood the process by which unconscious, obscure and confused representations are raised into clear and distinct consciousness, and thereby recognized by the soul as its own and *appropriated by self-consciousness*" (463).

Leibniz's philosophical descendants stressed that all of the contents of the mind, beliefs, attitudes and motives of every sort, germinated and developed unconsciously and remained unconscious, perhaps forever, unless and until they were apperceived.

For some of Leibniz's later followers, the coming to consciousness of unconscious mental states became a process of intellectual, psychological and spiritual growth. The domain of consciousness expanded with each elevation to consciousness of a previously unrecognized mental state. From a beginning stage in which it was blind to many of its own assumptions and predilections, the mind progressed by stages to a higher level of self-understanding. Where once it had been helplessly driven by unrecognized urges, it now could control and channel them; thereby it had achieved a new freedom. Windelband credited Leibniz with the realization that "the genetic process of the psychical life consists in the changing of unconscious into conscious representations or ideas, in taking up perceptions into the clearness and distinctness of self-consciousness" (463). Raising the unconscious to consciousness was thus an ideal long before Freud recommended it: "Where id was, there ego shall be" (*S.E.,* XXII: 80).

In Leibniz's psychology are found most of the elements that, once they coalesced, gave rise to a nineteenth-century theory of personality and personality development centered around the concept of the "self." Locke, taking up the question of personal identity, had asked what it was that constituted "the self." He proposed that since, as he believed, consciousness always accompanied thinking; it was consciousness "which makes every one to be what he calls self." Locke proposed that the self included, not only present consciousness, but also the states of consciousness that could be recalled: "as far as this consciousness can be extended backwards to any past action or thought, so far reaches the identity of that person." The self includes whatever can be consciously remembered (Locke, 1959, 449).

Leibniz took a different view; not only the feeling of identity, but the whole of a person's character, were products of assimilated experiences most of which could not be recalled. Nothing was ever totally forgotten, traces were preserved unconsciously: "something remains of all our past thoughts, none of which can ever be entirely wiped out" (1981, 113). The soul "retains impressions of everything which has previously happened to it . . . but these states of mind are mostly too minute to be distinguishable and for one to be aware of them" (239). "Previous states" did not cease to be effective even "when the individual himself has no sense" of them, i.e., "no longer has any explicit memory of them" (55). The feeling of personal identity, the sense of "self" (*sentiment du moi*) (236), was based upon such unconscious memory traces: "It is this continuity and interconnection of perceptions which make someone really the same individual" (239).

Dispositions, enduring attitudes and expectations were composed in the same way: "our customs and passions, which have so much influence when we do deliberate" come from "a conjunction of minute perceptions." Without them, "we would not have acquired these noticeable dispositions" (116). But not only the memories that went into the formation of dispositions were forgotten, the resulting dispositions themselves could be unconscious: "we are not always aware of our acquired dispositions" (52). Much of our character may lie beyond our ken: therefore we are often at the mercy of "insensible inclinations of which we are not aware" (194).

EXPERIMENTAL PSYCHOLOGY

Leibniz supposed that a continuum of degrees of consciousness existed in the animal world, a progression of shades of awareness that ranged from a low in primitive invertebrates that were perpetually unconscious to a high in human beings, who were conscious intermittently. This observation was supported by Leibniz's "law of continuity," according to which "nothing takes place suddenly, and it is one of my great and best confirmed maxims that *nature never makes leaps*" (1981, 56). In the human being, mental contents ranged from states of deepest unconsciousness upward by degrees without interruption.[3] Freud's coauthor, Breuer, echoed this postulate of Leibnizian theory when he said of ideas in *Studies on Hysteria* that "they form an almost unbroken scale, passing through every gradation of vagueness and obscurity, between perfectly conscious ideas . . . and those which never enter consciousness in waking life but only in hypnosis" (*S.E.,* II: 229).

Given such a continuum, there must be a particular point, a threshold, at which the transition from the unconscious to consciousness takes place. Leibniz used sensation as an example: a small amplification of a sound that had been too weak to be heard resulted in its coming to consciousness: "a noise which we perceive but do not attend to is brought within reach of our awareness by a tiny increase or addition" (1981, 134). The radical innovation in Leibniz's approach was his assumption that the noise of which we are not conscious may nevertheless be *perceived;* in the language of a modern hypothesis, it may be "unconsciously registered" or "subliminally sensed."

Leibniz explained his reasoning: when we stand by the seashore and are conscious of the roar of the surf, we are actually hearing an aggregate of sounds, each of the countless waves contributing to the sum. We would not be aware of the sound of *one* of these waves, or even of several but, at a certain point; enough sound accumulates for us to be able to hear it. Leibniz supposed that, before this point was reached, the sound, although not consciously heard, was nevertheless being registered; in Leibniz's words we "must be affected slightly"; we must "have some perception" of these noises; they must "touch the soul" outside of our awareness (54). Then a small increment makes possible the transition from perception to apperception: "a noise which we perceive but do not attend to is brought within reach of our awareness by a tiny increase or addition" (135); "the soul itself does not know the things which it perceives until it has perceptions which are distinct and heightened" (Leibniz, 1956, 1040).[4]

In this speculation were three ideas that, in the middle of the nineteenth century, were put to work by Gustav Theodor Fechner (1801–1887), progenitor of modern experimental psychology: the hypothesis of subliminal sensation, the concept of quantity, or magnitude of a stimulus, and the concept of threshold.

In a different situation, unawareness of a stimulus required a different explanation: a stimulus might be powerful enough but might nevertheless remain unconscious because it failed to capture *attention.* The roar of a waterfall, for example, could hardly be described as "minute" and yet it could disappear from consciousness if it was heard continuously. Leibniz pointed out that we become so accustomed to the clatter of a mill or the rush of water, after living beside them for a while, that we pay no heed to them. The sounds still strike the ear but "lacking the appeal of novelty, are not forceful enough to attract our attention and our memory, which are applied only to more compelling objects" (1981, 54).

The roar of the waterfall did not fail to reach consciousness because it was too feeble but because it had to give way to a more powerful rival for attention. With Leibniz's emphasis on the concept of *competition* between different elements of the mind, what would later become the theory of inhibition or repression put in an appearance. The sound of the waterfall does not cease "to strike on our sense-organs"; nevertheless, we are not aware of it because our attention is applied "to more compelling objects" (54). Along the same lines, Leibniz noted that sometimes we seem to be "selectively asleep" with regard to an object (115). He stated that "there are always objects which strike our eyes and ears, and therefore touch our souls as well, without our paying heed to them. For our attention is held by other objects, until a given object becomes powerful enough to attract it, either by acting more strongly upon us or in some other way" (115).

The concept of the competition between sensations and other mental states, leading to the repression of the weaker, had ancient origins, as did many of the theories of eighteenth-century philosophers. These scholars were steeped in the literature of the remote past, which they had often read in the original Greek. In this instance, Aristotle had observed that of two stimuli "the stronger always tends to override the weaker." This is why "persons do not perceive what is brought before their eyes, if they are at the time deep in thought, or in a fright, or listening to some loud noise. "Although a visual impression directly meets the eyes, i.e. presumably produces a sensation, because of a competing element, either a mental state or a physical stimulus, nothing is seen. It is effectively kept out of consciousness—"inhibited" or "repressed" in nineteenth-century language (Aristotle, 1984, 447a).

Leibnizian psychology typically stressed conflict in the mind. Even the simple failure to consciously hear a sound was pictured as the outcome of a rivalry; consciousness was the prize for which mental elements of all kinds competed. We have "perceptions of which we are not aware in our present state. We could in fact become thoroughly aware of them and reflect on them . . . if bigger ones [*le plus grande*] did not, obliterate them or rather put them in the shade" (134). The winner had to be "powerful enough" to deny consciousness to opponents.

In Leibniz's theory of motivation, the "minute perceptions" became "imperceptible little urges" and Leibniz imagined warfare between urges as they struggled for dominance. He supposed that numerous motives might be involved in such a conflict, conscious and unconscious, rational and irrational, and he compared a collision of this kind with a clash of physical forces with different directions and strengths. The final outcome of the struggle, the prevailing motive, would be arrived at by vector addition, a compromise between all of them.

UNCONSCIOUS MOTIVATION

Leibniz compared these imperceptible urges to the hidden springs that drive a watch. "These impulses are like so many little springs trying to unwind and so driving our machine along" (166). Because the imperceptible urges were constantly at work, no action, however trifling, was ever performed without an unconscious determinant. This dictum was related to Leibniz's general "principle of sufficient reason," which asserted that nothing whatever occurs without a reason. If no reason is evident, this does not signify that it does not exist; it is merely unknown, its absence being due to lack of information. A person with adequate knowledge would always be able to explain "why the thing is as it is and not otherwise" (Leibniz, 1956, 1038). Applied to the mind, the principle entailed that every mental event was explicable, in principle, if not in practice. If, as often happens, the reason eludes us, Leibniz observed, then this is because "what usually drives us are those minute insensible perceptions . . . that we cannot become aware of" (1981, 188).

When Leibniz put such thoughts on paper, he was playing with fire; he was denying "the freedom of the will" and thereby contradicting a sacrosanct doctrine of the church.

The very old problem of free will rose from the discrepancy between, on the one hand, the powerful, subjective feeling that acts of the will are not caused, and, on the other, the powerful, rational, conviction that every event has a cause. The argument that the will is free has sometimes been buttressed by appeals to personal experience; for instance, picture yourself, being under no constraint, deciding to move your finger to the right or to the left. You make a choice; the finger obeys. You feel certain that you could just as soon have made the opposite choice. You willed the decision, but nothing caused your will to make this decision. The act of your will was therefore an uncaused event.

The law of universal causation is thereby breached; the law to which the rest of the universe is subject does not hold for your mind. For many centuries, this was exactly the position defended by the church: the soul was immortal; an "immaterial substance," it stood apart from the rest of the created universe. When it freely exercised its will, then the will was not being determined by any condition: physiological, psychological or environmental.

In the seventeenth century, René Descartes was comfortably in agreement with ecclesiastical opinion when he defended the doctrine. We could *perceive* our freedom of choice; it was "self-evident," so clear that it could not be doubted. (1973, Vol. 1, 234–235). John Locke, in the following century, concurred. If he could, by a thought, direct the motion of his finger, "make it move when it was at rest, or *vice versa,* it is evident, that in respect of that I am free: and if I can, by a like thought of my mind, preferring one to the other, produce either words or silence, I am at liberty to speak or hold my peace: and as far as this power reaches, of acting or not acting, by the determination of his own thought preferring either, so far is a man free. For how can we think any one freer, than to have the power to do what he will?" (Locke, Vol. 2, 1959, 324)

Descartes and Locke were echoing the wisdom of centuries; Leibniz disagreed; his predecessors were mistaken, he declared. The absence of an unconscious motive could not be *sensed.* The *feeling* that one was making a free choice could *not* be trusted. However trivial the episode, we can never be sure that we are not under the influence of the minute perceptions which determine "our behavior in many situations without our thinking of them, and which deceive the unsophisticated with an appearance of *indifference of equilibrium*—as if it made no difference to us, for instance, whether we turned left or right" (Leibniz, 1981, 56).

Leibniz maintained that "when I turn one way rather than another, it is often because of a series of tiny impressions of which I am not aware but which make one movement slightly harder than the other" (1981, 116). He insisted that "the reason M. Descartes has advanced to prove the independence of our free actions, by what he terms an intense inward sensation, has no force. We cannot properly speaking be sensible of our independence, and we are not aware always of the causes, often imperceptible, whereon our resolution depends" (1985, 150). Leibniz drove the point home with an imaginative metaphor comparing the controlling power of an unconscious determinant with the magnetic force that governed the movement of a compass needle—which needle believed that it was moving of its own free will. "It is as though the magnetic needle took pleasure in turning towards the north: for it would think that it was turning independently of any other cause, not being aware of the imperceptible movements of the magnetic matter" (1985, 150).

Leibniz concluded with a reference to the new physical science, likening the actions of imperceptible thoughts with the invisible activities of matter. "If we do not always notice the reason which determines us, or rather by which we determine ourselves, it is because we are as little able to be aware of all the workings of our mind and of its usually confused and imperceptible thoughts as we are to sort out all the mechanisms which nature puts to work in bodies" (1981, 178).

Leibniz took pains to make clear that even the most trivial behaviors, the apparently unmotivated, seemingly accidental actions, were strictly determined. The "insensible perceptions" accounted for what seemed to be "involuntary": "all our undeliberated actions result from a conjunction of minute perceptions" (115). "Often it is an insensible perception which we can neither discern nor single out . . . which makes us lean one way rather than the other without being able to say why" (183). At all times "an infinite number of great and small motions internal and external concur within us, which generally we are not sensible of. And I have already said, that, when a man walks out of a room, there are such reasons which determine him to set one foot forward rather than the other, though he observes it not" (Leibniz et. al. 1956, 139).[5]

An experiment carried out a few decades ago might have been designed expressly to test Leibniz's dictum that even trivial behavior is governed by imperceptible inclinations. Subjects in this procedure were confronted with four pairs of nylon stockings lined up in a row from left to right and were asked to decide which pair was of the "best quality." In actuality the stockings were identical, the only difference between the pairs was their position in the row. Overwhelmingly, subjects picked the stockings which were farthest to the right, preferring these to those on the left by a factor of almost four to one. Obviously, they had been strongly influenced by the position of the stockings, but none of them was aware that an "imperceptible" inclination had given them a push (Nisbett and Wilson, 1977, 243–244).

Freud may have taken over Leibnizian postulates about unconscious mental functioning without giving them a thought; they were current in his day. It was only later that, woven into presentations of his own theories, they came to be regarded as his own inventions by those unfamiliar with their history. Thereafter, just these principles were often selected for special acclaim and hailed as Freud's greatest discoveries, the jewels in his theoretical crown. In his influential primer, psychoanalyst Charles Brenner, maintaining that psychoanalytic theory "comprises what are by far the most important contributions that have been made to human psychology to date," picked two of these as basic. Unaware that this was one of Leibniz's fundamental principles, he chose as the first "the principle of psychic determinism," the premise that "nothing happens by chance, or in a random way. Each psychic event is determined by the ones which preceded it. Events in our mental lives that may seem to be random and unrelated to what went on before are only apparently so." The second proposition was that "consciousness is an exceptional rather than a regular attribute of psychic processes" (Brenner, 1955, 11–12). Freud's studies had convinced him that "in fact the majority of mental functioning goes on without consciousness and that consciousness is an unusual rather than a usual quality or attribute of mental functioning." Brenner concluded that "this is of course, in sharp contrast to the view that prevailed before Freud's time that consciousness and mental functioning were synonymous" (Brenner, 1955, 24). However, Freud's supposedly radical insight did *not* contrast sharply with the previous view; it simply *was* the previous view.

As we will see, Leibniz's psychology endured. The principles of psychic determinism and the proposition that consciousness is an exceptional rather than a regular attribute of psychic processes—which the psychoanalytic writer regarded as Freud's and as "revolutionary"—would probably not have come as a surprise to any educated Austrian in 1900. Moreover, the conjecture had considerable currency elsewhere in Europe and in America as well. The general ideas which Freud claimed for psychoanalysis, the concepts that the unconscious is the fundamental part of the mind and that mental processes are largely unconscious, came as no shock to Freud's literate contemporaries. In fact, if you had asked them who had "discovered the unconscious," they likely would have told you that this had been Leibniz, in whose writings the principles which Freud and his followers have attributed to "psychoanalysis" are to be found. The voices of Freud's contemporaries attest to the recognition which was accorded this seventeenth-century philosopher: "Leibniz retains the glory of having been the first to affirm the existence of ideas of which we are not conscious and to recognize their vast importance" (Hartmann, Vol. I, 1893, 19) and he "deserves immense credit for instantly perceiving with the eye of genius the range of his discovery, for penetrating into the dark inner laboratory of human feelings, passions, and actions, and for recognizing habit and much else as effects of an important principle only too briefly expounded (Vol. l, 1893, 17). Strümpell said, "It was he [Leibniz] who first, with clear insight into the matter, pointed to the importance of the unconscious emotional life for the physical and mental economy of the conscious person" (1874, 121–122).

Friedrich Nietzsche, himself often erroneously identified as a "discoverer" of the unconscious, referred to "*Leibnitz's* [*sic*] incomparable insight—with which he obtained the advantage not only over Descartes, but over all who had philosophised up to his time,—that consciousness is only an accident of mental representation, and *not* its necessary and essential attribute; that consequently what we call consciousness only constitutes a state of our spiritual and psychical world . . . and is *far from being that world itself*" (Nietzsche, 1987, #357).

In 1892, Wilhelm Wundt, having launched the new science of experimental psychology, worried that his contemporaries were too much concerned with the unconscious and lamented that "the notion has become so popular that many philosophers and psychologists consider it much more interesting to learn what takes place behind the scenes, in unconsciousness, than what occurs in consciousness" (1892, 235).

Some remarks, such as the above by Wundt, reveal the extent to which the concept of the unconscious was taken for granted in the fields of psychology and philosophy in the pre-Freudian decades. In the following selections, italics have been added to passages which manifest this *general* recognition.

In England, George Henry Lewes noted this:

> Leibnitz [*sic*] pointed out that we have many psychical states which are unconscious states—to have an idea and be conscious of it, are, he said, not one but two states. The Consciousness by Descartes created into an essential condition of Thought, was by Leibnitz reduced to an accompaniment which not only may be absent, but in the vast majority of cases is absent. *The teaching of most modern psychologists is that Consciousness forms but a small item in the total of psychical processes. Unconscious sensations, ideas, and judgments are made to play a great part in their explanations.* It is very certain that in every conscious volition—every act that is so characterized—the larger part of it is quite unconscious (1877, 165–166).

In the United States, Oliver Wendell Holmes called Leibniz's insistence on the existence of unconscious thought "audacious":

> Do we ever think without knowing that we are thinking? . . . Are there any mental processes of which we are unconscious at the time, but which we recognize as having taken place by finding certain results in our minds? That there are such unconscious mental actions is laid down in the strongest terms by Leibnitz [*sic*], whose doctrine reverses the axiom of Descartes into *sum, ergo cogito* (I am, therefore I think). The existence of unconscious thought is maintained by him in terms we might fairly call audacious, and illustrated by some of the most striking facts bearing upon it. . . . It does not follow, he says again, that, because we do not perceive thought, it does not exist. . . . In one word, it is a great source of error to believe that there is no perception in the mind but those of which it is conscious. This is surely a sufficiently explicit and peremptory statement of the doctrine, which, under the names of 'latent consciousness,' 'obscure perceptions,' 'the hidden soul,' 'unconscious cerebration,' 'reflex action of the brain,' *has been of late years emerging into general recognition in treatises of psychology and physiology* (1892, 276–277).

Holmes adds:

> The doctrine of Leibnitz, *that the brain may sometimes act without our taking cognizance of it, as the heart commonly does, as many internal organs always do, seems almost to belong to our time.* The readers of Hamilton and Mill, of Abercrombie, Laycock, and Maudsley, of Sir John Herschel, of Carpenter, of Lecky, of Dallas, will find many variations on the text of Leibnitz, some new illustrations, a new classification and nomenclature of the facts; but the root of the matter is all to be found in his writings (Holmes, 1892, 278).

Another American, writing about Leibniz at the end of the century, noted that he "was the first to recognize the importance of the unconscious" and commented that "apart from their metaphysical garb, *the unconscious perceptions in Leibniz's system are virtually the same thing as the unconscious soul-elements in modern psychology and philosophy*" (Carlson, 1899, 72).

When Freud was already on his way to fame, a German editor of his acquaintance commented that "the theory [of unconscious mind] has found more and more disciples" and *"at the present time is probably supported by the overwhelming majority of writers . . .* an assumption of this kind can already be found in the works of individual writers in antiquity. However, only the presentation of the great thinker Leibniz is responsible for the fact that *the psychic unconscious never again disappeared from the purview of philosophers and psychologists"* (Löwenfeld, 1913, 1–2).

Leibniz was not an isolated thinker, a luminary who "anticipated" Freud but whose thoughts about the unconscious were then forgotten. He was the founder of a school of psychological thought; his principles were accepted, clarified and developed by followers. In Freud's youth, the psychology most widely recognized in his milieu was Leibnizian. He could not have avoided coming across the idea that he later claimed for "psychoanalysis," namely that "mental processes are in themselves unconscious and that of all mental life it is only certain individual acts and portions that are conscious" (*S.E.*, XV: 21). In the intellectual milieu in which he grew up, such Leibnizian concepts were taken in stride.

The unconscious mind was not, in fact, the conception of any one identifiable individual; Leibniz did not "discover the unconscious" either. Lancelot Law Whyte, who examined some of the origins of the idea in his *The Unconscious before Freud,* noted that an inkling of the concept seems to have existed almost from the dawn of history and, focusing upon western European writers, pointed out several who, around 1700, were publishing ideas which closely resembled modern conceptions. Leibniz was only one of a list which included Pascal, Spinoza, Cudworth, Malebranche, Norris, Vico, Shaftesbury, Wolff and Kames (Whyte, 1962, 97). Whyte also issued a warning which is too little heeded: we ought not to forget that, in addition to these relatively well-known individuals, who had published this: "there must have been a vastly greater number who shared this realization without recording their thoughts" (1962, 71).

We do not have to suppose that the idea of unconscious mentation, and every other psychological concept found in Leibniz's works, was newborn, a child of his brain. However, no one before Leibniz had so clearly recognized the importance of the concept of the unconscious mind. His contribution has been grossly underestimated because the whole pre-Freudian development of the theory has been largely ignored. Leibniz laid out the vineyard in which his successors labored during the eighteenth and nineteenth centuries, working out his theory of mental functioning. The paradigm which Leibniz bequeathed to his immediate follower, Christian Wolff, and through Wolff to Wolff's disciples, was based on the premise that unconscious mental activities are primary in that they precede and generate conscious activities. Thus, every conscious experience rises out of a previous unconscious state. Human beings are at the mercy of unconscious motives; believing that they are acting of their own free will, they are often caught in the sweep of purposes and passions of which they know nothing.

NOTES

1. Leibniz's "minute perceptions" have sometimes mistakenly been equated with the "monads" of his metaphysical speculation. The "minute perceptions," which Leibniz likened to Boyle's "corpuscles," were hypothesized as the real causes of psychological phenomena. "Monads," on the other hand, were immaterial substances, "souls" or metaphysical atoms. If Leibniz had intended to equate these concepts, he would have done so; he would not have had to invent the new expression "minute perception" to designate the psychological concept. The conflation of Leibniz's psychology with his metaphysics has often confused and obscured presentations of the psychology.

2. Leibniz, accepted "corpuscles," but often inveighed against "atoms." Although he espoused the theory that matter was composed of tiny particles, he disagreed with features attributed to "atoms" by Democritus and avoided use of the Greek expression for this reason.

3. It has sometimes erroneously been asserted that Leibniz did not have a theory of the unconscious at all; he supposedly had in mind only very low degrees of consciousness. His "minute perceptions," according to this view, were faintly conscious, not unconscious. This misjudgment rises from the role which consciousness played in Leibniz's metaphysical speculation. Leibniz supposed that infinitesimally small degrees of "consciousness" existed throughout the cosmos, not only in the organic, but also in the inorganic world. This did not mean that Leibniz supposed that *rocks,* for instance, were aware; the degree of "consciousness" they possessed was far too "minute" for this. Only when consciousness accumulated to a certain point, did awareness ensue. Therefore, a thing could be said to possess minute amounts of "consciousness" but not be capable of conscious awareness. This puzzling formulation must now strike us as peculiar, but it was an element in a metaphysical system which is still attractive to some because of its logical construction and to others because it is a dream of a world in which everything is related.

4. There is a fallacy in this argument that has been pointed out by such notables as John Stuart Mill, Franz Brentano and William James. Leibniz suggested that because the cumulative sound of all of the waves can be heard, we must be hearing each individual wave unconsciously. He reasoned that, if an individual sound made no impression at all, if its value was zero, then no accumulation of these sounds could ever be heard because adding zeros would never result in anything more than zero. His critics pointed out that this does not follow; it might be that nothing at all is registered, even unconsciously, until a certain volume is reached.

5. In the *New Essays on Human Understanding*, Leibniz was a consistent spokesman for psychic determinism. His introduction of unconscious motives into the old argument strengthened the position of the opponents of free will. However, on occasions he wavered. In the only book published during his lifetime, the *Theodicy,* he pulled back and offered a dubious defense of free will. Thereby he brought down on himself the scorn of at least two philosophers who condemned his inconstancy in no uncertain terms. Schopenhauer called him a "middle-of-the-roader" who "tacks back and forth" and "hides behind words" (Schopenhauer, 1985, 61). Bertrand Russell, although allowing that Leibniz was a genius, decided that he was not an "admirable" human being because what he published was "designed to win the approbation of princes and princesses" (Russell, 1948, 604). This may be true; the kindly Leibniz may well have wanted to reassure his good friend Princess Sophie of Brunswick and other readers about the freedom of the will. In the same book, Leibniz attempted to offer a comforting answer to the question as to how it was that God, supposedly good and omnipotent, could have created a world so full of pain. God did what he could, according to Leibniz. Given the logical constraint that he was under, he assembled "the best of all possible worlds." This notion evoked the amused contempt of Voltaire who proceeded to write *Candide.*

Chapter Two

Psychodynamics

In the 1950s, when the Golden Age of psychoanalysis was at its height and Freud's stature as an immortal of science seemed to be beyond question, two respected scholars examined the foundations of his theory in order to lay bare its ultimate principles. Psychoanalysts David Rapaport and Merton M. Gill—noting that "at some point in the development of every science, the assumptions on which it is built must be clarified"—said the time had come "to attempt to state explicitly and systematically that body of assumptions which constitutes psychoanalytic metapsychology"—the theory at its highest level of abstraction. Stripping the abstract theory of all but the bare essentials, they came upon a substructure which, although they did not know it, was essentially of pre-Freudian origin. Like excavators who find, beneath the pavement of a Baroque cathedral, an ancient Roman foundation which determined the cathedral's floor plan, so did these psychoanalytic scholars unearth the principles of the Leibnizian psychology which had shaped the thinking of Freud.

The "metapsychology," whose principles the scholars had come upon, was psychoanalytic theory in what was deemed to be its most scientific form. Some of its principles were those of "psychodynamics," the section of the theory that explained psychological phenomena as resulting from the interaction of motivational forces. By analogy, these were likened to the forces of physics. A motive, a "psychological force," impelled the mind in a certain direction; this principle was called the "dynamic point of view." A motive possessed a certain strength, or magnitude—a "psychological energy." This was the "economic point of view." According to Rapaport and Gill, both "dynamic" and "economic" points of view were needed by the theory "because psychoanalysis requires—just as physics does—both energy and force concepts" (1967, 796). The bedrock of psychoanalytic theory, the set of "assumptions on which it is built," was the hypothesis that motives, "psychological forces," defined "by their direction and magnitude" were pitted against each other in a conflict whose outcome was determined by the "composition law of vectoral addition" (800).

How was this supposed to work? Imagine that a person who had two equally strong but contradictory wishes: he or she would find that they canceled each other out. The predicament could be described in terms of the rules governing "bodies" upon which "two forces" were acting simultaneously. According to vector arithmetic, subtracting a wish to go due north from an equally strong wish to go due south would give a "resultant" of zero and the person so pushed in two directions would be unable to move in either. If the motives were conscious, the person might be regarded as irresolute, as weak-willed. If one of the motives was unconscious, the person would want to move but could not—a case of psychogenic paralysis.

In the more typical situation in which the two wishes were not absolutely contradictory or of equal strength, the same kind of calculation would apply. Freud explained that in such instances "these two opposing forces do not cancel each other out, nor does one of them . . . overpower the other. Instead, a compromise is brought about, somewhat on the analogy of the resultant in a parallelogram of forces" (*S.E.,* III: 307). (Freud's reference here was to a corollary of Newton's third law of motion.) Vector arithmetic in such instances produces a compromise. If a person wanted to go due north and at the same time was equally determined to head east, they would find themselves moving in a northeasterly direction. When several, or perhaps a great number, of motives are involved in a conflict, vector arithmetic will produce the "resultant," the compromise between all of them.

The cognitive psychologist, Matthew Erdelyi, plausibly suggested that Freud conceived of conflict "in terms of clashing force vectors, in line with nineteenth-century physics fascination with dynamics" (1985, 10). While there can be no doubt that Freud was influenced by physics, the dynamics in question were of interest, not to nineteenth-, but to seventeenth-century science, and the introduction of vector arithmetic into psychology was undertaken by Leibniz, a leading physicist of that time.

When Leibniz approached psychology, it must have been only natural that he would bring some physical conceptions with him. He was one of the pioneers who just then, in the age of Newton, was attempting to clarify concepts which would serve as foundation of the new science: hypotheses about gravity, matter, force, energy, momentum. As a major participant in these endeavors, he must almost intuitively have compared the conflict of human motives with the clash of physical forces.

Leibniz pictured this conflict as occurring between numerous motives, a conglomerate of reasonable aims and irrational passions, both conscious and unconscious, and compared the struggle to the collision of numerous, conflicting physical forces whose outcome was decided by vector arithmetic: "We always follow, in our willing, the result of all the inclinations that come from the direction both of reasons and passions, and this often happens without an express judgment of the understanding" (1985, 151).

In a conflict between aims, more powerful motives could suppress weaker ones; but also, the weaker could join forces, combine their strengths and overcome, by united action, an opposing urge which could not have been defeated by any one of them individually. "Various perceptions and inclinations combine to produce a complete volition. It is the result of the conflict amongst them. There are some, imperceptible in themselves, which add up to a disquiet which impels us without our seeing why. There are some which join forces to carry us towards or away from some object, in which case there is desire or fear, also accompanied by disquiet. There are some impulses which are accompanied by actual pleasure or suffering." Some may, others may not, be accompanied by memories of the past (1981, 192). "Since the final result is determined by how things weigh against one another, I should think it could happen that the most pressing disquiet did not prevail, for even if it prevailed over each of the contrary endeavours taken singly, it may be outweighed by all of them taken together" (Leibniz, 1981, 192–193). Once "the battle has been engaged . . . everything which then impinges on us weighs in the balance and contributes to determining a *resultant direction,* almost as in mechanics."[1]

The Leibnizian psychodynamic metaphor did not have to be rediscovered by Freud at the end of the nineteenth century for it was well understood at that time. This is clearly demonstrated by the description of it given by a number of philosophers, including the American, John Dewey. Dewey was obviously at home with the idea that motives could be unconscious; his comments serve as a nice example of nineteenth-century familiarity with the concept of unconscious mental functioning. In 1888, he wrote that some actions occurred "for an end which is unknown, or at best but dimly felt. Such action may be called blind, not in the sense that it is without reason, but in the sense that reason is not consciously present." We are, in fact, never aware of all of the reasons which motivate us: "We are never able to take complete account of the agencies which are acting upon us" (1888, 328). Dewey pictured a hodgepodge of conscious and unconscious motives, impulses, desires, memories and feelings and invoked vector addition to explain how, in this situation, the will could arrive at a decision: "In the concrete act of will there are contained impulses which push us towards some end whose nature is not known; there is desire both in its inchoate stage, where pleasure and pain are not in consciousness, and in its formed state, where the pain and pleasure are definitely presented. Mixed with these desires and impulses are images of past experiences which call up the feelings which were formerly attached to them, and thus there are aroused indirectly additional impulses and desires. Out of this complicated mass of impulses, desires, and feelings, both original and reproduced, comes the 'dominant effort' which constitutes complete will. But what governs the production of this prevailing or dominant effort, which we may interpret as the act of choice? The answer is simple: the result of the conflict of these various factors, the striking of the balance, *is* the choice. Some desire emerges from the confused complex, and that desire is the final determination of the will. This desire may not in all cases be the strongest in itself,—that is, the one whose satisfaction will allay the greatest 'uneasiness,' for the others, taken together, may outweigh it; it may, so to speak, have a plurality, but not a majority, of volitional forces on its side,—and in this case a fusion of opposing factors may defeat it. But in any event the result will be the *algebraic* sum of the various desires and impulses"[2] (1888, 330–331).

References to the vector addition of psychological forces were not rare in Freud's milieu. The psychiatrist Theodor Meynert, in whose laboratory Freud had worked, made casual use of the concept to explain which solution to a question would be "allowed over the threshold"—i.e., would become conscious. This "depends upon the synergistic and antagonistic ideas which are already sufficiently well laid in the ego" (Meynert, 1890, 43).

The classical psychoanalyst, Charles Brenner, describing this principle, stressed the significance of the comparison with physical science" "the sense of this principle is that in the mind, *as in physical nature about us,* nothing happens by chance. Mental phenomena are no more capable of . . . a lack of causal connection with what preceded them *than are physical ones"* (12, emphasis added).

In classical physics, every event was the consequence of a preceding or concomitant event; from the wheeling of the galaxies down to the dance of the smallest particles, nothing happened without a reason. There was never a break in the chain of cause-and-effect. When this rule is applied to psychology, no fleeting thought, momentary feeling or apparently aimless bit of behavior is assumed to be fortuitous. This "principle of psychic determinism" has routinely been attributed to Freud. However, it was a tenet of the psychology to which Freud was introduced in high school. His textbook assured Freud that mental events were as strictly determined as the physical, that not the least thought or feeling, conscious or unconscious, escaped the dominion of the universal law of causality (Lindner, 1872, 7).

NOTES

1. Leibniz made the same point about the powers of the soul using different physical metaphors: "A man has always so much the more difficulty of determining himself, as the opposite reasons draw nearer to an equality: just as we see a balance turn so much the more readily, as the weights in each scale are more different from one another. However, since there are often more than two ways which a man may take; we may therefore, instead of this

similitude of a balance, compare the soul to a force, which has at one and the same time a tendency many ways, but acts on that part only where it finds the greatest ease, or the least resistance. For example: air strongly compressed in a glass-receiver, will break the glass to get out. It presses upon every part, but at last makes its way where the glass is weakest. Thus the inclinations of the soul, tend towards all apparent goods; and these are the antecedent volitions: but the consequent volition, which is the last result, determines itself towards that good which affects us the most strongly" (Theodicy, 31, from Leibniz-Clark Correspondence, p. 139).

2. A modern physicist, Max Planck, taking exactly the position which Leibniz took, equating forces and motives as Leibniz had, remarked that "the role force plays in nature as the cause of movements is taken here in the world of the mind by motive as the cause of action." The will of a person "results from the convergence of a certain number of motives or impulses, which, in a way that can be conscious or unconscious, operate inside him with different strengths and different directions, and which combine to give a determined result, just as in physics different forces come together with a resulting determined force." This assumption was a necessary one for "there would be no question of universal causality if it were broken at any place, if consequently even the processes that take place in conscious and subconscious psychic life, feelings, sensations, thoughts and finally the will itself were not governed by the law of causality" (Bouveresse, 85; Planck, 154).

Chapter Three

The Light and the Dark in the Mind

The psychology of the German Enlightenment was the psychology of Leibniz. In accordance with the ideal of the age, devoted disciples labored to make his teachings available, not only to the intellectual elite but also to the less distinguished, less highly educated members of society.

The Enlightenment believed in progress; behind it lay a century of scientific achievement then-unparalleled in history. A series of discoveries beginning in the Renaissance and climaxing in the accomplishment of Isaac Newton had given the Western world a profound respect for the capabilities of the intellect. It had also raised the expectation that further advances were well-nigh inevitable, that the application of reason, free of prejudice, independent of authority and tradition, would eliminate obscurity and confusion everywhere, not only in the understanding of the natural world but also in human life. A science of psychology would come into being; people would be perfectible. Education would gradually eradicate tyranny, injustice and cruelty.

Heralds of this sanguine vision were the French "*Philosophes*," the spokesmen for reason. They were not philosophers in the usual sense; rather, they were men of letters who pitted reason against the repressive powers of authority—especially, church and state. Firing off essays, novels, satires and epigrams, they disseminated ideas and ideals that were destined to topple governments and recast Western society in a democratic mold. During the French Revolution, which the thought of the *Philosophes* had inspired, the glorification of "reason" reached its high point when a statue was erected in its honor.

The psychology of Leibniz was profoundly inimical to this enthusiastic faith in reason. Leibniz himself was a great optimist, a great believer in the possibility of the betterment of the world and a striver for universal peace. However, his teaching about the hidden powers of unconscious mental activities undermined the trust that reason, conscious reason, could lead humankind from one triumph to the next. Consciousness was simply not to be trusted; the freedom of the reasonable will could not be guaranteed since the possibility of an unconscious motive could never be ruled out. Beneath the elegant logic and the admirable, judicious opinion, primitive impulses could lurk. Reason might confidently point this way or that, and yet, its direction, like that of the compass needle, might be set by some unrecognized power.

The *Philosophes*, champions of reason, had little patience with such concepts; they assumed that they lived in a complicated, but comprehensible, well-lit world. The oddball idea that one could unconsciously perceive, think, feel and will, left most of them cold. Voltaire, an admirer of Locke, came out against the "romance" that "we always think, but we do not always perceive that we think. It might as well be asserted that we drink, eat, and ride on horseback without knowing it. If you don't perceive that you possess any ideas, how can you affirm that you have any?" (Voltaire, 1928, 224).

Enlightenment opinion was not monolithic, however, for the simple reason that it spread into Leibnizian territory. The Enlightenment had its beginning in France, but, since all of Europe looked to Paris for intellectual leadership, the influence of the *Philosophes* quickly spread to other countries. In this way, the Enlightenment turned into a movement as wide and as effective as the Renaissance or the Reformation. Falling on different ground, its thought naturally took different forms. Given the disparity in the histories, environments and circumstances of their countries, the French *Philosophes* and their counterparts, the German "Enlighteners" (*Aufklärer*) could not be expected to share identical outlooks and aims. There were, in fact, many interesting and important differences between them but only one of these need occupy us: while the *Philosophes* were followers of Locke, many of the Enlighteners were firm adherents of Leibniz. Just as intent on promoting the progress of civilization as their French colleagues, the Enlighteners were likely to assume that what the public needed was information about the unconscious mind.

The Enlightener who took charge of this mission was Christian Wolff, assiduous promoter of Leibnizian concepts, including the concept of unconscious mentation. Arbiter of all things philosophical in the German-speaking world for nearly half a century, he was a powerful supporter of the theory.

Wolff, a protégé of Leibniz, produced a series of philosophical books in which he aimed to capture all of human knowledge in a single, logically ordered conceptual scheme. For a long time his endeavor was regarded as having been successful. The system he produced has often been called "Leibniz-Wolffian," but this is actually a misnomer since the system was eclectic, incorporating principles derived, not only from Leibniz but also from Aristotle, Descartes and Spinoza. The name is more appropriate if it is limited to that portion of the system devoted to psychology; here, although other sources are utilized, the Leibnizian principles are dominant.

Scholars were attracted by the system's comprehensiveness and the logic of its organization. Wolff quickly acquired a following which adopted and taught his system and this school underwent "an almost unbelievable expansion," according to a German historian: "during his lifetime more than one hundred of the master's disciples worked at the development and the dissemination of the system" (Dessoir, 1902, 81). His prestige and authority were immense; it was said of him that what Confucius was for China or Aristotle for the Middle Ages, Wolff was for German philosophy in the first half of the eighteenth century (Grau, 1916, 197).

Wolff's popular success was most likely due to the fact that, never losing sight of the Enlightenment ideal, he wrote in a style accessible to a wider public, aiming to meet the needs of readers not only in the universities, but in the palaces of princes, the salons of the fashionable and in the modest homes of the bourgeoisie as well. He wrote simply—some would complain pedantically—often repeating himself, like a patient schoolmaster who has designed the lesson to accommodate the slowest learner in the class. The response was gratifying. His admirers said of him that, like Socrates, he had found philosophy in the heavens and had brought it down to the huts of the poor (Grau, 1916, 197). Among the ideas spelled out and given this wide dissemination was Leibniz's premise about the realm of the unconscious mind.

In his attempt to establish the foundations for what he designed as a formal system of psychology, Wolff put together whatever concepts he considered useful, regardless of their source. With great respect for Locke, he took from him the general concept of an "idea." An idea, according to Locke, was that which the mind "is applied about whilst thinking" (Vol. I, 1959, 123). As understood by Wolff, it was anything of which one might be conscious: sensations, representations, mental images, memories. The eighteenth-century definition of "idea," the German "*Vorstellung*," usually took in far more mental contents than the "representation" of today; it could even include images and feelings. When the Lockean idea was picked up by Wolff, it underwent a Leibnizian transformation and became the kind of thing that could be either conscious or unconscious. Wolff introduced the word "conscious" (*Bewusst*) into the German language and contrasted it, not with "unconscious," which still lay in the future, but simply with what was "not conscious." His pragmatic willingness to adopt any concept he deemed useful served as model for his followers; his practical approach to psychology paved the way for the fruitful synthesizing eclecticism of the rest of the century.

Wolff maintained that the reason that Cartesians had made the mistake of supposing that the mind contained nothing but conscious thoughts was that they had relied upon introspection. Looking within, they had discovered only conscious thoughts and had assumed that these constituted the whole mind: "Since I find nothing within myself except consciousness, that is, my thoughts, I do not count anything further as belonging to me. And so it came about that the Cartesians believed that consciousness constituted the entire essence of the mind, and that nothing could happen in it of which we would not be conscious" (1952, 110).

But what were these activities in the mind which were not "conscious thoughts?" How was Wolff to explain such strange novelties as that the mind contained contents that were not conscious—clarify them, moreover, not only for the sophisticated but for the relatively untutored? The great simplifier, Wolff reached for the comparison with vision and so gave the century its metaphor—.ideas which we could "see" when we peered into our own minds were "clear;" those which could not be perceived were "dark."[1] Here he had been inspired by Leibniz according to whom "the mind is an ocean in which there is an infinity of dark ideas and clear ideas are the islands which emerge from the ocean"[2] (Feuchtersleben, 110).

Wolff adopted Locke's concept of an "internal sense," an inner eye with which the contents of the mind could be scanned. Locke had maintained that, in addition to the five external senses, an internal sense permitted the observation "of the operations of our own minds within us," enabling us to detect such things as "*perception, thinking, doubting, believing, reasoning, knowing, willing*, and all the different actings of our own minds." This inner perception, Locke suggested, could be compared to external sensation: "though it be not sense, as having nothing to do with external objects, yet it is very like it, and might properly enough be called *internal sense*" (Vol. I, 1982, 123).

Wolff added to this concept the Leibnizian qualification that this inner eye cannot see in the dark and that most of the mind is not illuminated. For Locke, the mind had resembled a well-lit hall; one could look about in it and watch what was going on within it; reasoning, desiring and deciding were all visible. But Leibniz had turned out the light. The hall was dark; nothing could be seen but the activity in the hall did not cease: reasoning, desiring and deciding continued as before, albeit now invisibly. Yet the viewer had a lantern which, casting a narrow beam, could be moved about to illuminate a few things at a time. The light of this lantern was the light of consciousness.

Wolff explained that "some thoughts are of such a kind that we know very well what we are thinking . . . then we say that they are clear. . . . On the other hand, when we ourselves do not rightly know what we are to make of what we are thinking, then our thoughts are dark" (1982 110–111).

"This terminology is taken from the field of vision. For we say that vision is clear when we can distinguish what we see but on the contrary, a vision is dark, when we can no longer clearly make out what we see. Since when we see, we are conscious of what we see, and therefore also, of what we are thinking [we therefore] . . . use the same expression for both vision and thoughts. This is why I have given examples which are connected with seeing" (1982, 112–113). He adds, "Therefore we also understand expressions such as 'I am beginning to see the light' or 'I am still entirely in the dark about that,' and so on" (1982, 113).

Using the metaphor of light, Wolff carried forward from Leibniz the concept of repression. Leibniz had assumed that a stronger, more powerful, idea could drive a weaker "into the shade." Wolff pictured the struggle for dominance between mental elements as resembling a competition between lights of different intensities; a brighter light could make a weaker one invisible. The point was that the weaker light that could no longer be seen continued to exist with no diminution of its intensity. Sensations have different degrees of clarity, Wolff explained, and "the stronger sensation dims the weaker one" (Grau, 1916, 195). "One sensation can have more clarity than another to the extent that one cannot perceive the one for the other or can barely perceive it. Experience provides us with an example. The light of the stars provides a lesser sensation than the light of the sun to the extent that, during the day, we cannot see the stars for the sun" (1982, 125). He stressed that "this difference in clarity is found not only in sensations, but in all the other kinds of thoughts as well. And this is why so much happens in the mind, and also why so much is pictured, particularly by the imagination, of which we have no perception" (Grau, 1916, 195).

In spite of the line drawn between clarity and darkness, neither Wolff nor his immediate successors explicitly recognized the need for a distinction between the easily accessible and the relatively inaccessible unconscious. He described as outside of awareness both the sensation which was not being noticed at a given moment and the hidden mental content whose existence could only be surmised by inference, mentioning these states without being struck by the difference between them. So he noted that a person engrossed in reading a book "is not conscious of what he is hearing, even though the sound of the words enters into his ear just as it does at other times, and although it produces the usual changes in the ear" (1982, 455). Presumably the reader of the book could at any moment become conscious of the sound by a simple shift of attention.

On the other hand, Wolff insisted on the importance of *inference*, maintaining that the existence of contents outside of consciousness could only be deduced by reasoning from *evidence*. But what can only be discovered within us by means of inference is clearly the relatively inaccessible unconscious; it is not something of which we can become aware simply by paying attention to it; this distinction had yet to be made.

Wolff emphasized that the failure to recognize that one might legitimately make inferences from conscious to unconscious contents was the reason for the Cartesian error. "We cannot perceive anything more than what we are conscious of, [if] there is more to be discovered within us than we are conscious of, we will have to bring it out by means of inferences, and indeed, it must be elicited from that of which we are conscious, because we have no reason for it otherwise" (1982, 108).

Wolff realized that accepting the theory of unconscious mental functioning demanded a radical transformation of the classical theory of the mind in which prudent, conscious reason governed the conscious, impetuous appetites. This simple formula had somehow to be adjusted to make room for dark reasons and dark appetites. Wolff probably designed the very first mental model that aimed to accommodate the unconscious, both unconscious reason and unconscious appetite. In his bold, but awkward design, reason was called the "cognitive faculty" and was divided into higher and lower faculties. The higher cognitive faculty was the seat of clear ideas, the lower cognitive faculty that of the dark. The appetitive, or passionate, part of the mind became the "desiring faculty" and was similarly subdivided; the higher desiring faculty was the rational will; the lower that of the dark instincts, guided by the search for pleasure and the avoidance of pain. Conflict was pictured as occurring between the higher and lower desiring faculties (Drobisch, 1898, 302–306).

Wolff's unpretentious model is worthy of note as an early attempt to work the unconscious dimension into a picture of the mind. This simple design, in which contents outside of consciousness are given an integral role to play, was a precursor of the more elaborate models which followed it.

THE LEIBNIZ-WOLFFIAN SCHOOL

"The psychology of the Enlightenment is chiefly based on two notions borrowed from Leibniz, i.e. that the difference between darkness and clarity is the fundamental difference in psychical life, and that ideas are the constituent elements of this life," according to the psychologist, Harald Hoeffding (1955, Vol. 2, page 8). The paradigm of clear and dark ideas was indeed assiduously cultivated by the school of Wolff. Generally speaking, his disciples remained within the guidelines: ideas were divided into the clear and dark; dark ideas sometimes came to consciousness through insight; at other times their existence could only be inferred. More powerful ideas could force the weaker out of consciousness. The domain of dark ideas was vast; the soil from which conscious ideas sprang, it was "the foundation of the soul" (*Grund der Seele*). The illumination metaphor was standard; in an adventurous moment, a scholar divided the mind into a "Realm of Light" and a "Realm of Darkness" (Grau, 1916, 200).

At midcentury, one of the chief exponents of the psychology, Georg Friedrich Meier (1718–1777), gave clear expression to its tenets at that time.

Since there were no radical differences of opinion between members of the school, we can let Meier speak for them all. Dark ideas, Meier explained, were "the foundation of the mind because they constitute the basis for all human cognition." The development of a "science of the mind" demanded the recognition of dark ideas; this recognition was essential "if the nature of the mind is to be properly understood" (Grau, 1916, 204).

Meier made heavy use of the illumination metaphor; the mind's coming-to-consciousness was compared with daybreak: "Consciousness much resembles light in the physical world. In the midst of a completely dark night all of the objects around us are invisible. We cannot distinguish one thing from another. . . . We see absolutely nothing. Then the sun rises and its bright rays illuminate the entire visual field. . . . Consciousness is the light of the mind, or rather, the source of this light. So long as we are not conscious of our ideas, just so long are they are hidden in a dense darkness and obscurity in the foundation of the mind. . . . When we become conscious of them, day immediately breaks in the mind; the ideas become clear" (Meier, 1751, 74).

But this is a metaphor. How, in fact, do dark ideas ever emerge into the light? Elucidations have typically relied on a feature of the Leibnizian continuum of consciousness which ranges from the darkest, most inaccessible mental contents at one end to those closest to consciousness—almost conscious—at the other. Explanations of the shift from the unconscious to consciousness will naturally be easiest in those situations in which a dark idea is already on the brink of dawn.

The kind of example which Meier offered for dark thoughts whose presence could be detected remained popular until modern times. He noted that moods are produced by what we are thinking; cheerful and unhappy frames of mind give rise to corresponding emotional states. If we now find ourselves in a mood which we cannot explain, a mood which cannot be attributed to a mental cause, we may infer that the cause is a dark idea. Likely as not, a bit of reflection will bring this idea to light.

In 1895, Freud's coauthor in *Studies on Hysteria*, Josef Breuer, explained the effect of "current ideas that are unconscious" in a similar way. "If I have forgotten to make one of my medical visits, I have feelings of lively unrest. I know from experience what this feeling means: that I have forgotten something. I search my memories in vain; I fail to discover the cause, till suddenly, hours later perhaps, it enters my consciousness. But I have been uneasy the whole time. Accordingly, the idea of the visit has been all the time operative, that is to say present, but not in my consciousness" (*S.E.*, II: 222).

Explanations of this kind may well cast light on the origins of the theory of unconscious mental states. It seems likely that such humble instances, frequently experienced, suggested depths of the mind extending beyond the examples. Once it was recognized that minor, easily retrievable, forgotten incidents, remained emotionally effective, it might not have been difficult to infer that weightier events could similarly escape the conscious mind and yet continue to influence it.

Meier stressed that the coming-to-consciousness of an idea took place in two stages: every mental state or activity that appeared in consciousness went through a first stage in which it was unconscious; in Leibniz' language, it was "perceived" before it was "apperceived." Like other Leibnizian theorists, he maintained that perceptions were unconsciously registered and reached consciousness only if a second, independent action was taken. Not all perceptions were apperceived.

Meier often, but not always, replaced the traditional Leibniz-Wolffian expressions with his own; for him a "dark idea" was usually an "idea"; (*Vorstellung*) and a clear idea was a "thought" (*Gedanke*). A "thought" was an "idea" which had become conscious: "A thought always consists of two different principal parts, of an idea and of the consciousness of the idea. . . . It is immaterial whether I refer to an idea as clear, or whether I say that I am conscious of it. If an idea is to become a thought, then the idea of that thing must become clear" (1751, 131). He elaborates: "It is undeniable that, although all thoughts are ideas, there are ideas which are not thoughts. An idea can be hidden in such a thick and impenetrable obscurity and darkness that one is not conscious of it in this state; one does not even know that one possesses it; one does not become aware of it in the whole field of knowledge. An idea does not become a thought until consciousness is added to it" (1751, 74).

He brought this distinction to bear on the Cartesian definition of the soul as a "thing that thinks." "If one wants to regard a thought as an action of the thinking thing, then, without much reflection, one realizes that the thinking thing, in that it thinks, necessarily must undertake two different actions, one by means of which it represents the object to itself and the other, by which it becomes conscious of the representation" (Meier, 1751, 133).

The concept of two different actions, according to which an idea remains unconscious until it is apprehended by the internal sense, was adopted by Freud who averred that the two separate steps could be discerned during analysis: "Incidentally, this enables us to form a quite definite view of the 'essential nature' of consciousness; we see the process of a thing becoming conscious as a specific psychical act, distinct from and independent of the process of the formation of a presentation or idea; and we regard consciousness as a sense organ which perceives data that arise elsewhere" (*S.E.*, IV: 144).

At this time, Freud attributed to a contemporary Leibnizian philosopher, Theodor Lipps, the concept that the unconscious was the foundation of the mind; that all mental states were initially unconscious, that some of these remained unconscious while others rose to consciousness. "In Lipps words, the unconscious must be assumed to be the general basis of psychical life.

The unconscious is the larger sphere, which includes within it the smaller sphere of the conscious. Everything conscious has an unconscious preliminary stage; whereas what is unconscious may remain at that stage and nevertheless claim to be regarded as having the full value of a psychical process" (*S.E.,* V: 613).

Meier suggested, that in principle, the whole mind was implicated in the coming-to-consciousness of a single idea. That is to say, that every idea which reaches consciousness does so as a result of the interaction with *every* other idea in the mind at that moment, together with *every* idea that was there in the past. The "sufficient reason why an idea in the mind is clear must be sought in all of the ideas which are in the mind with it simultaneously, indeed, in all of the ideas which were in the mind previously." Thus, all of the "innumerable dark ideas" of past or present "contribute to each clear idea" (1751, 130).

The assumption here is that the mind consists of a network of ideas no element of which can be activated without some activation of the whole. The entire mind contributes to the occurrence of every mental event. This hypothesis, which served as the basis for the psychological theory produced by Johann Friedrich Herbart in the following century, incorporated a further premise—that no memory is ever entirely eradicated, that is to say, that even a memory that lies beyond recall, may continue to influence ongoing, conscious mental life (Meier, 1751, 226).

Consonant with the general Leibnizian emphasis on the activity of the mind, Meier saw a power struggle even in the association of ideas. In the classical view, ideas flowed in a series, each member evoking the next; according to Meier, each member of the series *pushed* its predecessor out of consciousness, that is to say, "repressed" it: "there is in every mind a succession of modifications [ideas] which repress (*verdrängen*) each other in an unbroken series" (Meier, 1751, 217).

DARK IDEAS IN POPULAR CULTURE

During the last decades of the eighteenth century and the first of the nineteenth, an intense interest in things psychological, attributed to Leibniz-Wolffian efforts, was manifested by the proliferation of journals devoted to the subject. The contributions to publications with names like *Magazine for Experimental Psychology* and *General Repertory for Empirical Psychology and Related Sciences* revealed a fascination with the inner life, particularly the aberrant inner life. Pastors, physicians and miscellaneous students of human nature contributed to these journals, submitting case histories and anecdotes aimed to shed light on the obscure corners of the soul. Nothing human was alien to these explorers of the mind who sought to understand the motives and emotions of the troubled. The lives of obsessives, alcoholics, misers, pedants, suicides, even murderers were examined sympathetically by these amateur clinicians. Results varied widely; superstition still held sway in dream interpretation; some items were simply foolish; some reports were merely the kind of sad or dramatic "human interest" stories which we now expect to find on television but at their best, the analyses reveal surprising insights which we now erroneously associate with our own time. Among the themes found in these publications was the existence of the "dark" part of the mind; this too was illustrated by anecdotes or personal reports. One such account, titled *Action without Conscious Motive, or the Power of Dark Ideas,* was contributed by a country doctor. The physician had felt very uneasy about a patient's health without being able to account for it. The patient's sudden demise, due to what had been an unsuspected "internal defect," seemed to justify the doctor's premonition which had apparently been based upon an unconscious but sound intuition (Moritz, 1786, Vol. 3, 158–165).

Such instances of the practical application of Leibnizian theory may facilitate the comparison between the eighteenth- and the twentieth-century psychologies. Freud persuasively confronted readers with the uncanny notion that the conscious self knew nothing about the unconscious life of its own mind, or, as he put it, "the ego is not master in its own house" but we find that readers in the eighteenth century were also told to take this consequence of Leibniz-Wolffian theory in stride.

In 1759, a dedicated Enlightener at the court of the King of Prussia, Frederick the Great, set out to make the fundamentals of Leibnizian theory available to ordinary folk. When he arrived in Berlin, the thirty-year-old Swiss philosopher, Johann Georg Sulzer, a man of relatively humble origins, having started life as a vicar, joined a glittering company. The king, aiming to revitalize the Academy of Science, had invited participation of savants from all of Europe. The promise of intellectual freedom, financial support and other amenities offered brought scholars as distinguished as Voltaire to the Prussian capital. The language spoken at the academy was French; academy publications appeared in the same language. To the satisfaction of the Prussian king, the academy shone as an outpost of French science and culture.

Sulzer had been invited to join this prestigious society, in spite of his modest background, because of the status he had achieved as a philosopher. A factor in his subsequent success in Berlin may have been his geniality. He had a gift for friendship and a propensity to think well of people. (In an argument with Frederick, he supported Rousseau and insisted that human beings naturally tended to be good. The king quashed this idea: "Ah, my dear Sulzer, you don't know this damned race," *Encyclopaedia Britannica*, 11th ed.,Vol. XI: 56).

A century before Freud was born, while the French and their Indian allies were fighting the Redcoats for the control of North America, Sulzer embarked on his project to make the concept of unconscious mind available to ordinary citizens. We may picture him sitting at his desk, in relaxed attire perhaps, having doffed the powdered wig of the court, the velvet coat, and the shoes with the silver buckles and, quill pen moving rapidly, taking readers through the basics and confronting them with the conclusion that the ego was not master in its own house.

NOTES

1. The Wolffian adjectives used to designate conscious and unconscious ideas are *klar* ("clear") and *dunkel* ("dark). An unconscious idea is thus a *dunkele Vorstellung*; I am translating it as "dark idea." In other translations, *dunkel* has been rendered as "obscure." Unfortunately, however, the meaning of the word "obscure" is itself obscure for it can signify either that something is not well *understood* or that something is not clearly *conscious*. Moreover, it completely fails to capture the illumination metaphor for consciousness and unconsciousness which was so important in the eighteenth century.

2. The original was in Latin: *Animus est instar oceani in quo infinita multitudo perceptionum obscurissimarum adest et distinctae ideae instar insularum sunt, quae ex oceano emergent.* Quoted in Ernst von Feuchtersleben, *The Principles of Medical Psychology*, London, Sydenham Society, 1847, Reprint Arno Press, Inc. 1976.

Chapter Four

The Power of Dark Ideas

Psychoanalysis sought to enlighten the conscious ego by pointing out to it that it was making a mistake, Freud declared (*S.E.,* XVII: 141). "You feel sure that you are informed of all that goes on in your mind if it is of any importance at all, because in that case, you believe, your consciousness gives you news of it. . . . Come, let yourself be taught something on this one point! What is in your mind does not coincide with what you are conscious of; whether something is going on in your mind and whether you hear of it, are two different things." Sometimes the ego senses this: "The ego feels uneasy; it comes up against limits to its power in its own house, the mind. Thoughts emerge suddenly without one's knowing where they come from, nor can one do anything to drive them away. These alien guests even seem to be more powerful than those which are at the ego's command.

> Psycho-analysis sets out to explain these uncanny disorders; it engages in careful and laborious investigations, devises hypotheses and scientific constructions, until at length it can speak thus to the ego: "Nothing has entered into you from without; a part of the activity of your own mind has been withdrawn from your knowledge and from the command of your will. That, too, is why you are so weak in your defences; you are using one part of your force to fight the other part and you cannot concentrate the whole of your force as you would against an external enemy (*S.E.,* XVII; 141–143).

Johann Georg Sulzer many years before Freud, also compared unconscious forces with a hidden foe; dark ideas could not be opposed by reason because, like invisible enemies, they administered blows whose source the conscious self could not locate. Addressing uninitiated readers, he led them methodically from the introduction of the concept of dark ideas to their power to influence moods, thoughts and motives, to their occasional pathological effects.

Sulzer began by describing a situation with which his readers were familiar, the disruptive consequences of *conscious* mental conflicts. For instance, when the wish to say one thing is countermanded by the powerful desire to say just the opposite, mastery of the tongue may be lost: "One wants to speak swiftly and speaks slowly, one wants to express everything clearly and instead one stammers and stutters." This situation is not puzzling. However, the same sort of verbal stumbling can occur when we are not aware of any conflict; we stammer, stutter and make mistakes when no contrary motive is in evidence. Under these circumstances, the opposition to the conscious will may be attributed to the invisible power of a dark idea (102).[1]

Sulzer noted that, in the past, conditions of this kind had been so bewildering that people had reached for supernatural explanations (103). By way of illustration, he cited a case of what would once have been considered to be demoniacal possession. In this kind of pathology, an apparently alien voice emanated from a person as though another entity was sharing the body, a parasite which, having taken over the vocal chords, expressed its own opinions, often hostile and mocking the most cherished beliefs of the helpless host. For centuries, such voices had been attributed to an invading evil spirit. This explanation was no longer acceptable in the mid-eighteenth century and, demons having been ruled out, it became natural to assume that the hostile voice was produced by something within the mind of the afflicted of which the sufferer was unaware. Sulzer emphasized the helplessness of the conscious will in such situations:

> In the case of a certain kind of melancholy [mental illness] one does things for which one has the greatest abhorrence at the very moment that one does them and this is so strange that a superstition attributed it to an evil and omnipotent spirit. I knew a man of integrity, very reasonable and experienced in philosophy who had the misfortune to fall ill of a melancholia caused by a manifold and enduring affliction. Although he sincerely venerated the highest Being, for a time he nevertheless could not hear the name of this Being, which he worshipped with his whole heart, without uttering some blasphemies against it. His hair stood on end with abhorrence as he did so and he made every effort to hide or make amends for the blasphemies through acts of prayer and he often told me that he could almost believe that two souls lived within him, one of which praised God at the very moment in which the other blasphemed. He could not understand how the same individual could at the same time do two things which were so exactly contrary to each other. This case alone sufficiently proves that upon occasion one acts against the most determined will without the least appearance of a reason (103–4).

About comparable situations, Freud remarked that "the patient is aware with astonishment of having a will which is resolute but powerless" (*S.E.*, I:

122). This powerlessness of the will was due to the existence of a unconscious "counter-will" which accounted for "patients' not being able to do something precisely when and where they want to most passionately, of doing the exact opposite of what they have been asked to do." They "itch to do the wrong thing, to appear to be ill just when they most want to be well." Patients under such compulsions were "the helpless victims of their antithetic idea" (*S.E.*, I: 126–127).

Sulzer, having argued that something hidden within us may be able to compel us to think and act against our most fervent conscious desire, compared the helplessness of a person in the grip of a powerful unconscious motive with the pitiful condition of a bird hypnotized by a snake in the legendary forests of America. A mesmerized bird, its eyes fixed on those of the voracious animal, realizes that it is looking into its own grave, but plunges toward the open mouth against its will. Shrieking desperately and making every effort to escape by jumping from branch to branch, the bird vainly resists the unknown force and drops into the jaws of the snake. "Whether true or false," Sulzer commented, "this story is a perfect example of the kind of slavery of which we have been speaking" (101–2).

Two questions required an answer, according to Sulzer: what was the source of these forces, which, although imperceptible, could enslave the conscious mind? And why did these forces always have the upper hand over the efforts of the conscious mind? With the demonological explanation a thing of the past, Sulzer invoked the invisible powers postulated by Leibniz.

> To answer these questions we must turn to the theory of dark ideas introduced by Leibniz and developed by his students—a very important theory without which a great many phenomena could not be explained. Here are the principle tenets that form the basis of this theory: in addition to clear thoughts, that is, those of which the mind is conscious and which claim its attention, there exists simultaneously a great number of other more or less dark thoughts which the mind either does not notice at all or else only so slightly that it cannot distinguish between them. These dark thoughts often produce very marked consequences (107).

As Freud proclaimed that "there is unconscious thinking and unapprehended willing," (*S.E.*, XV: 22) so Sulzer insisted upon the existence of "dark judgments" and "dark desire." He emphasized "that not only the representations of an idea, but all other actions of the mind can be dark as well. There are dark judgments which we make without being conscious of them, dark sensations, a dark desire and a dark aversion. These are the 'I don't know what it is' that everyone experiences at one time or another. In brief, all the powers of the mind can be expressed in two different ways: in a clear way so that we know what we are doing and can account for our behavior; or in a dark way so that we ourselves do not know what is going on within us. A single and actually very common observation will suffice as evidence for all of this: how often does it not happen that we feel well or ill, cheerful or cross, without knowing why? This occurs at such times because one is sensing, estimating, desiring or detesting something which is only darkly represented."

A conscious point of view could coexist with a contradictory unconscious opinion: "we must note that every situation can be viewed from several sides and that the opinion which we form about it depends entirely upon the side from which we regard it. Different points of view will produce different judgments. It is therefore quite possible that we will regard a situation from one side by means of clear ideas and at the same time regard it from the opposite point of view, by means of dark ideas and that therefore the two judgments which we will form will contradict each other" (109).

Early childhood was an important source for unconscious attitudes and motives; these retained their power even when their origins were completely forgotten, according to Sulzer.

> In the case of manifest passions the thoughts and feelings that are struggling with reason are not entirely dark, one can distinguish between them, more or less. However, these inclinations or disinclinations are frequently so dark that they are unrecognizable. This happens principally when the dark feeling is connected to things that happened in the remote past. People often have inclinations or disinclinations whose causes would be sought in vain because they relate to an idea or an event which, derived from the years of childhood, has been completely darkened by time. A great many paradoxes can be explained in this way. We are astonished at times that very reasonable and intelligent people harbor prejudices that seem unforgivable to us. These prejudices are unquestionably the very natural consequences of some dark idea that has been lying hidden in the depths of the soul. This is the origin of those dark forces of which we have been speaking (110).

Sulzer then turned toward the other question: given that they exist, "how is it that the forces that emanate from dark thoughts always gain the upper hand over the efforts of the will? Or, to express myself more precisely, why do the dark ideas have more power over us than the clear and distinct ones?" (110–1) His answer was that one cannot combat an enemy whose existence one does not suspect. This was true, for instance, when dark judgments were acquired early in life before the individual was capable of independent thought:

> There are a thousand things about which we heard others judge and decide on innumerable occasions during the years before we were capable of independent reflection. We have become so familiar with these judgments that whenever one of these things recurs we immediately remember what we heard about it and this happens so quickly that the entire representation seems to be

> an inner feeling. Now when we are supposed to do something related to this thing these dark motivations, consequences of these feelings, must necessarily be effective, regardless of reason. The situation resembles that of optical illusions which are almost irresistible. No matter how well we understand that the moon at its setting is no larger than it was at noon, the illusion nevertheless has the upper hand (116).

He then adds:

> Now if the illusion is this strong at the very moment when we realize where it is coming from, just imagine the power it will have in those instances when we haven't the slightest suspicion that we may be deceiving ourselves. This generally occurs when the judgment arises from dark thoughts which cannot be distrusted because they are not perceived (117).

Such dark inclinations could have the force of strong passions: "in vain do we seek to oppose them with the strength of reason. They are enemies who lie hidden in ambush: one is beaten by them and does not see where the blows are coming from. For this very reason it is impossible to simply defend oneself against them. The human being will always be a slave of his passions and his prejudices as long as he has nothing but reason with which to oppose them" (117). Sulzer sums: "If I am not mistaken, this is the true origin of the tyrannical power of prejudices, passions and preconceived notions and of so many other enemies of reason. They are located in the dark regions of the soul where we are not aware of their inimical activities and devious enterprises until it is too late to resist them and it is just this which almost always assures them an infallible victory" (117).

Freud made the same point about the power of unconscious motives: "the mental and somatic power of a wishful impulse . . . is far stronger if it is unconscious than if it is conscious. . . . An unconscious wish cannot be influenced and it is independent of any contrary tendencies, whereas a conscious one is inhibited by whatever else is conscious and opposed to it" (*S.E.*, II: 53). A conflict involving an unconscious wish was not to be confused with "a normal struggle between mental impulses both of which are on the same psychological footing," that is to say, both conscious. When one of the two powers is unconscious, "the conflict cannot be brought to an issue; the disputants can no more come to grips than, in the familiar simile, a polar bear and a whale" (*S.E.*, XVI: 433).

According to Sulzer, whole cultures were subject to tyrannies exercised by the dark part of the soul. "At first glance, nothing seems more strange to the assumptions of reason than certain opinions to which entire peoples, sects and orders are devoted. One finds that they run so contrary to healthy reason that one does not know what to make of those who have adopted them. This is equally true of various habits and customs seem to be so absurd that when one sees them one can hardly trust one's eyes" (118). He continues:

> All of this can be explained clearly enough in the light of what I have said about the power of dark thoughts. What one hears and sees before the age of reflection fixes itself in the understanding without encountering any obstacle. It is well known that one can convince children and people who do not think for themselves of anything one likes. Words without sense fill the imagination and judgment accepts many unproven or even contradictory propositions which have the appearance of truth and reality. Then whenever memory revives these words or propositions it also reminds us, although darkly, of the appearance of truth and reality which accompanied their original acceptance. This prevents us from subjecting them to test by reason (118).

Sulzer sums:

> No opinion or custom is so absurd that it cannot insinuate and assert itself against the rights of reason and healthy understanding. As soon as an error is incorporated into the mass of dark ideas it is extremely difficult to extirpate or drive it out of the understanding. This is the reason why it is difficult even for a wise person to give up national prejudices or the prejudices of the rank in which he was raised (119).

The mind cannot combat an invisible enemy precisely because it is invisible. Is the mind helpless then? Can nothing be done against the power of these dark ideas, dark desires and dark aversions with which we are afflicted?

Leibniz had maintained that the existence of dark ideas could be inferred. Yet an inferred idea is still dark; the question which remained was whether a dark idea, once inferred, could be induced to emerge from the shadows. Sulzer suggested that a dark idea might come to light if, instead of trying to recall it deliberately, one let the mind drift. It was an ancient wisdom that, if something could not be brought to consciousness by direct efforts, it sometimes emerged freely, "on its own," if direct efforts were abandoned. Sulzer described an occasion when he had successfully raised a dark idea to consciousness using this method. Having forgotten something, he suspected that this forgetting might be motivated:

> In my presence a group of people spoke about a very noble action carried out by a person of whom I knew very little and whom I was not able to recall properly. The action was so honorable that everyone competed in praise of it. Meanwhile, at the same time, I felt something—I didn't know what—which weakened or moderated my admiration. An unknown force seemed to prevent me from abandoning myself completely to it. . . . Since I was myself surprised about the kind of indifference which was preventing my applause, I made efforts to look for its cause. . . . I found myself in the situation of those who attempt to remember a name which escapes them; at every moment they be-

> lieve that it is on the tip of their tongue. After many efforts one remembers a letter of this name, then another, then a third and finally one grasps it altogether. In just this way I obtained the key to the riddle on this occasion. I finally remembered that long ago someone had spoken to me of this person as being of very mediocre intelligence. The dark memory of this was the cause which prevented me from lavishing my praise. And this is the way in which our dark ideas can have an influence upon our judgments (109–10).

Did Sulzer bring a dark idea back to consciousness by means of what Freud would call "free association?" Was the eighteenth century free-associating? It would seem so, judging from the instructions of a philosopher who, a generation after Sulzer, captured the process in a set of rules (see chapter 10).

HYPNOTIC CREATION OF UNCONSCIOUS MOTIVES

In 1889, when Freud visited France, he was deeply impressed by post-hypnotic experiments which supported the hypothesis that motives could be unconscious. In these procedures, hypnotized subjects were given instructions that were to be carried out after they were wakened from the trance. In Freud's presence, a man was told that, when cued, he would open an umbrella over the doctor's head. Wakened, consciously recalling nothing of the instruction, the subject nevertheless complied with the foolish suggestion and, when queried, offered the lamest excuses for his behavior. The subject was convinced that he had been acting on a peculiar impulse of his own, unaware that, like a Leibnizian compass needle, he had been obeying a hidden command. Freud commented: "It is clear to us spectators that he is in ignorance of his real motive. We, however, know what it is, for we were present when the suggestion was made to him which he is now carrying out, while he himself knows nothing of the fact that it is now at work in him." Anyone who witnessed such a demonstration, Freud declared, would receive on "unforgettable impression and a conviction that can never be shaken" that "there are such things as unconscious psychical acts" (*S.E.*, XXIII: 285).

Just such demonstrations were being offered in the 1780s and 1790s; doubtless, they were just as compelling then; then also they must have produced unshakable convictions about the actuality of unconscious motives. At that time, hypnosis was called "animal magnetism" and its practitioners were "magnetizers." In 1787, a French experimenter, Mouillesaux, gave spectators the same kind of evidence for the reality of unconscious urges. According to the report "this magnetizer told one of his patients while she was still in the crisis [trance] that on the next day she was to visit someone at a particular time and at a place which she ordinarily did not frequent. Although for personal reasons this instruction must have been very unpleasant for the patient, she nevertheless promised to follow it because her magnetizer wished it. Mouillesaux then woke the patient from her magnetic sleep and took every possible precaution to make sure that in the waking state she would not find out about the promise she had made. The next day, together with several of his friends, he arrived at the designated place before the time agreed upon. Punctually, as the clock struck, the patient appeared in front of the house. She walked back and forth several times, anxiously and indecisively, and finally entered the room with obvious embarrassment. Mouillesaux reassured her immediately by informing her of the whole proceeding, whereupon she told him that ever since she had opened her eyes that morning she had thought constantly of coming here at such and such a time. She had tried to talk herself out of it, and had suggested various alternative plans to herself, but all in vain. As the predetermined time approached, she was seized by an inner unrest and anxiety from which she could free herself only by setting out on her journey" (Kluge, 1818, 112).

Post-hypnotic suggestions at that time were already being given practical application, just as they were later, in Freud's day. In 1786, a magnetizer described its successful use in achieving weight control. The magnetizer, an Alsatian nobleman, Count de Lützelbourg, treated a patient, a "very pious, but also very irascible" clergyman who was unable to stick to a diet: "by means of this [magnetic] power, I put him on a diet which he himself had specified and from which he has to date had neither the desire nor the ability to deviate, no matter what attempts are made to seduce him away from it" (DuPrel, 277) The clergyman did not realize he had been given a command while hypnotized and remained unaware of it, even as he continued to be influenced by it.

The same magnetizer also reported using the method successfully with a mentally unstable patient. This man, apparently during anxiety attacks, would run out into the street. Hypnosis was induced and the man was commanded never to do this again. After that, whether alone or with other people, he obeyed the post-hypnotic suggestion, even when seized by unreasoning terror. He was unaware of the suggestion but knew of it when rehypnotized.

Lützelbourg relieved a woman of a phobia; until treated hypnotically, she had been terrified of mice. On another occasion, the help which he extended turned out to be excessive. When she had been unable to remember the expression "solar plexus," he drummed it into her memory under hypnosis but "I imprinted it in her brain to such an extent that I afterwards found it necessary to put her back into somnambulism [hypnotic state] in order to prevent her using this expression at every opportunity, which is what she had been doing for three days" (DuPrel, 1889, 279).

Were eighteenth-century magnetizers like Lützelbourg and Mouillesaux engaging in experiments which had never been carried out before? It seems unlikely; trance states have been reported from the earliest times. Hypnosis is a natural condition which can be induced without difficulty in susceptible subjects, of whom there are quite a few. In superstitious times, most likely, hypnosis would have been regarded as a form of magic; it may be that the occult literature of that era contains references to phenomena which could be recognized as hypnotic. The question is interesting because if hypnotic evidence for unconscious mental activity was available earlier, then philosophers like Leibniz might have come to know of it. In Leibniz' case, the possibility is intriguing. For one thing, Leibniz was just the man to have been attracted by the subject for he was fascinated by such things as alchemy, occultism and theosophy (Leibniz, 1981, xlv). Moreover, he was acquainted with the Flemish physician and occultist Franciscus Mercurius van Helmont (1614–1696), studied his writings and had "pretty intimate" conversations with him (1981, xlv). Van Helmont was a healer, a practitioner of "occult medicine," which typically involved suggestion (1981, xxxvi) In all likelihood, he was a magnetizer also. His father, the famous scientist Joan Baptista van Helmont, (1579–1646) discoverer of gas, had made use of magnetism and had had to defend himself against the Inquisition on that account (Pagel, 1982, 2). Given this background, it is plausible that in his "intimate" conversations with Leibniz, the younger Van Helmont described, perhaps even demonstrated, some of the peculiarities of magnetism. If this was the case, it could account for Leibniz's apparently serene conviction that "thought need not stop just because one is not aware of it"[2] (113).

THE CONCEPTUAL PROBLEM OF DARK IDEAS

The concept of unconscious mental activity did not sweep through the philosophical psychology of the eighteenth century without controversy; critics spoke up and arguments ensued. However, if one were to attempt to assess the number of adversaries encountered by the Leibnizian premise, one could not simply count up the number of those "opposed." A distinction would have to be made between those whose objection was psychological and those who dissented on philosophical grounds. In the first group would be those who denied the psychological hypothesis that people could be unaware of their own thoughts, feelings and motives; the second category would be made up of those who protested against unconscious cognition as conceptually incoherent: these typically rejected as contradictory the definition of the "dark idea" as an "unthought-thought."

The conceptual problem was serious: if an "idea" is defined in the Lockean sense as that which the mind "is applied about whilst thinking," then it is nonsensical to describe a "dark idea" as one which is not being thought about. If an idea is identified as that of which we are conscious when we think, then a "dark idea" becomes "that of which we are conscious when we think—when we are not conscious of it"—a clear absurdity.

One way out of the problem of the "unthought thought"—a way also to avoid the whole notion of "unconscious thinking"—was preferred by those who, agreeing that one might have an idea without being aware of it, nevertheless wanted to insist that all ideas were "in consciousness." They maintained that an idea might be "in consciousness" but that it might not be "noticed." It might be "absolutely unnoticed;" it might even be altogether "unnoticeable."

The response to this solution was that it was a mere playing with words. An idea "outside of consciousness" and an "unnoticed" idea meant exactly the same thing, according to the eighteenth-century scholar, J.G.E. Maass. "Some philosophers maintain that there is no such thing as an idea without consciousness but that in some cases the consciousness is completely unnoticeable. One might agree with these philosophers but it would be beside the point. In that case, one would simply be taking what I am calling consciousness to mean a *noticeable* consciousness" (Maass, 1797, 63). Maass and the philosophers with whom he was disagreeing were not at odds about the psychological hypothesis; the argument was not about the facts, but about the language.

In spite of such early attempts at clarification, the conceptual argument did not wither away but survived until modern times. Therefore, any attempt to understand the position of a philosopher on the subject of unconscious thought must always begin with a differentiation: is the philosopher concerned with the facts or with the conceptualization of the facts? A failure to make this distinction is likely to result in the misapprehension that a particular scholar opposed the psychological hypothesis when he actually accepted it and was critical only of the terminology.

The psychological hypothesis fared well during the eighteenth century and held its ground during the nineteenth. Writing about the history of the concept in 1913, Freud's acquaintance, Leopold Loewenfeld, the editor of a neurological-psychological journal, commented: "For reasons of space, we are unable to cite the long series of philosophers who, after Leibniz, defended or denied the occurrence of unconscious psychic activity. During the discussion of the subject carried on in the eighteenth century, the concept of unconscious ideas won over ever more supporters so that the actual argument had to do less with the actual existence of the unconscious than with its relationship to consciousness" (Loewenfeld, 1913, 2).

NOTES

1. Freud made a similar point about this condition: "Stammering and stuttering," he maintained, were, like slips of the tongue, small behavioral lapses which, although generally disre-

garded, were actually determined by "an internal conflict, which is betrayed to us by the disturbance in speech" (*S.E.*, VI: 101).

2. Leibniz's having watched demonstrations of hypnosis might explain an otherwise puzzling passage in which he referred to a person as being in a "coma" and described a condition which resembled a somnolent hypnotic state: when a man "is reduced to a state where it is as though he were in a coma, and where he has almost no feeling, he does lose reflection and awareness. . . . Nevertheless, his faculties and dispositions, both innate and acquired, and even the impressions which he receives in this state of confusion still continue: they are not obliterated though they are forgotten. Some day their turn will come to contribute to some noticeable result" (1981, 139). In the original French, Leibniz used the word *lethargie* to refer to this condition. *Lethargie* can be translated either as "coma" or as "trance." Nineteenth-century French hypnotists used *lethargie* to designate a trance state in which the subject seemed to be unconscious, as in a "coma," having lost "feeling," "reflection" and "awareness." However, in fact, such subjects remained in touch with their surroundings, registered what they heard and could act upon it afterward. Leibniz could have been referring to post-hypnotic effects when he averred that "impressions" received in this state "are not obliterated though they are forgotten" and would some day contribute to a "noticeable result."

Chapter Five

The Leibnizian Brain

As the eighteenth century approached its end, Leibniz's postulates were pushed as far as they could go by Ernst Platner, philosopher and physician. We are always thinking, desiring and willing, Leibniz had said. Platner, taking him at his word, offered a vision of an unconscious mind that almost completely paralleled the activities of consciousness. Platner's unconscious could form judgments, make decisions and set goals. It was capable of foresight, of planning and of executing plans. It was pleased by success and disappointed by failure and reacted accordingly.

Platner had been one of the leading philosophers of Germany before the publication of Kant's *Critique* cast a shadow over his eminence. Thereafter, he became one of Kant's foremost critics. In psychology, he was an unabashed eclectic and an imaginative innovator. He replaced the expression "appetite" with the more modern "drive," postulated a theory in which an instinct was driven by the pleasure-pain principle and gave this theory a biological underpinning by speculating about the conscious/unconscious dimension as it was represented in the brain.

Platner's drive was a thrust for self-fulfillment, for actualization of potentialities: "Every living being has a basic drive [*Grundtrieb*]. . . . It always strives to function in keeping with its nature, that is, to express its basic potency" (1790, #607). When a creature "is functioning in accordance with its nature," that is, "freely expressing its basic potency," then "it is conscious of a satisfaction of its basic drive." On the other hand, when it is "not functioning as its nature demands, or when this functioning is inhibited, it is conscious of non-satisfaction" (#612). It was obvious, and did not need to be proven, that consciousness of satisfaction was pleasure and consciousness of non-satisfaction was unpleasure (#613).

Having summarized this version of the standard psychological theory which maintained that motives were determined by pleasure and unpleasure, Platner moved the whole of this concept down into the unconscious; whatever happened in the clear light of the upper realm could also take place in the darkness below. A desire might be unconscious, but also the setting of a goal, the formulation of a plan, the attempts to carry out the plan, the achievement of the goal and the subsequent satisfaction—this whole sequence of events might take place outside of awareness.

The search for drive satisfaction could take place entirely in the unconscious because unconscious pleasure or unpleasure were "analogous to conscious pleasure or unpleasure" and the unconscious striving to which they gave rise was analogous to conscious striving. When people consciously foresee future satisfaction or frustration of the basic drive, they experience hope or fear and take appropriate action, engaging in "desirous" or "aversive" strivings. But there were also "unconscious premonitions of state;" people could unconsciously foresee that a given course of action would lead to the one or the other result and this foreseeing, giving rise to the analog of conscious hopes and fears, resulted in unconscious strivings. Of these, there were two kinds: the desirous and the aversive.

Platner, who has been credited with coining the word "unconscious" (which did not come into general use in Germany until much later) propounded all of this in a serious but tedious, axiomatic fashion: "All desirous strivings aim, with or without consciousness, to bring about . . . the fully developed pleasant sensation which rises out of the satisfaction of the consciously or unconsciously active drive" (#1626). Moreover, "all aversive strivings aim to bring about, with or without consciousness . . . the avoidance of the fully developed unpleasant sensation which can rise out of the lack of satisfaction of the consciously or unconsciously threatened drive" (#1627).

In this scheme, an idea, whether derived externally, from sensation, or internally, from the mind's own workings, was originally unconscious. Once formed, it could be raised to consciousness, "turn into a concept," in Platner's terminology. It could remain unconscious; in that case, it could either satisfy or not satisfy the basic drive. If it was unconsciously satisfying, it produced unconscious pleasure. If it was not satisfying, it caused unconscious unpleasure which stimulated an unconscious attempt to rectify matters to obtain satisfaction.

As this summary of his theory shows, Platner was a dedicated scion of Leibniz, a convinced exponent of the thesis of unconscious mind. His treatment of the British doctrine of association therefore illustrates the reception accorded this teaching when it reached the philosopher-psychologists of Central Europe.

Careful readers of Freud have sometimes noticed what seem to be British empiricist influences in his writings. His associationism particularly has attracted attention and it has been asked whether he was familiar with the writings of Locke and Hume. He may have been, of course, but the question overlooks the fact that the ideas of these philosophers had been imported into Leibnizian thought long before Freud and it was with this thought that he was undoubtedly acquainted. Moreover, the ideas of Locke and Hume, once imported, underwent a great sea change as they were assimilated. What Freud encountered was British associationism as transformed by such Leibnizian philosophers as Platner. What they had added to what they had received was the unconscious dimension.

Platner pictured the conscious train of ideas as flowing through the mind constantly accompanied by two unconscious streams emanating from two different sources. One of these was memory. The mind was continuously being stimulated by impressions rising from memory traces which, according to Platner's theory, were never entirely quiescent. This source therefore consisted of "the sum of all of the material ideas [traces] of the entire memory, unconsciously affecting the mind at every moment" (#1165).

The other source was the body. Platner, a physician, gave full weight to a factor not always fully appreciated by philosophers, the individual's physical condition. The body's influence upon the mind was unintermittent, he maintained. The mind was at every moment under the influence of "the presently existing stimulations and changes of the entire nervous system."

Conscious thought was always under the influence of these two unconscious trains. "In the conscious state, the train of thoughts is a series of clear ideas which are partly surrounded and partly interwoven with dark ones." There was therefore never a moment during which a person's thought or behavior was not being shaped by past experiences and the momentary state of the body. The two unconscious, ever-flowing trains were also the basis of an unconscious sense of identity; they produced "an always enduring dark sense of self" (#1166).

Unconscious thought was the source of all conscious ideas. Impressions from the external world registered by the senses, as well as products of the mind itself, were unconscious before they became conscious. All remained unconscious unless endowed with sufficient strength to reach consciousness (#1166). Platner imagined that the mind was full of ideas which, originating externally or internally, remained dark indefinitely, often permanently.

A PHYSIOLOGICAL THEORY OF THE UNCONSCIOUS

As a physician, Platner was not content to offer merely a psychological hypothesis of mental functioning. He supposed that conscious and unconscious states and activities must be manifestations of concomitant brain states and activities and he therefore supplemented his psychological hypothesis with a physiological theory. He may have been the first theoretician to suggest that conscious and unconscious mental functioning must be ascribable to different nervous activities and conditions of the brain and to offer a hypothesis about the nature of the difference. The theory he proposed resembled Freud's hypothesis in the particular that mental functioning depended upon an energy which flowed through the mind as though in channels and which, being dammed up, could accumulate and which could also be diverted and dispersed.

The notion that something, a substance or a force, traveled in the nervous system and was active in the brain was not new. More than a century earlier, Descartes had assumed that "animal spirits" were responsible for the creation and reactivation of memory traces and Platner's theory echoed that of Descartes. Descartes, in turn, had borrowed from a tradition which dated from ancient times.

The traditional trace concept accounted handily for remembering and forgetting. Whenever an experience produced a conscious impression, an alteration was made in the physical substance of the brain; this alteration was the trace. The trace remained dormant until it was reactivated, at which point the memory returned to consciousness. Thus, two sets of conditions were envisaged: activated trace/conscious memory and inactive trace/no memory. This scheme had no place for unconscious memory, nor, indeed, for unconscious thought of any kind. Platner therefore had to come up with an alteration to the scheme which would accommodate the continual flow of unconscious memories which he postulated. It occurred to him that the solution to his problem might lie in the traces, then called "material ideas," i.e. ideas embedded, or preserved, in matter: "since the mind also has unconscious ideas . . . the question arises: how are the material ideas of conscious thoughts different from the material ideas of unconscious thoughts?" (1790, #526)

Platner created a Leibnizian physiological model by suggesting that memory traces were never entirely dormant. A memory trace, he supposed, might consist of a permanent low degree of activation of a nerve fiber. Every trace was therefore continuously giving rise to an idea, but to an *unconscious i*dea. The consciousness or unconsciousness of an idea depended upon the degree of activation of the trace. Only when activation was increased to a certain point did the trace produce an idea capable of breaking through into consciousness. Activation depended upon a substance which he called "nerve spirit" (not in the sense of "spiritual," but rather in the physical meaning of "essence" or "vapor"). He did not imagine, as Descartes had, that it resembled a liquid going through tubes but rather as being a very fine substance which permeated the nerves. It had already been suggested that the action of the nerves was electrical but, believing that this hypothesis had not yet been definitely established, Platner remained faithful to a more conservative hypothesis (#143).

The nerve spirit moved through the nervous system in the brain, traveling from one part to another, activating a succession of material ideas, thereby giving rise to a train of conscious thoughts. Nerve spirit varied in quantity; the greater the quantity affecting a trace, the higher the degree of consciousness attained by the idea: "the degree of strength with which an idea can be stimulated in the mind depends upon the degree of strength with which the corresponding material idea affects the mind" (#529) and "since the material ideas are movements of the brain fibers produced by the nerve spirit, it follows that, in the end, the consciousness and unconsciousness of an idea depends entirely upon the amount of movement of the nerve spirit" (#530).

Platner's theory provided a physiological underpinning for the ceaseless mental activity of Leibniz' vision: "in dreamless sleep and in all other physical unconscious states, the activity of the nerve spirits in the material ideas is below the degree of strength needed for consciousness. Therefore all of the ideas are unconscious, even though the material ideas of the memory are not completely at rest" (#531).

> When one says that a material idea of the memory is now being awakened and presented to the mind this does not mean that previously it had been entirely at rest, but rather, that it is now being excited with a greater degree of activity of the nerve spirit, so that the mind can become conscious of the thought which results. This is because all material ideas of memory, including those described as resting dispositions of the brain fibers, constantly affect the mind, although not all of them do so, all of the time, with the degree necessary for consciousness (#488).

Later he adds,

> In the waking state also, only some of the material ideas that are continuously being formed, partly by the senses and partly by the imagination, ever are linked with consciousness; and this is because the remaining ones lack the required degree of strength (#532).

Platner's nerve spirit hypothesis could explain some pathology and here the resemblance between his spirit and Freud's flowing excitation, the "psychic energy" of his later theory, becomes most apparent.[1] Platner supposed that obsessive thinking, the unremitting rumination about a particular subject, then known as "fixed idea," occurred when an inordinate amount of nerve spirit attached itself to the trace of a thought. At such times, the nerve spirit "tended entirely" in the direction of a trace and, as a result of this unidirectional flow, accumulated around it and kept it in a state of constant activation. At the same time, the amount of nerve spirit available for other traces diminished. Clinically, the state was manifested by an almost constant concern with the idea in question and a relative loss of interest in everything else. Platner noted that "persons who have a fixed idea are almost entirely deprived of reflection and memory, indeed, even of the conscious use of their senses, and think of nothing, or feel nothing, except of what is connected with the fixed idea. At the same time, however, also because of the lack of sensation and lively activity in the animal parts, their entire state of health is weakened and disturbed" (#507).

This explanation can be compared to Freud's elucidation in psychic energy terms of a situation such as mourning when a person's mind is occupied with just one thing. Psychic energy, like the nerve spirit, traveled between ideas, or "mental representations." It also attached itself to these; such attachment was known as "cathexis." When an inordinate amount of energy was fixed upon a representation, a "hypercathexis" came into being. At such times the person was mentally occupied with a single subject and the rest of his or her mental life was accordingly impoverished.[2]

Platner's treatment of a fixed idea consisted of attempts to disperse the nerve spirit and to induce it to resume its normal flow. "All psychological and physical means" were to be used, "all kinds of spiritual and physical stimuli" were to be employed "to draw the nerve spirit away from the material idea upon which it is fixed and distribute it evenly in the brain and nervous system" (#507).

Platner had nothing to say about the concept of repression which, however, was well understood at the time. In the previous century, Blaise Pascal, had already touched upon it. He had famously commented on the power of the unconscious in his aphorism: "the heart has its reasons which reason does not know" (277). "Reason," for Pascal, was clearly at the mercy of the heart: "all our reasoning comes down to surrendering to feeling" (216 and 530). "Reason may object in vain, it cannot fix the price of things" (39, no. 44). The dupe of the heart, or the "will," reason was not even allowed to become conscious of something if the will decided against it: "When the will likes one aspect more than another, it deflects the mind from considering the qualities of the one it does not care to see. Thus the mind, keeping in step with the will, continues to look at the aspect preferred by the will and judges by what it sees there" (Pascal, #539, 218). What goes against the heart is prevented from entering consciousness; Pascal's description clearly satisfies Freud's definition of repression: "*the essence of repression lies simply in turning something away, and keeping it at a distance, from the conscious*" (*S.E.*, XIV: 147).

At the dawn of the nineteenth century, J.G.E. Maass, author of two notable books on psychology made much the same point. The unconscious will, he maintained, could evoke associations it desired and suppress those it disliked, causing this interference "through a turning away of the [mind's] attention" (1797, 164).

It is hard to imagine a more complete unconscious mind control than that envisaged by Maass; every thought that surfaced in the conscious mind appeared because the will desired it; thereafter, having determined the idea that emerged, the will governed the ensuing flow of associations at every step (164–165). Like Pascal, Maass identified the "will" with the "passions."

> The passions often suppress the intellect by darkening its ideas entirely or in part, or at least by rendering them ineffective. Those ideas of the intellect . . . which oppose the passion, or which represent the satisfaction of the passion or the means to achieve it, as impermissible or as unwise, or which show the object [of the passion] in a form different from that which sensuality desires, are easily darkened. For passion calls attention to what harmonizes with it, that is to say, to what promises, or seems to promise, satisfaction, and, for the same reason, it draws [attention] away from the intellect's opposing ideas to such an extent that these are either darkened entirely or are so weakened that they cannot influence action and are unable to prevent the passion from reaching its goal (Maass, 1805, #16, 104).

The passions, however, could do more than merely suppress thoughts and deflect the mind, they could interfere with the process of reasoning itself: "the power of the passions can not only suppress the intellect and darken its thoughts completely or in part, but it can go even further in that it can mislead the intellect into making false judgments" (1805, #19, 129). Thus this power was responsible not only for what today is called "motivated forgetting," it could also create false memories: "since the faculty of memory is a branch of the power of judgment which, in turn, is part of the intellect in a larger sense, it is clear that the passions necessarily have the capacity to disturb the faculty of memory. But memory is not merely disturbed by passion; it is also often misled into recalling incorrectly. When a false idea harmonizes with a passion and intensifies the aspect in which it sees the object, memory is misled into recalling incorrectly" (1805, 135–136).

It was sometimes suggested that a thought had to be conscious before it was repressed. Maass denied this. In order to make a decision about an idea, it was not necessary for the idea to have clarity: "I can decide to suppress the feeling of envy as soon as it stirs, without now being conscious of this hateful feeling. Indeed! Without having it at all" (1805, 164)

It is not difficult to find resemblances between some of the thoughts of Platner, Maas and Freud. Does this signify that he must have been acquainted with their publications? Not necessarily—but the question is not far-fetched. They were major psychological theorists and, although the eighteenth century seems remote to us today, it was not so in Freud's time. Temporally and culturally, Freud was no farther removed from Platner and Maass than we are today from William James. Given his wide reading, Freud may well have looked into the works of these distinguished philosopher-psychologists.

The theory that the mind was equipped with inaccessible mental contents that could wield enormous power over the conscious mind naturally brought with it the question as to whether this inaccessibility could not somehow be circumvented.

Sulzer provided an instance of such an escape. He had teased a memory out of the darkness by giving up mental control and letting thoughts flow through his mind spontaneously. Sulzer was not unique. At the end of the century, a philosopher formalized a procedure which, he maintained, was widely in use.

NOTES

1. The resemblance is closest when Platner's theory is compared with Freud's original hypothesis, which was an attempt to account for mental phenomena by means of the flow of neuronal excitation. Freud abandoned this effort and in later theories replaced the physical neuronal excitation with a mental "psychic energy." See "Project for a Scientific Psychology," *S.E.*, I: 283-397.

2. For a long time, psychoanalytic theoreticians insisted on the value of this Freudian notion. According to the Laplanche and Pontalis dictionary: "Whatever the difficulties presented by the concept of cathexis, psycho-analysts would certainly find it hard to do without it, essential as it is in accounting for a large number of clinical data, and in assessing the progress of the treatment. There are certain pathological conditions which seem to leave us no alternative but to postulate that the subject draws on a specific quantity of energy which he distributes in variable proportions in his relationships with objects and with himself. In a state such as mourning, for example, the manifest impoverishment of the subject's relational life is to be explained by a hypercathexis of the lost object, and from this we can only infer that a veritable balance of energy holds sway over the distribution of the various cathexes of external or phantasied objects, of the subject's own body, of his ego, and so on." Later, other analysts denied the usefulness of a purely hypothetical energy, a notion borrowed from physics, in the explanation of psychological events. The concept of psychic energy has now been abandoned.

Chapter Six

Dark Ideas and Free Association

In 1795, Ludwig Heinrich Jakob described a method by means of which "absolutely dark" ideas could be raised to consciousness. The procedure advocated closely resembled the "free association" method of Freud.

Jakob pictured the mind as consisting of a flow of associated ideas, almost all of them dark. In his version of the illumination metaphor, mental activity consisted of a constant stream of ideas that moved through the mind like a perpetual, invisible parade. Here and there a few of them glowed; a few shone brightly, and it was these glowing or shining ideas which the inner eye could see. Jakob asserted that there was no doubt that many ideas never affected the inner eye at all.

Jakob was interested in the factors which impeded or facilitated the coming-to-consciousness of an idea. Using the "inner eye" metaphor, he believed that he had identified three of these. To begin with, there might be variations in the acuity of the inner eye. What we see of the outer world depends upon the condition of the eye; what we perceive of the sphere within may be contingent on the state of the internal sense. Presumably this would explain why some individuals suffer from a sort of myopia for their inner landscapes.

Then, the degree of consciousness of an idea depended upon its strength, or "intensity." Continuing the comparison with external vision, it is assumed that just as an object in the external world must have a certain degree of brightness if it is to be perceived by the eye, so must the inner object, the idea, possess sufficient intensity if it is to register internally. An idea may not be perceived simply because it is too weak.

Finally, consciousness depended upon the outcome of a conflict between ideas with different degrees of intensity. Even immense power did not guarantee that an idea would achieve consciousness; stronger ideas repressed those which were even marginally less strong, however luminous the latter might be. Recalling Leibniz's suggestion that "bigger" perceptions will put the weaker "into the shade," and echoing Wolff's metaphor about the sunlight blotting out the light of the stars, Jakob stated that the inner eye will not be able to perceive the idea which is cast into darkness by one which has more intensity.

He distinguished between two classes of dark ideas, the "relatively" and the "absolutely" dark. The relatively dark were those of which we were not conscious but whose existence we could obscurely sense. These could be brought to consciousness by mental effort, a focusing of attention. (Jakob apparently had in mind those situations in which one says to oneself: "something is bothering me" and in which a certain amount of reflection can bring this "something" to light.) The absolutely dark were those which could not be sensed; their existence could sometimes be inferred—presumably by a person's behavior.

Jakob took for granted that ideas outside of consciousness retained their power to influence the mind but he stressed that this influence might not be direct, that is to say, he warned that one should not imagine that each dark idea had one, and only one, effect. Dark ideas, like those in consciousness, could interact in complicated ways and the results of this interaction might be the determinants of inexplicable phenomena: "It is not unlikely that the dark ideas themselves have an effect on each other and that . . . because of this interplay of dark ideas many mental phenomena are developed and emerge in clear consciousness which we are altogether unable to explain because of our ignorance of these depths of the human mind. Many a dreary or happy mood, many a quick decision, many a passion, and so forth, may be the work of this unknown interplay of dark ideas which never reach the light of day except in their effects and thereby make the human mind so completely inscrutable" (1795, 267).

Although such ideas were absolutely dark, when appropriate means were used, some of them could be induced to emerge into the light, according to Jakob. An idea could be raised to consciousness by a process which entailed "reawakening ideas associated with it." He remarked, unfortunately without further elucidation, that the method was being employed by people in a number of fields: "Raising dark ideas to clarity is the affair of several disciplines, particularly of psychology" (238).

Since "raising dark ideas to clarity" was the aim of free association, the technique Freud used to explore the unconscious mind, let us review his recommendations for its use before looking at Jakob's rules. Freud asked the patient to do two things: "abandon reflection," that is, give up the critical, purposive thinking which normally regulates thought and then, pay attention to and report the ideas that subsequently emerge "of their own free will." Freud explained that when voluntary thought is given up, "involuntary ideas," will arise; the self-observer will find that "innumerable ideas come into his consciousness of which he would otherwise never have got hold" (*S.E.*, IV: 101). To promote concentration, it was advantageous for the patient on the couch "to lie in a restful attitude and shut his eyes" (*S.E.*, V: 528).

The analyst could facilitate the uncovering of an unconscious idea if, after having himself inferred what it was, he shared this information with the patient. He provided the patient with a "conscious anticipatory idea," letting the individual know, in advance, what he or she could expect to find (*S.E.*, XI: 142). The similarity between the idea suggested by the analyst and the patient's unconscious idea, even when the similarity was imperfect, made it easier for the unconscious idea to become conscious.

When Freud introduced his free association method, he put quotation marks around the words "voluntary" and "involuntary," indicating that these were customary expressions. He was alluding to the traditional distinction between "voluntary" and "involuntary" thought, the voluntary, controlled by the "will," or by "reason," and the involuntary, the uncontrolled, lawless. The understanding that the voluntary control of thought could be deliberately relaxed to permit the free flow of the involuntary was old, as was the assumption that this mental relaxation made possible the emergence of contents otherwise not easily available, or not available at all.

The most common use of this method of mental relaxation, recommended already by Aristotle in "On Memory," is found in the search for temporarily mislaid memories. For instance, when a name cannot be recalled, one gives up the deliberate attempt to retrieve it and permits names to occur spontaneously. These are likely to be associations to the name sought and are apt to bring it to mind (452a1).

The mental relaxation which facilitates such humble retrievals is essentially the same as the liberating act which opens the sluice gates to the domain of the involuntary. When we give up voluntary, logical thought to recall a name, we are switching to the involuntary mode. The creative artist, the writer and the inventor, seeking inspiration, make the same move, abandoning strict reason to give the untrammeled mind room to play.

"All remembering occurs through the association of ideas," Jakob explained (295). It is the task of recollection "to awaken a multitude of associated ideas, in order to provide the necessary clarity to the memory that is being sought, so that it may be recognized." He suggested six rules and conditions for the process which raised the dark idea by stirring up ideas associated with it.

1. A deliberate attempt should be made; just as the will could sharpen the external senses, so also could it heighten the sensitivity of the internal sense. This suggestion corresponds to Freud's recommending "an increase in the attention [the patient] pays to his own psychical perceptions" (*S.E.*, IV: 101). Jakob supposed that facility would be enhanced

by practice for "the more often one attempts to raise dark ideas to clarity . . . the greater the ability to accomplish this becomes"

2. The activity of the external senses should be reduced; presumably this rule entailed finding a quiet place or in some other way ensuring undisturbed peace: "the less the external senses are active or engaged, the greater is the receptivity of the internal sense. Therefore, many dark ideas become clear as soon as the external senses rest or are not engaged". Freud's patient relaxed on a couch in a quiet room, in a restful attitude, with closed eyes (*S.E.*,IV: 101).
3. The mind should be cleared of other thoughts. Just as Freud enjoined the patient who would free associate to "abandon reflection" (*S.E.*, V: 531) so did Jakob advise that "the less the other powers of the mind are occupied with other ideas, the more clarity is gained by the inner sense".
4. If the association between the dark idea being sought and another idea already in consciousness is close, the dark idea will be easier to raise: "a clear idea clarifies a dark one which is closely related to it. Therefore, the clearer the already existing ideas are, the more light they cast upon the remaining dark ones." It was on this basis that Freud provided the patient with "conscious anticipatory ideas"; the similarity between the suggested idea and the unconscious idea facilitated the latter's rise to consciousness (*S.E.*, XVI: 437).
5. If deduction has already suggested the presence of a particular dark idea, then that dark idea will more easily come into consciousness: "when reason determines, via inferences, that certain definite dark ideas exist, then they can be raised to clarity, and can be made even clearer, partly by the deliberate effort of the inner sense (attention) and partly by new inferences." Freud delegated the making of inferences to the analyst. Having inferred the existence of a particular unconscious idea, the analyst informed the patient about it, in order to help it reach consciousness (*S.E.*, X: 104).
6. The stronger an unconscious idea becomes, the more likely it is that it will break through into consciousness: "when the ideas themselves become more powerful, they are more easily perceived by the inner sense. Therefore, everything which strengthens the ideas and enhances the conceptualizing power which produces the idea, also illuminates the ideas of the inner sense" (1795, 238). Freudian theory also assumed that a powerful unconscious idea could more easily make its way into consciousness than a weak one. Unconscious ideas could be strengthened by alliance with related ideas, such as the conscious anticipatory ideas furnished by the physician (*S.E.*, XI: 142).

That eighteenth-century efforts to make the unconscious conscious by free associating were not uncommon is indicated by a warning against the practice issued by none other than Immanuel Kant. In 1798, in the *Anthropology from a Pragmatic Point of View,* Kant took a negative view of the attempt to examine one's inner life by observing "the involuntary flow of one's thoughts and feelings" (1978, 17). He elaborates:

> To scrutinize the various acts of the imagination within me, when I call them forth, is indeed worth reflection, as well as necessary and useful for logic and metaphysics. But to wish to play the spy upon one's self, when those acts come to mind unsummoned and of their own accord (which happens through the play of the unpremeditatively creative imagination), is to reverse the natural order of the cognitive powers, since then the rational elements do not take the lead (as they should) but instead follow behind. This desire for self-investigation is either already a disease of the mind (hypochondria) or will lead to such a disease and ultimately to the madhouse (170).

Kant issued a warning which Freud would have done well to heed: free association was likely to lead to deceptive results. Observation of the inner life by the inner sense should not be confused with observation of the external world by the external senses, he urged. When one attempted to "play the spy upon one's self," one was likely to find what one expected to find. This was because "without noticing it, we here make supposed discoveries of what we ourselves have introduced into our own minds" (17).

Kant's warning was prescient: the criticism that self-analysis by means of free association could not deliver the kind of evidence of the inner life which Freud expected of it has been one of the persistent objections to his mode of mental exploration. Freud was wont to compare the efforts of the psychoanalyst with the work of the archaeologist; both were in search of something hidden. But the comparison was dangerous. The archaeologist's expectations and hopes will not affect the discovery: either the ancient city will be there or it will not. The self-analyzer who possesses a theory, indeed, anticipations of any kind, is not in the same position. He is not free to wonder: "If I dig into my mind, will I find support for my hypothesis? If I let my thoughts emerge freely, will I come upon evidence for infantile sexuality?" The expectations accompanying the act of self-exploration will almost invariably evoke thoughts or feelings related to what is expected.

So far as Kant's foreboding is concerned, his worry that letting thoughts come to mind unsummoned and of their own accord, might lead to madness, some therapists today would agree that, in the case of people whose mental balance is already very precarious, free association might aggravate the imbalance.

In a note published in the *International Review of Psycho-Analysis*, the writer commented on "Kant's precise description of free association." Alan

A. Stone remarked that "Kant's description of spying on the self, written two centuries ago, suggests the futility of trying to determine exactly who discovered free association and how Freud and/or his patients came to this method. It is tempting to suggest that free association was a product of German philosophy's preoccupation with the nature of human subjectivity. . . . But that, if plausible, is not definitive. No doubt free association has been discovered and rediscovered throughout human history, it seems to be part of the repertoire of experiences of consciousness of self" (Stone, 445).

Given that the principle was understood, is it likely that free association, or something close to it, was used "throughout human history" for purposes of self-exploration? This seems unlikely, if for no other reason than that, through the long Christian centuries, "involuntary" thought was regarded with deep suspicion. The unleashed mind may indeed come upon much that is novel and beautiful, but it may also wander into sin.

In Medieval thought, the critical difference between voluntary and involuntary thought was that the soul was responsible for the first, but not the second. Human nature being what it was, souls were often beset by involuntary unholy thoughts, by unforeseen, sudden temptations, for instance. Such thoughts had to be squelched immediately. Voluntarily allowing the thought further entry into the mind, voluntarily indulging it, dwelling on it with "concupiscence"—this could be a ticket to hell, enjoyable rumination about a sin being as culpable as committing the sin itself.

This attitude toward the liberated flow of ideas outlasted the Middle Ages. At the dawn of the Enlightenment, Leibniz, commenting on "involuntary thoughts," noted that "even when we are awake we are visited by images . . . which come to us unbidden as in dreams. In German they are called *fliegende Gedanken*, meaning "flying thoughts"; they are not within our power, and they are sometimes full of irrationalities which provide upright people with moments of moral unease, and provide much work for casuists and directors of consciences" (1981, #177).

It seems likely, therefore, that letting go of rational control in order to deliberately open the door to such "flying thoughts" could not have been a recommended practice during the long Christian era. The pious had to keep close watch on what they allowed into their minds. Only when the fear of hell-fire had lost its grip would people have been able to let down their mental guard to permit "flying thoughts" to enter freely. It seems likely therefore that freely associating to explore the hidden reaches of the mind was an innovation of the Enlightenment. This would explain why instances of it turn up, apparently suddenly, during this era.

Free association was not forgotten thereafter. Perhaps the most serious pre-Freudian treatment of the subject was that of Eduard von Hartmann, who discussed it in his *Philosophy of the Unconscious*, a book published in 1869 which came out in a series of editions thereafter. Freud denied that he had taken the concept from Hartmann (see chapter 10).

By the middle of the eighteenth century, the Leibniz-Wolffian philosophy was faltering. It was given the coup de grace in 1781 when Kant published *The Critique of Pure Reason.* With its rigid structure, dogmatic principles and oversupply of meticulous classifications, it was brushed aside as irrelevant by the rebellious spirits of the early Romantic age. And when it died, the Leibniz-Wolffian philosophy died for good; it was not destined to surge to renewed life at a later time as other philosophies, shelved for a while, had done. Philosophers, when they have thought of it at all, have dismissed it as insignificant.

However, if we dislodge the psychology and pluck it out for separate evaluation, the picture changes. Wolff then must be accorded a modest but honorable place in history, the history, not of philosophy, but of psychology. The distinction between the philosophy and the psychology explains the different treatments accorded to Wolff by philosophers and by those few psychologists who have paid any attention to him, notably D.B. Klein (1970, 467–475). This historian regarded Wolff as an important contributor to the development of a psychological discipline, noting, among other things, his recognition of the distinction between a philosophical and a scientific psychology. These lines were not strictly drawn in Wolff's time, nor did he firmly draw them, but he succeeded in rousing interest in the question.

Wolff's greatest service to psychology was undoubtedly the support he gave to the concept of the unconscious. His treatment of it as an empirical hypothesis and his promulgation of the central premise in the language of common sense, made it attractive to the host of his disciples. These, in turn, through voluminous writings, assured the survival of the idea. By the time Wolffian philosophy died, the psychology had achieved a life of its own and was firmly anchored even in the minds of those who were otherwise Wolff's opponents. This was the case with Immanuel Kant. When he turned his attention to psychology, he went back to the concept of clear and dark ideas and to the irresistible comparison of these ideas with objects either sparkling in the sunshine of consciousness or shrouded in blackest night.

It was in a Leibniz-Wolffian spirit that Kant wrote:

> To have ideas and still not to be conscious of them seems to be a contradiction; for how can we know that we have them unless we are conscious of them? This objection has already been raised by Locke, who on that account rejected the existence of such a type of ideas. Nevertheless, we can be indirectly conscious of having an idea, although we are not directly conscious of it. . . . Sense perceptions and sensations of which we are not aware but whose existence we can undoubtedly infer, that is, obscure ideas in both man and animals, constitute an immeasurable field. . . . It is as if just a few places on the vast map of our mind were illuminated. This can inspire wonder at our own being;

> for a higher power would need only cry, "Let there be light" and then, without further action . . . there would be laid open before the eyes half a universe (1978, 19).

Kant's picture of the mind as a great dark map lit up only here and there by points of light joined the metaphors that contrasted something huge and unknown with something known but exceedingly small: the little islands in the enormous sea, the tip of the iceberg and its hidden mass, the thin surface of the earth and its dark interior. It differed from these, however, in reflecting its era: it was an instance of the ubiquitous illumination metaphor.

Chapter Seven

The Cartesian Unconscious

Descartes has long been regarded as the philosopher who limited "thought" to "conscious thought." When he said "I think, therefore I am," what he meant was "I think *consciously*, therefore I am.

He has come in for some negative appraisals on this account, the assumption being that his theory had retarded recognition of unconscious mental states. One critic suggested that Descartes may have committed "one of the fundamental blunders made by the human mind" (Whyte, 1962, 23). Another added that "the Cartesian catastrophe . . . the *identification of 'mind' with conscious thinking*" was responsible for "an impoverishment of psychology which it took three centuries to remedy even in part" (Koestler, in Whyte 1978, Introduction).

It seems, however, that Descartes could dispense with the unconscious *mind* because he had at his disposal—the unconscious *brain*. Consider, for instance, Descartes's explanation of an emotional response that would now typically be attributed to the unconscious mind. In *Passions of the Soul*, he writes:

> Joy proceeds from the belief that we have of possessing some good, and sadness from the belief that we have of possessing some evil or defect. It often, however, happens that we feel sad or joyful without being thus able distinctly to observe the good or evil which are the causes of it; e.g. when this good or this evil *form their impression in the brain without the intermission of the soul,"* that is to say, without the intermission of consciousness (italics added; 1973, 373).

As an instance of the soul's unawareness of its own motives, Descartes suggested the risk-taking behavior of young people: they perhaps supposed that they loved danger for its own sake. In reality, however, they might be motivated by the unconscious association that being fearless is considered admirable. Passions may be "excited by the things good and evil which the soul does not notice even though they belong to it" (374).

Memories imprinted on the brain persisted, Descartes assumed. This persistence explained how it was that infantile traumas could have a lifelong, unrecognized influence. Descartes offered this explanation for mysterious phobias: "It is easy to reflect that the strange aversions of certain people which prevent their being able to endure the scent of roses or the presence of a cat, or things of that sort, only proceed from the fact that at the beginning of their lives they have suffered much unpleasantness through some such objects . . . the scent of roses may have caused a severe headache to a child while still in the cradle, or a cat may have terrified him without anyone having been aware of it, or of any memory remaining of it afterwards, although the idea of aversion which he then had for these roses or for this cat remain *imprinted on his brain* to the end of his life" (italics added; 391).

In this passage, Descartes was clearly describing the kind of symptom which would be recognized, at the end of the nineteenth century, as phobic: the memory link between cause and effect had been severed; the cause was forgotten but continued to operate, producing inexplicable behavior. In the one case, nausea caused by the heavy scent of roses resulted in a permanent antipathy to the aroma, in the other, a trauma experienced in the cradle brought on a phobia, a lifelong fear of cats.

Not only stressful memories survived to produce effects in later life; pleasant memories could be just as potent as the painful; sympathies as well as antipathies could rise from events that were beyond recall. Descartes attributed a strange attraction that a certain kind of woman had held for him as having been due to what would later be called "transference."

Descartes reported that he himself had for a long time been attracted to women who unconsciously reminded him of a love of his early years.

> When I was a child I loved a girl of my own age who had a slight squint. Because of that, the impression made upon my brain by the sight of her crossed eyes so closely joined itself to that [impression] which aroused in me the feeling of love, that for a long time afterward, in seeing cross-eyed persons, I felt myself more inclined to love them than others, only because they had this defect; nevertheless, I did not know that was the reason. On the contrary, since I have reflected upon it, and recognized it was a defect, I have no longer been affected by it. Thus, when we are drawn toward loving someone without knowing the cause for it, we can believe it stems from the fact that there is something in them similar to what was in another

> object we loved previously, although we do not know what it is (1978, 263).

Descartes was not alone in this assumption. Malebranche and Locke also assumed that attitudes, positive and negative, or what were frequently called "sympathies and antipathies," were frequently transferred.

PERSISTENCE OF INFANTILE MEMORIES

Nicolas Malebranche, a follower of Descartes, arguing that some childhood memories could not be effaced, suggested that *all* of the unique sympathies and antipathies whose origins a person could not recall, originated in childhood:

> If men would seriously reflect upon what occurs within themselves, and in their own thoughts, they would not lack evidence for proving what has just been said. They would ordinarily recognize secret inclinations and aversions in themselves, which others do not have, for which it seems that we can give no other explanation than these traces from our earliest days. For since the causes of these inclinations and aversions are particular to us [as individuals], they are not founded in the nature of man; and since they are unknown to us, they must have acted upon us at a time when our memories were not yet capable of retaining the settings of things, which would have enabled us to remember them. This time could be no other than our most tender infancy (1997, 126).

Astonishingly, John Locke went along with this. We are unaware of the source of most of our inclinations, he maintained; forgotten memories, but also unremembered fantasies, can have powerful effects; they can produce strange, anomalous behavior which is inexplicable because its cause is unknown. It is almost as perplexing to find such ideas entertained by Locke as it is to discover them in Descartes. Locke too is generally regarded as having equated mind and consciousness; in fact, he firmly proclaimed his opposition to the notion of unconscious thought, and yet, here we find him, apparently happy in company with Leibniz (1959, Vol. 1, 527–535).

Locke believed that peculiarities of behavior, such as inexplicable sympathies or antipathies, were usually caused by associations that could not be recalled, or, in later parlance, unconscious associations. In a very influential essay on the association of ideas, Locke began by stressing the power with which association could link even the most irrational and peculiar thoughts. A child warned that goblins lurked in the dark might ever afterward fear the dark, the ideas being so firmly joined. Ideas could "come to be so united in some men's minds that it is very hard to separate them; they always keep in company, and the one no sooner at any times comes into the understanding, but its associate appears with it" (529). A man watches a friend die in a particular room; although the event and the room have nothing to do with one another, "yet when the idea of the place occurs to his mind, it brings . . . that of the pain and displeasure with it; he confounds them in his mind, and can as little bear the one as the other" (532).

These fusions explain some bizarre behavior; because of the associations they evoked, "there are rooms convenient enough, that some men cannot study in, and fashions of vessels, which, though ever so clean and commodious, they cannot drink out of" (533). These aversions could be explained so long as the disagreeable ideas associated with the rooms of the vessels were known. The situation changed when the associated ideas were unknown: the behavior then became incomprehensible.

Mysterious behaviors were often attributed to the person's innate constitution, Locke noted. They were considered to be "natural" peculiarities with which he or she was born. In fact, however, he declared, most of these anomalies were probably acquired, the associations that caused them being forgotten. He furnished an example: suppose that "a grown person [at one time] surfeited with honey no sooner hears the name of it, but his fancy immediately carries sickness and qualms to his stomach, and he cannot bear the very idea of it, other ideas of dislike, and sickness and vomiting, presently accompany it, and he is disturbed; but he knows from when to date this weakness, and can tell how he got this indisposition. Had this happened to him by an overdose of honey when a child, all the same effects would have followed; but the cause would have been mistaken, and the antipathy counted natural" (1959, 531). The person would have gone through life feeling sick whenever he so much as heard the word "honey" and, not recalling the original incident, would have blamed it on his "constitution."[1]

Boldly, Locke concluded that there were such wrong associations in most minds "and to this, perhaps, might be justly attributed most of the sympathies and antipathies observable in men, which work as strongly, and produce as regular effects as if they were natural" (1959, 530). Some antipathies, of course, really were constitutional, "but a great part of those which are counted natural, would have been known to be from unheeded, though perhaps early, impressions, or wanton fancies" whose causal connection to the later behavior could have been recognized "if they had been warily observed" at the time (531).

One might suppose that Locke's proposition that "most" of our inclinations, positive and negative, are attributable to memories that remain effective even though they are inaccessible, would move Locke into the camp of philosophers who supported the concept of unconscious mind. However, this would be a mistake. Consider Locke's explanation for the development of a phobia. It begins with an event which has an impact on the mind. No thought is required to produce this impact. Thereafter, association produces the phobia; but associations are automatic; they are not mental actions; they happen;

no thought is required. What Locke has given us is an explanation of unconsciously determined events which can be accepted by opponents of unconscious thought.

Locke's description of the acquisition of "sympathies and antipathies," with its homely examples, apparently contributed to the acceptance of the concept. Locke's prestige in Britain and on the Continent was enormous; the German physiologist, Johann August Unzer, more than a century after Locke, may have owed more to the English philosopher than he did to Leibniz when he wrote about the effects of both conscious and unconscious associations: "a certain person always faints during the operation of venesection (bloodletting). Some time afterwards, he meets the surgeon in the street and becomes faint," the faintness being due to the foreseeing of future bloodletting. "We sigh at the sight of a person who is like another, with respect to whom we have had sorrowful sensations." He adds: "A person sees a visionary image of a figure and becomes pale with fear. It is the resemblance of an individual who long ago caused him bitter vexation. The pallor comes on before it is remembered whom the figure resembles, and simply from the repeated sensation, without the recognition. How often in such cases we hear persons say: "this appearance terrifies, effects, and calms me, without my knowing why; some subordinate ideas, which I cannot remember, must be the cause." When the person whose figure we have seen actually appears, no other actions result than as stated above, we become pale as before, but now we know why" (Altschule, 60). Unzer's remark about the frequency with which people expressed the opinion that an emotion had an unconscious cause, indicates that the premise was rather widely recognized at the time.

A century after Unzer, apparently commonplace, the concept was expounded in the psychology textbook which Freud studied as a teenager. Here, the definition of "sympathies and antipathies" stressed that they were unconscious. Students were advised that consciously understood feelings of empathy or dislike "must be distinguished from those of sympathy and antipathy, that is, from feelings of unconscious attraction or aversion with respect to living or inanimate things. We feel sympathy or antipathy towards people whom we meet but once in our lives, towards parrots and apes, towards landscapes and cities, without being able to give definite reasons why. . . . These feelings are based upon obscure ideas that are associated with the idea of the object in question and [these ideas] produce in us positive or negative feelings. . . . The man who makes such a strong claim to our sympathy may perhaps bear a facial feature that vaguely reminds us of beloved people; the valley that so moves us may bear a resemblance to the open fields and meadows of our native land, etc." (Lindner, 1872, 166). Presumably Freud became acquainted with the concept of "transference" at this time, if he had not learned it earlier.

The expression "transference" was apparently in general use. Friedrich Jodl, influential Viennese psychologist, used the expression as synonym for "sympathies or antipathies" in his textbook in 1903. He explained that "every experience that has a particular emotional value *transfers* (*übertraegt*) this value to what is associatively connected with it, according to the general laws of association. . . . Phenomena otherwise regarded as inexplicable, the so-called instinctual *sympathies or antipathies* (*Zuneignung oder Abneigung*), idiosyncrasies of every kind, are rooted in such *transference* of feelings" (italics added; 1903, 125).

Years later, the old expression survived in one of Freud's expositions of his theory of neurosis: "What children have experienced at the age of two and have not understood, need never be remembered by them except in dreams; they may only come to know of it through psychoanalytic treatment. But at some later time it will break into their life with obsessional impulses, it will govern their actions, it will decide their *sympathies and antipathies*, and will quite often determine their choice of a love object, for which it is so frequently impossible to find a rational basis" (italics added; *S.E.,* XXIII: 126).

Some evidence that sympathies and antipathies may have unconscious determinants has already been supplied by modern cognitive psychologists; John F. Kihlstrom has commented that "in the social domain, speakers may like one face more than another, while being unable to say exactly why they have that preference. A large number of social judgments and inferences, especially those guiding first impressions, appear to be mediated by such unconscious processes." These "automatic processes are themselves unconscious in that the person has no introspective access to their principles of operation—or even the fact that they are in operation at all" (1987, 1447).

More controversial, and probably also more difficult to explore, is the auxiliary hypothesis that determining events may occur at an extremely early age and that, moreover, a single event may have long-lasting, unfortunate consequences. Freud's "seduction theory" was based on this idea. He suggested that a sexual experience, occurring at the age of one-and-a-half, or even less, could be responsible for neurotic repercussions later in life. This assumption was also very old; we have seen that Descartes supposed that a child in the cradle, frightened on one occasion by a cat, might go through life with a cat phobia. Leibniz, sharing this opinion, noted that, although usually associations between ideas are formed as a result of numerous experiences, a single trauma could produce the same result: "a single very strong impression, may, by its very intensity, instantly have as much effect as could be had by a repetition of mild impressions over a long period of time; and so this intensity may etch into the imagination as deep and vivid an image as prolonged experience produces." This could happen even in infancy; Leibniz recalled that "there was a gentleman who could not stand to see a badly fastened pin without feeling faint, because he had once been hurt by one, perhaps when he was a baby" (1982, 271–272).

Malebranche was bolder than anyone else when he anticipated the theory of Freud's disciple Otto Rank by proposing that one dreadful early experience was universal: the birth trauma. Malebranche empathized with the infant who, emerging from the darkness and comfort of the womb, encountered light for the first time, felt the cold of the outside air and was confronted with a whole world of terrifying unknown objects: "the tears and cries with which it consoles itself are infallible signs of its pain and fear." It is true that confusion, pain and injury suffered then are generally healed by time: "This is what generally keeps all men from being mad from birth. But that does not keep some impressions from being so strong and deep they can never be erased, and so they remain with us throughout our lives" (1997, 125–6).

Phobias about roses or cats, inexplicable nausea and vomiting, fear of pins, would have been regarded as hysterical symptoms by those late nineteenth-century medical researchers who were willing to assume that a very early trauma could have lasting consequences. They did not, however, attempt to subject the hypothesis to experimental investigation.

Such an investigation was undertaken in 1920 by behaviorist John B. Watson who, most likely without being aware of it, tested Descartes' hypothesis about traumatized babies, using a white rat instead of a Cartesian cat. He successfully induced a conditioned fear response in a nine-month-old infant, subsequently identified in the literature as "little Albert." Watson supposed that the conditioning of Albert was likely to last. He believed that, with this experiment, he had successfully challenged the Freudian emphasis on infantile sexuality as determinant of adult behavior. He had proved that "fear is as primal a factor as love in influencing personality." With apparent amusement, he speculated that "twenty years from now," the irrational fear of a fur coat might bring the grown-up Albert to Freudian analysis (1920, 14).[2]

THE POSSIBILITY OF PSYCHOTHERAPY

Benedikt de Spinoza affirmed the power of unconscious determinants as decisively as any of his contemporaries; but notably, he suggested that the tyranny of the unconscious might not be inescapable. Leibniz's comparison of the conscious mind with a compass needle moved by a magnet implies that people are helplessly driven by their unconscious proclivities. Spinoza, however, supposed that relative freedom could be attained by a mental clarification that has been compared to Freud's bringing the unconscious into consciousness. Because of this premise, Spinoza has sometimes been acclaimed as the latter's precursor. One of Freud`s disciples, the writer Lou

Andreas-Salomé, dubbed him "the philosopher of psychoanalysis" (Neu, 1977, 150).

Spinoza refused worldly positions and safeguarded his philosophical independence by making a modest living grinding lenses. A Jew, he was expelled from the synagogue for his unorthodox views. However, admirers broke into his isolation; one who visited his Amsterdam abode was Leibniz who was influenced by his psychology, deriving from him, for instance, the metaphor which compared the heedless, unconscious action of an instinct with the fall of a stone. During his lifetime, many reviled Spinoza as an atheist; his influence spread only slowly. Then, however, a century after his death, it mushroomed, particularly in the German-speaking nations. An historian, surveying the period, noted that "the rise of Spinozism in the late eighteenth century is a phenomenon of no less significance than the emergence of Kantianism itself" (Beiser, 1987, 48). In the last quarter of the eighteenth century, almost all of the intellectual leaders had become enthusiastic followers of Spinoza (Beiser, 44).

Spinoza's psychology, like most others, was founded on the traditional plan in which sober reason, governed, or attempted to govern the impetuous appetites but, like Leibniz, he added to it the dimension of the unconscious. "Appetite" was what it had always been: "the essence of man," consisting of "all those endeavours of human nature, which we distinguish by the terms appetite, will, desire, or impulse." However, as he saw it, appetite was unconscious; when it became conscious, it was called "desire." He asserted that "between appetite and desire there is no difference, except that the term desire is generally applied to men, in so far as they are conscious of their appetite, and may accordingly be thus defined: *desire is appetite with consciousness thereof* (italics added; 1955, 137). He added "I recognize no distinction between appetite and desire, for whether a man be conscious of his appetite or not, it remains one and the same appetite" (173).

From appetite sprang the emotions which ruled the mind; the passions, not reason, dominated thought and action. Emotion was the factor "by the presence of which the mind is determined to think of one thing rather than another" (1955, 185). However, emotions did not always determine thought in a uniform direction because they often conflicted: "By conflicting emotions I mean those which draw a man in different directions" (1955, 191). The intellect alone was helpless against the force of emotion, for "the emotion which we undergo can only be checked or destroyed by an emotion contrary to, and stronger than, itself." As a result, "a man is necessarily always a prey to his passions" (194–195).

Like his contemporary, Locke, Spinoza assumed that an object could stir powerful feelings merely because it was associated with something else which was the real source of the reaction. There are objects "which affect us unpleasurably or painfully, simply because they resemble other objects which affect us in the same way (1955, 141). Therefore "we understand how it may happen that we love or hate a thing without any cause for our emotion being known to us" (141).

The principle of unconscious determinism was espoused by Spinoza in no uncertain terms; the belief in free will was erroneous. "In the mind there is no absolute or free will; but the mind is determined to wish this or that by a cause." Free will was an illusion. "Experience teaches us no less clearly than reason, that men believe themselves to be free, simply because they are conscious of their actions, and unconscious of the causes whereby those actions are determined." However, some relative freedom was attainable. Spinoza believed that being at the mercy of overwhelming passion always involved some degree of ignorance. To heighten one's awareness, to put order into the confusion of thoughts, was to weaken the passion and thereby to escape its domination: "An emotion, which is a passion, ceases to be a passion, as soon as we form a clear and distinct idea thereof." He adds, "An emotion therefore becomes more under our control, and the mind is less passive in respect to it, in proportion as it is more known to us" (1955, 248).

A psychoanalytically oriented scholar, Jerome Neu, remarked about this concept that "the movement from confused ideas and passive emotion to more adequate ideas and active emotion through the 'correction of the understanding' is very much like the movement towards freedom and self-determination through making the unconscious conscious" (1977, 148–151). In the following century, it would be suggested that the "correction of the understanding" could be implemented by deliberately attempting to bring unconscious contents into consciousness and the method recommended would be the free association of ideas.

NOTES

1. That Locke's position on unconscious thought was inconsistent was pointed out soon after his book was published. In 1690, the English Platonist philosopher, John Norris, noted that Locke had insisted that nothing could be "imprinted" on the mind without the mind's having first consciously perceived it. However, he had also speculated that children might acquire some ideas very early, perhaps even in the womb, before they were born. Norris commented caustically "and if before they are born, then certainly before they are conscious of them" (1978, 8).

2. In 1916, Watson said of himself that he had been "for some years an earnest student of Freud" and that he was "convinced of the truth of Freud's work." He welcomed dream interpretation (Watson, 1916a, 590 and 592). Agreeing that slips of the tongue could reveal suppressed wishes, he analyzed the slips of his acquaintances (1916b, 481 and 483). He explained that he was trying "in a popular way to rewrite the essentials of Freud's theory in terms of behavior" (1917a, 92). He appreciated Freud's concept of "transference," but explained that it was "nothing more or less than habit formation" (1917b, 168).

Chapter Eight

The Demonic Unconscious

The discovery of repression, the power that constrains innate human savagery, is still often mentioned as one of Freud's greatest achievements. It is admired as a unique psychoanalytic contribution to psychology, a contribution made possible by the exploratory method he had devised. Use of the method supposedly enabled him to descend to previously unsuspected depths of the mind. Here he was brought face-to-face with crude, instinctual desires which, clamoring for satisfaction, were held in check by an opposing moral force. It has been suggested that, were it not for Freud's use of the analytic method, the phenomenon of repression might have remained forever undetected. Freud himself was certain that this was so; repression, he declared, was "a concept which could not have been formulated before the time of psychoanalytic studies" (*S.E.*, XIV: 146).

Freud was appalled at what he believed he had found in the mind's lowest region: the "evil in the constitution of human beings" (*S.E.,* XV: 146). He pulled no punches in his condemnation of the loathsome desires he thought he had discovered: "Lusts which we think of as remote from human nature, hatred, raging without restraint, "wishes for revenge and death directed against those who are nearest and dearest in waking life." These monstrous appetites were kept out of the conscious mind during waking hours; they made their presence known, however, in dreams. It was then that sexual desire "chooses its objects without inhibition, and by preference, indeed, the forbidden ones; not only other men's wives, but above all incestuous objects, objects sanctified by the common agreement of mankind, a man's mother and sister, a woman's father and brother" (*S.E.,* XV: 142–143). Freud declared that "these censored wishes appear to rise up out of a positive hell (*S.E.,* XV: 143).

The "positive hell" was the unconscious—the "unconscious system" of his first theory and the unconscious "Id" of the second. Between this monstrous unconscious and the conscious moral self lay the protective wall provided by repression.

According to Freud's basic definition, "the essence of repression lies simply in turning something away, and keeping it at a distance, from the conscious" (*S.E.,* XIV: 147). For repression to occur, there must be a force "which is seeking to express something and another which is striving to prevent its expression" (*S.E.,* II: 14). The appearance in consciousness of unacceptable desires when repression failed was referred to as "the return of the repressed." During sleep, when the repressive force weakened, repressed desires could make their way into dreams where their presence could be detected.

The very assumption that the mind was divided and that conflict occurred between these divisions, notions upon which the concept of repression rested, has been attributed to Freud. According to the eminent psychoanalyst Charles Brenner (1982, 5), "the concept of psychic conflict was one of Freud's earliest discoveries." Freud had supposedly realized, while treating neurotic patients that their symptoms were caused by a clash of antithetical motives. This insight had given rise to the model designed to explain the occurrence of inevitable mental storms and stresses.

But ideas this basic are usually not new; certainly they are not uniquely Freudian. A researcher, looking for their origins, traveling back into the past, will come upon a supposedly "Freudian" idea in seventeenth-century France, then, continuing, will find it in fifteenth-century Germany. Thereafter, it can be followed through the Renaissance and the Middle Ages and finally, by an easy hop, to antiquity. The lesson taught by such a trip is that all of these ages shared one psychology and that the fundamentals of this psychology tend to be Greek. Therefore, no mere antiquarian interest takes us back to the remote past. We may gain a sense of psychology's continuity and may come to recognize the futility of arguments about the priority of some of our most important ideas.

Mental conflict has always been recognized. Everyday human experience mandates a theory that partitions the mind, one that acknowledges its constant, often painful, struggle to harmonize disparate intentions and colliding desires.

No one has explained the connection between the sensing of inner division and the classical theory of mental functioning more simply than Plato in *Republic*. Plato described a minor conflict taking place between the wishing and the restraining forces of the soul. The wish blindly demanded satisfaction: "The soul of the thirsty then, insofar as it thirsts, wishes nothing else than to drink and yearns for this and its impulse is towards this." This being so, then, "if anything draws it back when thirsty, it must be something different in it from that which thirsts and drives it like a beast to drink." Therefore, since people sometimes refuse to drink, even though they are thirsty, we must conclude that "there is a something in the soul that bids them drink and a something that forbids." Having concluded from this fact of inhibition that two principles are necessarily involved, one desiring, the other restraining, he decided to name "that in the soul whereby it reckons and reasons the rational, and that with which it loves, hungers and thirsts, and feels the flutter and titillation of other desires, the irrational and appetitive" (439a–c).

Here, in the fourth century before Christ, we have the essential split between two mental powers that will serve as the fundamental principle of Western psychology—confirming Alfred North Whitehead's assessment that "the development of European philosophy consists of a series of footnotes to Plato" (1979, 39). Since psychology was a part of philosophy until modern times, this appraisal applies to psychology as well.

In this view of human nature, *reason*—called variously "the soul," "intellect," "will," or "ego"—will conflict with the *irrational*—designated as the "passions," "appetite," or "animal instincts." Reason, prudent and capable of foresight aimed to control the irrational passions which demanded the immediate gratification of urges, including the sexual and the aggressive.

These features are essentially those of the "ego" and the "id" of Freud's later and best-known theory. The id is the irrational, instinctual component, origin of all motivational energy. The rational ego evaluates conditions and anticipates consequences, aims to restrain and channel expression of the id. Freud himself was aware of these ancient antecedents of his theory, noting that "the ego represents what may be called reason and common sense, by contrast to the id, which contains the passions. All this falls into line with popular distinctions which we are all familiar with" (*S.E.,* XIX: 25). Freud did not originate these concepts, nor did he maintain that he had originated them. He forgot, however, that the belief that the passions could be repressed was just as familiar. Let us return to Plato.

Having introduced the concept of conflict between appetite and rationality with reference to an imperative urge to drink and the restraining control which forbade drinking, Plato went on to apply the distinction to the management of sexual desire. The theory of "subjugation" that he developed was essentially identical with Freud's postulate of "repression."

In a famous metaphor in his *Phaedrus*, Plato pictured the conflict engendered in the soul dealing with a serious, sexual temptation as the struggle of a charioteer to control one of a pair of horses. The charioteer and the well-behaved white horse are moral forces. The black horse, however, deaf, ugly, hot-blooded and wanton—clearly the counterpart of the Freudian Id—is in full rebellion. The driver manages to draw him back for a moment but he then immediately rushes forward again—"struggling and neighing and pulling," he "shamelessly plunges on." And this "happens time and again" (253d).

It would seem that the black horse could be tamed only temporarily; the immoral instincts were subdued with difficulty and their subjection would always be temporary. However, Plato had second thoughts. In a work which scholarship attributes to his later years, he concluded that the sexual appetite was not only controllable but was, in actuality, subject to widespread taming.

Plato offered his *Laws* (837b–838b) as suggestions for the improvement of society. As the elderly philosopher looked about him, it seemed to him that human beings might well be happier under other arrangements. The adoption of his proposals might bring about a better world. He hesitated, however, when confronted with the difficulty of regulating sex.

Uncontrolled sexual desire was undoubtedly responsible for much of the strife, misery and grief which afflicted humankind. Governing this passion would certainly be beneficial. But what law would be able to contain the "fierce and furious" sexual drive? The problem might have seemed hopeless, but for one thing: evidence that the sexual passion could be subdued was offered by the paucity of incest.

This rarity was perplexing: how was it that the imperious sexual urge was quiescent, just where one might imagine that its activity could have been at its height? One might have supposed that it would run rampant in the close confines of family life. And yet, this did not happen: the father did not sexually enjoy the daughter; the mother did not have intercourse with the son. Brothers and sisters, however sexually attractive they might be, lived together in affectionate but unerotic intimacy. Typically they did not even have to ward off temptation; they did not even experience it.

Plato decided that the urge for sexual satisfaction with near relatives, although it was an inborn passion, had been forcibly suppressed in early childhood, so "subjugated" that it disappeared from the conscious mind. The complete conquest of the forbidden desire was accomplished by means of a terrible and total taboo against incest with which the child was confronted from the beginning of life. Everywhere, these lusts were condemned as "unhallowed, abominations to God, deeds of black shame." "All of us," Plato declared, "from our very cradles, are constantly hearing the same report of them from all quarters," and we never hear of a contrary opinion (*Laws*, 838c). When a law, albeit unwritten, is given support such as this "the minds of all will be subjugated" (839c). Therefore, "even today . . . lawless as most men are, they are very effectually deterred from cohabitation with the fair [relatives], and not against their own will either, but with their full and entire consent" (838a). "The same law [that protects siblings] . . . proves a complete safeguard of son and daughter—so much so that no one lies with them, openly or covertly, or approaches them with any familiarities of that sort." When subjugation is complete, "the very wish for such congress never so much as enters the mind of the ordinary person" (838b). This did not mean, however, that the subjugated wishes no longer existed. "Subjugated" did not mean "eliminated"; it implied survival. Plato assumed, as did Freud, that these desires were merely kept out of awareness but that they retained their strength and were forever ready to escape when the moral pressure against them slackened. When this happened during sleep, they were "freed from restraint" and made their way into dreams (*Republic*, 574d).

In the dreams described by Plato, satisfaction was accorded to both incestuous desires and wishes for murder: "there exists in every one of us, even in some reputed most respectable, a terrible, fierce, and lawless brood of desires, which it seems are revealed in our sleep" (*Republic*, 572b). Then "the rest of the soul, the rational, gentle and dominant part, slumbers, but the beastly and savage part, replete with food and wine, gambols and, repelling sleep, endeavours to sally forth and satisfy its own instincts. You are aware that in such case there is nothing it will not venture to undertake as being released from all sense of shame and all reason. It does not shrink from attempting to lie with a mother in fancy or with anyone else, man, god, or brute. It is ready for any foul deed of blood; it abstains from no food, and, in a word, falls short of no extreme of folly and shamelessness" (571c).

Condemning both unbridled sexuality and ruthless aggression, Plato compared humankind to a herd of bovines dominated by two primordial urges—which we recognize as Freud's two basic instincts, sex and aggression: "with eyes ever bent upon the earth and heads bowed down over their tables they feast like cattle, grazing and copulating, ever greedy for more of these delights, and in their greed kicking and butting one another with horns and hoofs of iron they slay one another in sateless avidity" (*Republic*, 586b).

In normal, waking life, these passions were tamed. If they were not, the human being acting under these impulses would be "the most evil type of man." Such a one would "refrain from no atrocity of murder nor from any food or deed, but the passion that dwells in him as a tyrant will live in utmost anarchy and lawlessness" (*Republic*, 574e). He would, in waking hours, manifest the savagery otherwise found only in the dream state (576b).

Plato's "subjugation" clearly meets Freud's definition of "repression," namely that "the essence of repression lies simply in turning something away, and keeping it at a distance, from the conscious" (*S.E.,* XIV: 147). Both Plato and Freud assumed that what had to be kept "at a distance" were incestuous and murderous desires and both believed that these desires were revealed by dreams.

The Platonic conception features the essential hallmarks of the Freudian theory: the mind's division into moral and immoral powers, the two instincts, the resulting psychic conflict, the conquest of the immoral by repression. Moreover, the theories are identical in their assumption of what might be called an "economic" principle: both can be expressed in terms of mental "forces" possessing varying degrees of strength. An instinctual desire is a force which, attempting to break into consciousness, is restrained by a stronger, moral force. In sleep, the balance of forces changes; the moral is weakened but the instinctual retains its strength and is then in a position to overcome the restraint. Both theories assume the continuing existence of desires outside of consciousness, that is to say, they accept that a portion of the mind is unconscious. They hold that a mental content can become unconscious, can retain its vitality in this state, and, given the required relationship between forces, can return to consciousness. I assert that any theory which features these principles, regardless of the language in which it is expressed, must be recognized as a "repression" theory.

TWO FUNDAMENTAL APPETITES

The continuity between the ancient past and the present may be illustrated by the survival, over the centuries, of Plato's two troublesome urges, the passions for copulating and killing. Picked up by St. Augustine in the fourth century of our era, they appeared in Christianity as the two fundamental "appetites." Following Plato, Augustine insisted on the perverting effect on the soul of these two drives which he called the "dyad" of lust and anger (1986, #15). He contrasted the unity of the soul, which entailed goodness and rationality, with the disunity brought about by the troubling dyad, "anger that leads to crimes of violence and the lust that leads to sins of passion" (1986, #15).[1]

Eight centuries later, another great theologian, St. Thomas Aquinas, taught the doctrine of "irascible" and "concupiscent" appetites in *Summa Theologica,* and as such they remained basic components of Christian psychology down to modern times. However, Aquinas qualified the theory; he suggested that the concupiscent and the irascible appetites were not on a par, the latter being in the service of the former. The irascible appetite did not aim at destruction for its own sake; it destroyed where need be, in order to safeguard the interests of the concupisible appetite (1945, 773).[2]

In the seventeenth century, Descartes was tired of the two old appetites. Why, he asked in *The Passions of the Soul*, should all of human motivation be explained in terms of only two drives? His comments indicate how entrenched the two-appetite hypothesis was, for he remarked that "in this I know well that I am parting company with all those who have written on this subject before." All of these writers, he asserted, distinguished two appetites in the soul, which they name the concupiscent and irascible respectively . . . this seems to me to signify nothing but that [the soul] has two faculties, the one of desire, and the other of anger, and because in the same way it has the faculties of wondering, loving, hoping, fearing, and thus of receiving in itself every other passion or else bringing about actions to which these passions urge it, I do not see why they have desired to refer them all to concupiscence or anger" (1973, 362). However, in spite of Descartes's protest, the two appetites endured.

In the twentieth century, Freud, after having experimented with a variety of instincts, settled for a time on the sexual and the aggressive as fundamental; in this "dual instinct" theory, they were outfitted with their own energies, the sexual and the aggressive. The repression theory in which they appeared, however, was the direct descendant of a conception that had been described by Plato.

ORIGINAL SIN

What remains to be explained is the almost unbelievable longevity of repression theory. How is it that one can dip into history, from one age to the next, and consistently come up with the belief in the existence of a moral force which pushes and keeps the immoral, instinctual out of the conscious mind? What we find is that much of the staying power of the theory is due to its having been the perfect auxiliary for the doctrine of "original sin" which burdened the people of Europe for many centuries. According to this terrifying doctrine, a single unconfessed transgression could doom the soul to the everlasting flames of hell. The dread of damnation, easy to incur, hard to avoid, burdened entire populations, in the opinion of French historian Jean Delumeau. The "Western guilt culture" condemned "an entire civilization" to a preoccupation with original sin. "It is no exaggeration to assert that the debate over original sin and its diverse by-products . . . came to be one of the prime obsessions of Western civilization, a concern of all people, from the theologians to the most modest peasants" (1990, 250 and 248).

The doctrine of original sin was the teaching of Augustine, saint and founding father of the church, of whom it has been said that he was one of the most influential men who ever lived, his opinions carrying weight for at least a millennium and a half.

According to his teaching, the infant was born in a state of sin, having inherited this condition from Adam and Eve; the guilt accrued by their eating the forbidden fruit was passed onto their descendants in perpetuity. Temporary relief from guilt could be obtained by confession but the state of innocence lasted only up to the moment when the next sin was committed. The temptation to sin meanwhile welled up unceasingly from the soul's wicked foundation. Conflict was therefore inescapable; the soul had to defend itself perpetually against the welling up of its own inclinations. The person dying in a state of sin was dammed.

THE UNCONSCIOUS SIN

Given his harsh, uncompromising doctrine, what must have been Augustine's horror when, as a result of his self-analysis in *Confessions*, he discovered that he himself had been harboring an unconfessed sin, a sin which he had been unable to confess because he had not been aware of it. According to his own principle, that a sin was unconscious would not exculpate the sinner; it could doom him as certainly as would the most conscious, deliberate depravity. He realized that he had been deceiving himself; having sworn to put aside all worldly ambitions and to serve only the Lord, he found that he had assiduously been seeking the approval of his fellow men. Praying to God, he admitted that "in heart and tongue alike I am guilty of falsehood in your presence for I cannot easily deduce how far I am cured of this disease, and I have a great fear of offending you unaware by sins to which I am blind, though to your eyes they are manifest" (1986, 245).

"Sins to which I am blind" -Augustine explicitly acknowledged that the mind had an unconscious dimension; "though no one can know a man's thoughts, except the man's own spirit that is within him, there are some things in man which even his own spirit that is within him does not know" (211). The mind was not transparent, self-scrutiny was limited. He might therefore have any number of unrecognized fatal faults for which he could be doomed. Could a sinner ask pardon for an unknown sin? Could he ask for the remission of who knows how many other concealed transgressions? Augustine solved the problem for the church for all time by deciding that this was possible. He asked forgiveness for all of his transgressions, those with which he was familiar and those which lay beyond his ken. Throwing himself on God's mercy, he declared that "I shall therefore confess both what I know of myself and what I do not know." It is interesting that Augustine did not find it necessary to offer his readers any further explanation for this phenomenon: "There are some things in man which even his own spirit that is within him does now know." He apparently assumed that this would be understood and we need not doubt that it was. Not only his contemporaries but his readers through the millennia may have had a good grasp of the concept of the "unknown sin."

Although he readily condemned himself for unconscious sins committed while he was awake, Augustine in *City of God* did not blame himself for sexual transgressions in his dreams. His understanding was that the dream had not been a creation of the responsible soul; it had been produced in a part of the mind that was beyond the soul's purview. The dream scenario was not something that had been "done" by the soul; it was something which "had been done" to it. This premise enabled Augustine to awaken from a sexual dream with "a clear conscience" (1986, 234). But the ascetic ideal that he, and innumerable men and women after him, followed, demanded the vanquishing of such desires. Leading a blameless life entailed not only resistance to sexual urges but, optimally, to the suppression of the urges themselves" (1986, 233–234).

Augustine prayed, therefore, that God would "quench the fire of sensuality" which provoked him in his dreams so that his soul would no longer commit even in sleep "these shameful, unclean acts inspired by sensual images, which lead to the pollution of the body" (1986, 234).

This was a prayer which the very devout would repeat in centuries to come. In monastic communities, members aimed to achieve ever-higher degrees of spiritual purity. One rule formulated steps which would take a monk in this direction, beginning with his avoiding sexual experience in waking life, progressing through a stage in which the sight of women no longer aroused him and culminating in his no longer responding to the seduction of feminine images even in dreams. A continuing dream response to such images was evidence that "cupidity" was still "located in the marrow." Anthropologist Charles Stewart explains that "dreams potentially represented the last unruled part of the self and the goal of ascetic practice was to colonize even this dark recess with the force of the will" (Stewart, 48–49).

During the era of the Western guilt culture, the pious regularly searched their dreams for unrecognized sins. Dreams, which supposedly could plumb the depths of the soul, could detect germinating wickedness before it emerged in the conscious mind. The dreamer, having been warned, was more likely to be able to resist a temptation which had been foretold. The dream was therefore a valuable resource in the attempt to avoid transgression.

SEEKING SANCTITY

Sweeping the mind clear of sinful thoughts was a full-time occupation for those who had not reached the heights of sainthood. A serious threat was posed by "involuntary" thoughts, those tempting thoughts, or perhaps images, that come unbidden when one is least looking for them. They were not sinful in themselves; no harm was done if they were banished without delay. On the other hand, if they were allowed to linger, if, perhaps imperceptibly, they were allowed to slip from the "involuntary" condition to the "voluntary" and were then savored, the soul had entered into a state of sin.

The ideal was an asexual mind, a mind no longer threatened by temptation, filled only with holy thoughts. In pursuit of this goal, prodigious efforts had to be made to construct an impenetrable wall, a barrier which would keep even the slightest hints of a sinful thought out of the conscious mind. This mind-watching endeavor, which permitted no momentary respite, which was never-ending, must have been exhausting. Contemporary critics charged that it was also unhealthy. They believed that sexual deprivation resulted in a damming up of desire which raised it to a dangerous pitch. It was to be expected that the repressive wall would sometimes crack. It could then happen that a person who was convinced that all sexual thoughts had been banished from the mind, engaged in peculiar behavior which bystanders attributed to the repressed inclination.

When the wall was seriously breached, the repressed sexual desires could return in the form of delusions and hallucinations. The afflicted persons could imagine that malicious spirits were attempting to seduce them. Sometimes they believed that they were actually seeing these persecutors in the form of attractive human beings; at other times, as vicious demons threatening to attack them. In the worst condition, it seemed that a demon invaded and inhabited the body of the victim, causing the person to shout obscenities and blasphemies, to dance around madly, to roll on the floor, screaming. In the sixteenth and seventeenth centuries, in Germany and in France, virtual epidemics occurred in religious houses, one individual setting off another until most of the community was infected.

In the nineteenth century, such behavior had become rare. Medical historians diagnosed it as having been a consequence of hysteria, or of hysterical insanity, brought on by the religious fanaticism of those long-gone times. The internationally recognized medical authority, Wilhelm Griesinger, while attributing the attacks to a breakdown of repression, believed that they occurred only in cases of mental illness. Only then could the "non-satisfaction of the sexual functions and continence" cause erotic outbursts. At such times, "the long-repressed desire readily now shows itself as amorous and sexual delirium, sometimes ideal, sometimes unconcealed (Griesinger, 1965, 198). Some physicians were still of the opinion that the relatively mild hysteria they encountered in their practices was sexual in origin; others demurred.

Then, as the century neared its end, hysterical women on the ward of a hospital in Paris experienced attacks that two or three hundred years earlier, would have called for exorcism. These seizures were often accompanied by unmistakable signs of sexual excitation. In the winter of 1885–1886, when Freud visited the French capital, expecting to study the brain under the tutelage of Jean-Martin Charcot, he found the world-famous neurologist and his team probing the records of the exorcists, looking for parallels between the demoniacal attacks of the past and the paroxysms of the present, assuming that both were manifestation of hysteria. Freud joined these physicians in the recognition of resemblances between the erotic apparitions which had tormented the pious in religious orders and the sexual hallucinations of the modern Parisiennes.

Freud was undoubtedly as aware as other physicians of the tradition that attributed hysteria to repressed sexual desire. He would have been forcefully reminded of this tradition when he witnessed the sexual acting-out of hysterical patients on the wards of the hospital in Paris.

AUGUSTINE AND FREUD

Can Augustine's harsh doctrine be compared to the Freudian theory to which such notions as sin and damnation were utterly foreign? Freudian teaching did not consign sinners to the fires of hell; nevertheless, resemblances between the theories are not trivial and they are interesting, suggesting as they do that psychoanalytic theory was produced under the influence of the ancient tradition. Three of these similarities stand out: the concept of inheritance, the ineradicable nature of innate immoral inclinations, and denial of environmental influence.

Augustine taught that the child was born in sin; according to Freud, the Oedipus complex, with the boy's fear of castration by the father and the unavoidable aggressive urges that accompanied it, was a phylogenetic inheritance. This signified, for instance, that a boy who had been threatened with mutilation only by females, or had never been threatened at all, would nevertheless fear castration by his father. Freud declared that "instinctual wishes . . . are born afresh with every child. . . . Among these instinctual wishes are those of incest, cannibalism and lust for killing" (*S.E.,* XXI: 10).[3]

For Freud, psychic conflict was as inescapable as it was for Augustine. The instinctual desires of his theory welled up as persistently as did the sinful inclinations of Augustine's doctrine. Prohibitions imposed by society forbade the expression of instincts much as the ordinances of God forbade the satisfaction of prohibited desires. Yet sin and instinct welled up persistently and could not be abolished. Temptation was therefore constant and had to be countered by lifelong efforts. No single act of repression, no single sacrament sufficed to remove it. Because the forces of the forbidden unceasingly clashed with moral demands, conflict was interminable. Finally, whatever efforts were made, success would be partial at best and humans were doomed to a less than happy condition, the state of sin on the one hand and at least some degree of neurosis on the other.

Both men were resolute nativists. The environment did not enter into either the ecclesiastic or the psychoanalytic account as a prime cause of aberrations. For Augustine, it could provide only an "occasion" for sin. He did not believe that a child properly brought up would be free of moral stain. Parents might lead a child to God but it would inevitably lapse because temptation surged from within. Similarly, Freud presumed that good parenting could not prevent neurosis. The child was inevitably propelled into the Oedipus complex; it had to incestuously love one parent and murderously hate the other. Ironically, Freud is now widely regarded as an environmentalist and credited with bringing into focus the importance of parent-child relationships, the significance of which, it is supposed, was unsuspected before his time. Freud did not altogether ignore the environment, but his stress was upon the innate, biological urges which he assumed were critical determinants of the child's development. The kindest, most intelligent and loving upbringing would not prevent the welling up of forbidden urges which would necessitate repression. And, finally, both Augustine and Freud believed that, in sleep, these urges could escape repression and make their way into dreams.[4]

Recognition of parallels between Freud's ideas about human nature and some traditional beliefs may help explain the rapidity of the spread of psychoanalysis. Freud always stressed the difficulties which his theories had encountered and insisted that psychoanalysis had had to make its way against a host of implacable enemies. That there were such foes is not to be doubted. However, it is at least equally true that Freud's hypotheses were easily and even enthusiastically accepted by a great many people, only a small minority of whom could have been influenced by personal experience with psychoanalysis. They seem not to have been disturbed by the assumption that human beings were born with antisocial propensities, that the basic instincts were impersonal lust and destructive aggression, that toddlers had monstrous desires, and that neurotic unhappiness was due to guilt acquired without understanding, before the age of reason. Nor were they bothered by the proposition that their dreams were prompted by lusts and hatreds which rose up out of a "positive Hell." Surely these notions are not self-evident; how then are we to account for their uncritical, cordial reception?

If we bear in mind that ideas quite similar to these are part of our cultural inheritance, then perhaps the welcome they were given can be partially explained. By the end of the nineteenth century, religion had lost its hold over many intellectuals who had, however, been raised in, or near, the old faith. The tradition probably lingered among those who no longer believed. When such people came upon apparently new theories, they were actually meeting old, familiar notions in a novel and seemingly scientific dress. Instinctual gratification had taken the place of sin, the two wicked appetites reappeared as dual "drives," the ego, instead of the soul, was embattled. Salvation was now to be sought in this world, instead of in the next. So far as the dream was concerned, the evil to be found in it remained unchanged; responsibility for the appearance of repulsive wishes simply devolved from the Devil to the id, his modern incarnation. Freud remarked about the Devil that he "is certainly nothing else than the personification of the repressed unconscious instinctual life" (*S.E.,* IX: 174), But it might be just as accurate to say that Freud's theory of the repressed unconscious instinctual life was the reincarnation of the Devil.

PLOTINUS

An entirely different concept about the morality of the unconscious mind had been offered almost a century before Augustine. Plotinus (204–270 A.D.) the last of the great classical philosophers, was the ancient thinker who most clearly recognized unconscious mental activity and who made extensive use of the concept in the development of his system. His thought, like that of Aristotle and Plato, permeated the intellectual life of the Middle Ages and of the Renaissance, and when the "modern" era of philosophy began, in the seventeenth century, it was available to the men who laid the foundations for the discipline of today. It is well to keep in mind that certain "modern" ideas which seemed to surface suddenly during the Enlightenment had roots in the distant past. For instance, in the seventeenth century Benedict de Spinoza distinguished between conscious and unconscious desire. He referred to the latter as "appetite" and commented that "I recognize no distinction between appetite and desire for whether a man be conscious of his appetite or not, it remains one and the same appetite" (1911, 173). This will seem less startling if it is recalled that in the third century after Christ Plotinus had already dealt with unconscious desire: "not all that occurs at any part of the Soul [his capital letter] is immediately known to us; a thing must, for that knowledge, be present to the total soul; thus desire locked up within the desiring faculty remains unknown except when we make it fully ours" (1911, 364).

Plotinus understood the everyday unconscious. He illustrated it with homely examples from everyday life, the same examples that turned up again in the nineteenth century: the unconscious that takes over the performance of habitual activities, like walking (1911, 292), the unconsciousness of the deeply absorbed reader who is oblivious to the surroundings (1911, 41), and the lack of awareness of danger by a person engaged in a courageous action (1911, 41). He supposed that a memory, when unconscious, could be more powerful than one which was conscious (1911, 289) and believed that some actions could be more perfectly carried out unconsciously, consciousness having a "blunting" effect (1911, 41). He assumed that unconscious mental action was continuous although rarely perceived. He compared the conscious soul's access to the unconscious with that of a person who could only get a glimpse of certain activities by using a mirror. When the mirror was improperly placed, or absent, as was usually the case, the person could not see what was going on, although the activities did not cease (1911, 40).

To this vision of the personal unconscious, Plotinus added ideas that were to play an important role in the future. He conceived of the unconscious, not merely as a collection of unconscious mental contents, but as a separate, hidden part of the mind, ordinarily inaccessible to consciousness, ceaselessly active and possessing its own distinct mode of cognition. Further, he thought of this unconscious part of the mind not only as superior to consciousness, but as related to the divine.

Plotinus blended the philosophy of Plato with concepts derived from Aristotle and other earlier thinkers and created his own system, now known as "Neo-Platonism." This system came into being during the time when Christianity, already well established but not yet triumphant, and paganism, still powerful, competed for the minds of the uncommitted. Paganism was no longer what it had been; faith in the ancient gods had faded long ago and philosophy had turned mystical to replace this faith. Neo-Platonism was a religious doctrine, many of whose principles, absorbed by Christianity, gave rise to Christian mysticism.

Plotinus taught that the world had come into being, not through an act of creation by God in such a fashion that it was separate from God, a product of his activity, but rather that it had emanated from "The One." Each human soul was an extension of the One, the cosmic soul; it was individuated when it sank into matter, into the body. Thus captured, it forgot its divine origins; however, it did not forget them completely, for one part of the soul, escaping individuation, was never caught by matter and remained forever in touch with the transcendental realm. Of this part of the soul, the person was ordinarily unaware. On occasion, however, in a mystical experience, he or she could escape individuation and could ascend for a time to be at one with the cosmic soul. In Plotinus's psychology, therefore, the traditional rational and irrational parts of the soul were joined by a third, hidden element: "spirit," or the Neo-Platonic unconscious.

Plotinus's conception of the hidden part of the soul was antithetical to Freud's unconscious in respect of their natures. Plotinus's unconscious was the highest and best part of the soul; Freud's was the lowest and the worst; Plotinus thought that our everyday selves concealed the god within us; Freud supposed that what we kept out of sight was the demoniacal Id. Plotinus supposed that life could be lived on different spiritual levels but that on whatever conscious level a person was situated, he or she received guidance from the unconscious level just above. The aim of the life of a human being was to become actually what he or she already was potentially; in this endeavor, the unconscious could be a reliable and powerful ally.

The pagan Plotinus and the Christian Augustine were at odds on the subject of innate human evil. Having accepted much of Plotinus, Augustine rejected his belief that the soul was fundamentally decent. Paganism on the other hand had no use for the Christian idea that the human soul was essentially corrupt, that it could not achieve salvation on its own and that it could escape hell-fire only through the intercession of a divine Redeemer. Plotinus recognized evil but he maintained that it was something that approached the soul from without; it was not an innate constituent of the soul which, he insisted, "is not an evil Kind" (1911, 59). The church, however, condemned this opinion as heretical The victory thus went to Augustine and to the theory of original sin.

Augustine was also challenged in his own time. A contemporary, the British monk Pelagius, denied the whole hypothesis of original sin: man was not born corrupt, he declared. The sin of Adam and Eve was not transmitted because sin cannot be inherited; human beings were not doomed to conflict and unhappiness by their own nature. On the contrary, human misery could be blamed upon the environment and upon the upbringing of the individual and could be redressed by human effort. The optimistic Pelagius was sure that the human lot and humanity itself could be improved (Brown, 1967, 352). The "Pelagian heresy" was condemned by church council during his lifetime. Thereafter, from the fifth to the seventeenth century, a series of councils—nine in all—denounced the notion that humankind was basically good.

NOTES

1. See also *City of God*, 577–589.
2. See also, Vol. I, 774–775 and 783–785.
3. Two psychoanalytic historians, Alexander and Selesnick, remarked upon this similarity of approach between Freud and Augustine and, hailing the latter as a "forerunner" (81) of psychoanalysis, noted that he was "fully aware of the asocial forces of mind" (84). They noted that Augustine had buttressed his theory with empirical evidence garnered from the study of infants. Augustine's observations of babies, perhaps the first recorded instances of infant studies, seemed to him to confirm his hypothesis that they were not naturally good. Augustine had watched angry babies and he noticed that an infant in this state would "work himself into a tantrum against people older than himself . . . and try his best to strike and hurt others . . . including his own parents, when they do not give in to him and refuse to pander to his whims . . . this shows that, if babies are innocent, it is not for lack of will to do harm, but for lack of strength." Augustine also noticed sibling rivalry and this behavior seemed to him to be another indicator of the infant's intrinsically selfish nature. "I have myself seen jealousy in a baby and know what it means," he stated. "He was not old enough to talk, but whenever he saw his foster brother at the breast, he would grow pale with envy." This was "common knowledge," Augustine asserted, adding that "surely it cannot be called innocence" (*Conf.* 1, 7). The Freudian historians, sharing Augustine's basic point of view, noted with approval that "Augustine did not believe in the angelic innocence of infants" (84, Alexander and Selesnick; *The History of Psychiatry*).
4. The resemblances between the theory of the analyst and the doctrine of the ecclesiastic have prompted the surmise that Freud may have been influenced by Catholic thought during his childhood. His parents were Jewish but when he was very small, he had a Roman Catholic nanny, a strict, devout old woman who took him with her to church and filled him up with religious stories. His mother told him later that when he got home from church, he would "preach and tell us what God Almighty does." It has been suggested that the lessons may have taken deep root in his unconscious and helped shape the theory he created years later. It should be remembered however, that Freud grew up in a Roman Catholic country, that the influence of the church was pervasive and that in this atmosphere he could have absorbed elements of the doctrine almost anywhere. See Paul C. Vitz, *Sigmund Freud's Christian Unconscious*, New York, Guilford Press, 1988.

Chapter Nine

The Romantic Imagination

When Immanuel Kant finished the *Critique of Pure Reason*, he believed that he had set limits to what could be achieved by metaphysical speculation. But, he warned, "this domain is an island, enclosed by nature itself within unalterable limits. It is the land of truth—enchanting name!—surrounded by a wide and stormy ocean, the native home of illusion, where many a fog bank and many a swiftly melting iceberg give the deceptive appearance of farther shores, deluding the adventurous seafarer ever anew with empty hopes, and engaging him in enterprises which he can never abandon and yet is unable to carry to completion" (Kant, 1965, 257). This was the cautious sentiment of the declining Enlightenment.

A generation later, we hear the voice of the Romantic era as the ebullient young Friedrich Schelling declares that he does not intend to be stuck on an island.

> Of course those systems which continue to float between earth and sky and lack the courage to press forward to the ultimate point of all knowledge, are far less likely to fall into dangerous errors than is the system of the great thinker, whose speculation takes the freest, most daring flight, who risks everything and wants either the whole truth, in all of its grandeur, or nothing at all, and who he who is not daring enough to follow truth to its ultimate height, may touch the hem of her dress here and there, but will never win her. A more just posterity will far more highly rank the man who, not willing to accept merely tolerable errors, daringly had the courage to seek truth, above the fearful who, in order to avoid the reefs and sandbanks, preferred to remain forever at anchor (Beckers, 1875, 14–15).

During the early decades of the nineteenth century, philosophy was thriving as three intrepid metaphysicians, ignoring Kant's warning, braved his "wide and stormy ocean." For all their differences, Fichte, Schelling and

Hegel had in common the vision that behind the reality perceived by common sense, lay another, transcendent reality. According to historian Frederick Copleston, their combined efforts produced "one of the most remarkable flowerings of metaphysical speculation which have occurred in the long history of western philosophy." For each of these philosophers professes "to solve the riddle of the world, to reveal the secret of the universe and the meaning of human existence." They were convinced "that the nature of reality was at last clearly revealed to human consciousness. And each set out his vision of the Universe with a splendid confidence in its objective truth" (Copleston, 1965, 15–16).

The Romantic philosophers, in their ambitious search for the meaning of the universe and the purpose of human life, did not share their eighteenth-century predecessors' lively interest in the theory of the personal unconscious. Yet Romantic philosophy has long been regarded as the primary source of the concept of the unconscious. This is puzzling because examination of the literature of the time does not support this belief. In 1956, a medical historian, Werner Leibbrand, noted that the assumption that "the unconscious was really discovered by Romanticism has become almost a platitude." Logically, he continued, connections between the Romantic concept and the therapeutic methods (Freud, Adler, etc.) supposedly based on it ought not to be hard to find. Surprisingly, just the opposite was true; evidence for such a connection had to be called "scanty" (Leibbrand, 294).

Evidence will continue to be scanty because the seekers for a connection have been unaware that the expression "unconscious" has been used to refer to two different concepts. A distinction is sorely needed.

Much of Romantic philosophy was metaphysical in the sense that it was engaged in the exploration of a realm that lay beyond all experience. This transcendent reality could be reached by reasoning alone. The unconscious of the Romantic philosophers was a metaphysical construction. The theory of the personal unconscious, on the other hand, is a scientific hypothesis whose validity depends upon support obtained by observation or experiment.

As an instance of a metaphysical system, consider an early version of the "Nature-Philosophy" of Friedrich Schelling, the "Prince of the Romantics," as introduced by the American philosopher Josiah Royce. "This theory is that the whole universe, including the physical world also, is essentially one live thing, a mind, one great Spirit" (Royce, 1983, 17). For Schelling, "Nature" was a mind, or spirit which constituted the cosmos. This cosmic mind, called variously the "World Soul," "Nature" or the "Absolute," unconsciously actualizing itself, had brought the world into being. It took form first as inorganic nature, then it appeared in the life of plants and animals and finally it came to consciousness in the human being, that is to say, in human consciousness, for the conscious mind of the World Soul consisted of the conscious minds of human beings. We are related, therefore, not only to other living beings, but to the inanimate world as well. Whatever *is*, is a constituent of the World Soul.

In this view, evolution is guided by an intelligence, not the intelligence attributed to the traditional God, the creator who is separate from his creation and remains outside of it, but an intelligence inherent in Nature itself. Moreover, this cosmic mind differs from that of the Judeo-Christian deity in that it is unconscious; it works its wonders and builds the world without knowing it. Finally, having worked blindly to create the non-mental world, it achieved conscious reason, self-contemplation and a new mode of expression in the human mind (Royce, 186–189).

In this grand scheme, our individual conscious minds protrude like islands from the vast unconsciousness from which they have sprung. The unconscious mind of each individual is a part of the cosmic unconscious, its roots anchored in the world mind of which it is a part. The unconscious generative power of that mind is now active within the individual mind: its creativity becomes ours and the source of all of our creativity remains unconscious.

The "unconscious" as conceived here is a constituent of a metaphysical system and is metaphysical itself. It does not appeal to evidence for its validity. This unconscious is not the personal unconscious, the unconscious of thoughts, feelings and motives attributed to individuals. To put it in practical terms, the unconscious of the Spirit that created the world is not identical with the unconscious of the man who was not aware that he was looking forward to the death of a rich relation. (An example taken from Schopenhauer.) Identification of the concept of the personal unconscious with the unconscious of the philosophers of the Romantic era, rests on a confusion between the two concepts.[1]

Schelling's system has an aesthetic appeal which has attracted people who are otherwise not committed to Romantic metaphysics. Even today, a philosopher can respond to it as a poetical conception of the cosmos: "Schelling's vision of the universe is ultimately a vision of God as the great creator, not bringing the world into existence *ex nihilo* at some ancient time, but continuously creating it (and Himself) through time. We are not only part of that process; we are its consciousness and its instruments of expression. Poets and philosophers are not simply expressing themselves; they are expressing—and realizing—the movement of the Absolute. It was a grand image, a living universe growing and developing through history in which we ourselves played an essential, creative part" (Solomon, 1988, 54).

Early in his life, Freud himself had responded to this appeal. He recalled that, just before leaving secondary school, he had been thrilled to hear a Nature-Philosophical essay then mistakenly attributed to Goethe, "it was hearing Goethe's beautiful essay on Nature read aloud at a popular lecture . . . that decided me to become a medical student" (*S.E.,* XX: 8). The

"Nature" of this poetical essay was at one with Schelling's "World Soul" which creates the inanimate and animate realms and comes to consciousness and self-expression in the human mind.[2] "Endlessly she creates new forms." "All human beings are in her and she is in all." "She is the only artist—each of her works has its own nature . . . and yet everything constitutes but one unity." "She has thought and thinks constantly, but not as human beings do, but as Nature does." "She has neither language nor speech but she creates tongues and hearts through which she feels and speaks." "She is everything" (Hemecker, 1991, 145–146).

That this hymn to a Nature-Philosophically conceived creative cosmic spirit touched Freud deeply suggests that it may have appealed to a latent, perhaps invincible, Romanticism in his soul.

It would not be surprising if this intellectually adventurous teenager found a kindred spirit in the equally adventurous young philosopher, barely out of his teens when he appeared on the philosophical stage. Omnivorous reader that he was, Freud might have plunged deeply into Schelling's *The World Soul*. Jones reported that Freud "passed through a brief period of the pantheistic *Naturphilosophie*" but later "swung to the opposite extreme and became for a while a radical materialist" (Jones, 1953, 43).

If Freud had arrived at the university still a Romantic at heart, he would likely as not have been deeply shocked. He would have found that the assessment of Schelling's Nature Philosophy had plummeted, due to its debasement decades earlier. The fanciful style of speculation that had produced Nature Philosophy had slipped out of philosophy and had penetrated into other domains, notoriously medicine, where it wreaked havoc. The expression "Nature Philosophy" could still signify the metaphysical theory of Schelling but, used pejoratively, as it so often was, it referred to the disastrous developments which had produced the grotesqueries of "speculative medicine."[3]

As a young materialist, Freud had fared well. He had achieved a secure position in the scientific milieu of Vienna and had won the respect of some of the most eminent men in the medical field. He seemed to have laid out a path which would take him to the top of the profession. Then, however, he cast this well-earned reputation to the winds and began speculating in a fashion which horrified his erstwhile mentors. During the 1890s and in the first decade of the twentieth century, his approach to science changed dramatically. Giving up the cautious, logical, evidence-bound mode which had characterized his work until then, he embraced something quite different, a style of conjecture that was intuitive, imaginative, and relatively unfettered by demands for proof. The transformation was so drastic, the new mental set and the new methods adopted so strange, that some critics have charged him with turning from science to charlatanism.

In his own time, however, a different diagnosis was offered. It was suggested that Freud's way of thinking had regressed to the mode of an earlier period, that the faults imputed to his style of theorizing were those common in the Romantic era when German physicians, embracing speculation, had brought progress in their science to a halt. Among Freud's critics, the most august was Wundt. In 1911, by then the revered founder of a well-established experimental psychology, Wundt published his verdict. In his textbook, the official organ of the profession, he opined that 1) Freudian thought closely resembled that of Schelling and 2) psychoanalysis was unmistakably related to the regrettable speculative medicine of bygone times (Wundt, 1911, 636–637).

Here then are two specific objections to the Freudian enterprise coming from a respected contemporary. What are we to make of them? First, did Schelling's thought in any way seriously influence the development of psychoanalytic theory? Then, was Freud in any sense a speculative physician? Could he have imported a long defunct style of theorizing into the twentieth century?

Henri Ellenberger, author of *The Discovery of the Unconscious*, has suggested that a search for a link between the theorizing of Freud and Schelling might begin with an examination of their dependence on "polarities" (1970, 203–204).

Freud routinely framed his theories around polar opposites. Each theory was constructed upon a foundation in which two antithetical concepts confronted each other. Commenting on this "peculiar feature of Freud's thinking throughout his life, his constant proclivity to dualistic ideas," Jones noted that "any kind of pluralism was quite alien to him. Someone once said facetiously that he had never learned to count beyond the number two" (1955, 320). This characteristic "was most pronounced in Freud's basic classifications: love-hunger; ego-sexuality; auto-erotism-heteroerotism; Eros-Thanatos; life-death, and so on. . . . But the same fondness for pairs is found again and again: love-hate, exhibitionism-scopophilism, etc. It is as if Freud had a difficulty in contemplating any topic unless he could divide it into two opposites, and never more than two" (1955, 422).

Unable to explain this anomalous behavior Jones ventured the psychoanalytic hypothesis that "the dualism must have sprung from some depths in Freud's personality, from some offshoot of his Oedipus complex, perhaps the opposition between the masculine and the feminine sides of his nature" (1957, 266–267).

Certainly this strange proclivity was not driven by empirical facts. Freud behaved almost as though he was acting under a kind of duress, as though some unstated, constraining axiom required the establishment of polarities. It cannot have been the easiest way to construct a series of theories, to have to search, with each change, for a new polarity on which to hang the structure. It certainly does not look like good science either; establishing a polarity would require the constant forcing of facts into one of two compartments, regardless of fit. The method of polarities would be justifiable only on the supposition that psychological reality was really subdivided in this way, that facts naturally always fell into two classes, and that these classes were always in opposition. Could Freud have believed something of the sort?

Indeed, he could have believed just this, had he been a follower of Schelling. Perhaps, as he went his dualistic way, he was hearing the admonishing voice of Schelling, who, in *The World Soul*, proclaimed his axiom: "It is the first principle of a philosophical doctrine of nature to *go in search of polarity and dualism throughout all of nature*" (1988, ix).

Standing behind Schelling was an awe-inspiring authority, Isaac Newton, equipped with the ultimate polarity—attraction and repulsion. In Schelling's time the near veneration with which attraction and repulsion were regarded was due to Newton's stunning achievement. At the end of the seventeenth century, he had explained phenomena as disparate as the fall of an apple and the paths of the planets by way of a single great polarity. In the introduction to his *Principia,* Newton had expressed the hope that the search for polarities would continue. He might almost have been encouraging the Nature-Philosophers of the future when, after noting that he had deduced "the motions of the planets, the comets, the moon and the sea" from these forces, he continued: "I wish we could derive the rest of the phenomena of nature by the same kind of reasoning from mechanical principles for I am induced by many reasons to suspect that they may all depend upon certain forces by which the particles of bodies, by some causes hitherto unknown, are either mutually impelled towards one another and cohere in regular figures, or are repelled and recede from one another" (Newton, 1934, xviii).

In the Romantics' immediate past, Kant had suggested that reason alone could show that the forces of attraction and repulsion were necessary constituents of the physical world. For consider, if only the attractive force existed, then matter would condense to infinity, ending up as a mathematical point and the world would be empty. If only the repulsive force existed, matter would fly apart to infinity and again the world would be empty. However, the world was not empty; matter existed; the existence of matter therefore demonstrated the action of the two conflicting forces; it was the product of the equilibrium between them—requiring the joint efforts of uniting and disuniting forces (1985, xviii-xix; 40–60).

This argument could be interpreted as signifying that reason alone, reason without experiment or the use of mathematics, might enable an intrepid philosopher, a philosopher of genius, to discover important truths about the ultimate structure of Nature. Schelling set out to be that philosopher. Supremely confident and ambitious, he assumed that the same forces of attraction and repulsion must be at work at some deep level in each of the different physical sciences. Basing himself on the premise that the sciences were essentially related, the cosmos being one, he surmised that beneath the various explanatory theories there must lie a more fundamental explanation, one which they all shared. This, he assumed, would be grounded on polarities. In a speculative tour-de-force, a work of undeniable ingenuity, Schelling supplied this ultimate explanation. By the use of bold hypotheses and cogitation of a kind which would later be deplored as misguided, Schelling deduced light, the composition of the air, electricity, heat, magnetism and chemical processes from the solitary premise that the phenomena of each science were the result of the action of the opposing forces of attraction and repulsion.

The creation of this "speculative physics" did not involve the philosopher in a painstaking search for facts. Observation, experiment, measurement, mathematical analysis—all of these could be left to the scientist. The philosopher accepted these facts as reported, reasoned about them and by sheer reasoning discovered the substructure which had eluded the scientist. With the brashness of the very young, Schelling declared that it had been his intention to provide "wings for our slow-moving physics" (Schenk, 1966, 179).

The same "wings," the wings of pure thought, might be expected to speed progress in other fields. Schelling's speculative physics interested people who regarded it as a spectacular new metascience. He had apparently arrived at profound and important truths about the universe by thought alone. He had penetrated the manifold of physical explanations and had discovered their common foundation. Biologists saw no reason why they too should not ruminate in this fashion; physicians were not slow to join them and speculative medicine was the result.

To make a name for himself in this new enterprise, the speculative physician did not have to spend time with the sick; he did not have to exert himself looking for causes or cures of physical or mental lesions. All he had to do was *think*. But he had to think on a grand scale. Taking off from humble clinical generalities, he could only attain the longed-for distant reaches of the universe by donning the seven-league boots of speculation. So Henrik Steffens, follower of Schelling, linking the laws of psychology with the great principles of physics, compared mental stability with the order of the physical universe and likened madness with the "ancient chaos" which supposedly had filled the cosmos before order was established (Leibbrand-Wettely, 1961, 467)

Medicine in Germany seemed for a time almost to have become a branch of philosophy as diseases were explained by philosophizing about them. A historian has noted that "it was a strange period, that period of romantic medicine," for "while French physicians were observing patients in the hospital and performing autopsies in the laboratory, while English doctors were engaged in clinical investigation, the Germans sat at their desks and wrote big books on the nature of disease and on the world at large" (Sigerist, 1944, 40). A medical book published in 1817 devoted 130 pages to general diagnosis, but only twenty-four of these were concerned with actual observations, the rest were devoted to speculation about the significance of symptoms in relation to the general nature of disease, with emphasis on polarities (Schenk, 1966, 180).

SPECULATIVE MEDICAL THEORY

When physicians fell under the spell of Nature-Philosophy, they needed a polarity, a polarity which could be regarded as the analog, in the biological realm, of attraction and repulsion in the physical. An obvious important duality lay ready to hand, biology could claim the momentous polarity of life and death. Life could be equated with attraction because both were cohesive forces. Attraction pulls things together and makes them stick; life combines substances to build up the organism which consequently grows. Repulsion, on the other hand, is a disintegrating force; it causes things to come apart. Death similarly breaks up and destroys cohesion and is responsible for dissolution.

In order to complete the analogy to attraction and repulsion, the life and death poles had to be postulated as continuously in operation. In the physical world, matter was a product of the uninterrupted action of two opposing forces; in biology, therefore, existence had to be similarly explained. Therefore, the theory had it that life and death were at war in every living being at every moment; the death force was ceaselessly striving to bring about the dissolution of the being, the life force was endlessly counteracting it to ensure survival. Alexander Haindorf compared the life of the individual to a galvanic process acting between positive and negative poles; forces of composition and decomposition, or creation and destruction, were ceaselessly at work. Physical health depended upon the achievement of a harmonious equilibrium between them (Leibbrand-Wettley, 1961, 468 and 664).

An additional polarity lay ready to hand. Love and hate could similarly be compared to the great physical forces. Love brings people together; it unites, creates and heals. Hate destroys relationships; it separates and ruins. This theory also demanded a continuous interaction between love and hate.

Speculative physicians who set out to construct a model of the mind had available to them the venerable classical theory. This theory, with its higher, rational, and its lower, irrational elements, lent itself handily to incorporation with poles of love and hate. The amalgamated pole of reason-and-love strove to govern the pole of irrationality-and-hate which ceaselessly tried to break free. One such theory was that of Gustav Blumröder who should be noted for the skill with which he endowed his concepts with picturesque labels. The lower, irrational pole, an obvious relative of Freud's id, was the "blood essence," or "blood principle." It propelled the soul into action; it was instinctual and possessed a capacity for sadism. The higher, rational pole, corresponding to Freud's ego, was the "brain essence," or "principle;" it played the usual governing role. The conflict between the principles of "blood" and "brain" was perpetual; the defeat of "brain" by "blood" was the cause of mental illness. Blumröder's theory also featured life and death instincts, as did that of Freud, but he did not go to the Greeks for names; he turned to an ancient eastern religion. Instead of Eros and Thanatos, therefore, we have "Ormuzd" and "Ahriman," "Ormuzd" being the Zoroastrian cosmic spirit of light, "Ahriman" the spirit of death and darkness (Leibbrand-Wettley, 1961, 470).

In the twentieth century, Freud initially believed that he had discovered the polarity of life and death. Subsequently, when he found a polarity that resembled his own in the writings of Empedocles, a philosopher who lived five centuries before Christ, he recognized that the ancient Greek's "Love" and "Strife" were the same, "in name and function" as his own life and death instincts (*S.E.,* XXIII: 244–245). He maintained that he was pleased to find a conception so like his own which had reemerged "after two and a half millennia" However, Freud need not have traveled so far back in time to find a conception congenial to his own. Such cosmic fantasies were waiting for him in his own backyard.

In a letter to Albert Einstein, in 1932, Freud recalled the original polarity when he explained that psychoanalysis recognized two instincts, this being no more than a "theoretical clarification of the universally familiar opposition between Love and Hate which may perhaps have some fundamental relation to the popularity of attraction and repulsion that plays a part in your own field of knowledge" (*S.E.,* XXII, 209).

Given Freud's early enthusiasm for Schelling's Nature Philosophy, it seems more reasonable than not to suppose that his life-long adherence to polarities stemmed from a conviction acquired at that time. He himself, however, may have been unaware of this connection. We are therefore left with the probability that Freud's dedication to polarities was derived from a reading of Schelling.

But what of Wundt's other complaint that Freud had returned to the fantasizing of the Romantic era doctors—that he was, in fact, a twentieth-century speculative physician? A comparison with a genuine member of this species may be informative. We can liken Freud's medical theories with those of successful, well-known and well-liked Gotthilf Heinrich von Schubert. Personal friend of Schelling, practitioner of therapeutic magnetism, enthusiastic Nature-Philosopher, he had proposed, for his doctoral dissertation, the thesis that "the same laws of motion, the same harmonies of space and time which Kepler discovered in the planetary system, should also be found in the inner vital motions of the organisms, for instance, in the circulation of the blood" (Merkel, 1913, 20). His mentors persuaded him to lower his sights and accepted as substitute the case history of a patient whose deafness (presumably hysterical) he had cured by hypnosis.

Schubert was a gentle, kindly physician who, albeit he had had some success with hypnotic treatment, could not make a living practicing medicine because he could not bear to take money from poor people. Friends persuaded him to give up the profession and to join philosophical acquaintances in Dresden. Here a lecture series enticingly called "Views of the Night-side of the Natural Sciences," based in part on his familiarity with animal magnetism, quickly brought him to the attention of the avant garde. Encouraged by this success, Schubert steeped himself in ancient Greek and Indian philosophy and in the metaphysics of French and German mystics and, fusing the conceptions obtained there with the ruminations of his Romantic contemporaries, produced his book. In *The Symbolism of the Dream,* which appeared in 1814, he maintained that dream symbolism was the language with which God and humankind had communicated in happier times before relations between them had deteriorated. The book was a success and Schubert enjoyed several years of fame. Schubert's model of mental functioning, appeared in this book in support of his dream theory.

At that time, medical science was progressing rapidly outside of Germany. In France, M.F.X. Bichat was inaugurating a new epoch in biology by examining the symptoms of living patients and following these up with post-mortem studies. He was focusing on the nervous system with its two divisions, the cerebrospinal and the sympathetic, the first linked with sensory and motor functions, the second with the functions of organic life (Bréhier, 1987, 42).

Schubert decided that the two systems being investigated by Bichat constituted a "polarity" for which he could find a place in his theory. The cerebrospinal and sympathetic nervous systems seemed to him to be two mutually opposing poles; the first was the pole of the senses and the organs responsible for voluntary movement, the second that of the organs of the chest, the abdomen and the blood vessels (1968, 100–101).

Schubert made an imaginative leap and decided that the higher and lower parts of the soul were located in these two physical systems. He associated the cerebral system with consciousness, with voluntary control and with morality, the sympathetic, (which he called the "ganglionic"), with the unconscious, the involuntary and the instinctual. In Freudian terminology, the ego was in the cerebral, the id in the ganglion system.

The unconscious ganglion system resembled the roots of a plant that sucked nutriment from the earth to sustain the conscious cerebral system which resembled the branches and leaves of a tree. The tree metaphor was long-lived: in 1895, in the *Studies on Hysteria*, the book which launched psychoanalysis, Freud's coauthor Breuer made use of the same figure of speech: "when we speak of ideas which are found in the region of clear consciousness and of unconscious ones which never enter the full light of self-consciousness, we almost inevitably form pictures of a tree with its trunk in daylight and its roots in darkness" (*S.E.,* II: 228).

THE UBIQUITY OF CONFLICT

Nowhere was Freud more Romantic than in his assumptions of perennial human ambivalence giving rise to ceaseless mental conflicts, both conscious and unconscious, and the existence of two fundamental instincts, that of love and that of hate, forever in opposition. Early in his career, when his theory was still in the early stages, when the "big problems" were still wholly unresolved and everything was "in flux and dawning," Freud wrote to his friend Fliess that he was catching sight of "an intellectual hell, with layer upon layer; in the darkest core, glimpses of the contours of Lucifer-Amor" (Freud, 1985, 421). But Freud was discovering what he expected to find, the tradition that the soul was rooted in the antithesis between hate and love being part of his heritage.

Schubert's Romanticism appeared in his emphasis on the complexities and above all, the ambivalences or polarities of the soul, which he depicted as ranging from the gentle alternation of moods to the fiercest antagonism between love and hate. Such conflicts could be unconscious; in the war between sorrow and joy, love and hate, desire and guilt, one combatant could be entirely hidden from the view of the conscious soul, revealing its presence only in dreams. Human nature could be compared to the classical god Janus who had two faces which looked in opposite directions. We are "Janus-faced," and therefore "conscience stings in the midst of the pleasures of the sensual world, in such satisfactions of sensuous inclinations it lets us find no peace. On the other hand, our higher peace is constantly interrupted and our better powers are always being challenged to renewed combat. One face of Janus begins to laugh as the other starts to cry, when one is wide awake and dominant, the other slumbers and continues to speak only in the dream" (1968, 69).

The conflict was often a moral one. Schubert recalled that Socrates had always heard a good voice which warned him against evil. There is such a voice of conscience in all of us, Schubert stated. However, another voice is also heard which, with an altogether opposite intention, attempts to prompt us to wickedness. These opposing voices never leave us alone. Echoing Plato, Schubert compared the inner conflict with a struggle between horses: "Both natures demand their rights. Neither wants to sacrifice himself for the other. Like a linked pair of horses, one pulls in one direction, the other in the opposite, and the unhappy individual is in the middle, torn in two directions, often torn apart by the obstinate pair." When would this "old contradiction" end, Schubert asked himself. When would we ever be free of the "monster" who would "boldly break into laughter when we stand at the bier of our most dearly beloved?" (1968, 70)

For Schubert, the perfect representation of this human duality was the half-human, half-animal sphinx, the upper portion of a human being in calm contemplation, the lower portion a lion capable of tearing everything apart. The passions most likely to tear everything apart were lust and destructiveness, the old dyad of Augustine, Freud's "Luzifer-Amor." These urges were closely coupled, according to Schubert, as they were to Freud. Freud remarked that "love is with unexpected regularity accompanied by hate . . . hate is frequently a forerunner of love" and that "in a number of circumstances hate changes into love and love into hate." He stated that "the history of human civilization shows beyond any doubt that there is an intimate connection between cruelty and the sexual instinct" (*S.E.,* VII, 159). Schubert was of the same opinion. In antiquity, religions which had begun with the loftiest principles had been corrupted when they were infiltrated by those two closely related vices, "lust and bloodthirstiness." Their once-pure ceremonies were turned into debaucheries of lasciviousness and cruelty (1968, 72).

Both Schubert and Freud believed that sexuality and hatred could be so tightly linked that they could achieve simultaneous satisfaction; they could cooperate to such an extent that the sexual and destructive urges, expressed at one and the same moment, could not be distinguished. As an instance of such joint discharge, both cited cannibalism. Schubert asserted that lust and hate "lie so close to each other here that, in certain instances (in animal nature, for example), it is impossible to determine from which of the two sources the expression derives." He adds, "The tremendous hatred and violent attraction emerge from the same base, and very often (when, for example, the male predator eventually mauls the female, whose favor it has long courted in vain, and devours her with inordinate fury, or when the female of many insects kills and dismembers the male immediately after mating, the sensuous attraction appears to be merely a fierce hatred that has appropriated the mask of love and vice versa" (1968, 32).

Schubert's Romantic daring seems to have faltered at this point; he did not go on to speculate about the cooperation between lust and hatred in human beings. Freud was less timid. He was aware of the sexual behavior of certain insects; he assumed that death and copulation coincided in some of the lower animals but he located this simultaneous action in human behavior also (*S.E.,* IXX, 43). Cannibalism was clearly a manifestation of hatred, but it was also an expression of love: "the cannibal . . . has a devouring affection for his enemies and only devours people of whom he is fond" (*S.E.,* XVIII,

105). The act of eating was aggressive because it resulted in the destruction of the individual; it was sexual because it aimed at the most intimate union" with the person who was eaten (*S.E.,* XXIII: 149).

NEUTRALIZATION

Freud and Schubert were thus in agreement about the nature of the unconscious roots of the psyche. For Freud, cruelty and the sexual instinct, rising in the id, were the basic urges. Schubert similarly supposed that the "shameful part" of the soul situated in the ganglion system was motivated solely by lust and bloodthirstiness: The theories of Freud and Schubert manifestly relied upon the concept of repression; they followed the ancient model in which the civilized, prudent part of the mind must subdue the unruly and immoral and must vanquish it not merely once but must maintain subjugation by continuous effort. Freud and Schubert both compared the condition of the repressed with that of the slave.

Schubert likened the repressed "shameful part" with an imprisoned felon, locked in a dungeon into which only enough light filtered to permit it to work. Fettered in the ganglion system, it was forced to labor like a galley slave, responsible for the nutrition of body and soul. Thus employed, it was harmless, unable to manifest its wicked nature. The maintenance of rationality and morality depended upon the continuing ascendancy of the cerebral system (1968, 118) The slave in the ganglion system was peaceable only so long as it was kept in chains: "The murderer, so long as he spends the whole day working and, deeply tired, sleeps all night, does not seem to be what he really is. However, let some naive, well-meaning individual set him free, then he would immediately show himself in his true nature as the lascivious and blood-thirsty creature he was"[4] (115).

The preservation of civilization demanded that the relationship between the higher and lower parts of the soul had to be that of master and slave; further, it required ceaseless vigilance on the part of the master. Just as Schubert cautioned that the galley slave set free would immediately reveal his sexuality and destructiveness, so did Freud warn that "the ruler's throne rests upon fettered slaves. Among the instinctual components which are thus brought into service, the sexual instincts, in the narrower sense of the word, are conspicuous for their strength and savagery. Woe if they should be let loose! The throne would be overturned and the ruler trampled underfoot" (*S.E.*, XIX: 219).

The slaves in both of these theories were evil, in both, they performed a service. But how could an evil servant benefit the psyche? Because of the similarity of their models, Freud and Schubert came up against what might have been a theoretical roadblock. However, the theories being works of imagination in the first place, the theorizing imagination could easily enough extricate itself from the difficulty which it had put in its own path. The two model-builders could have been trapped by their postulate that the energy sources of the mind were evil but saved themselves by reaching for metaphors and declaring that the noxious properties of these energies could be nullified. Their descriptions of the processes responsible for this cancellation of the lust in sexuality and the destructiveness of the aggressive urge, although very different, were yet based on the same core concept: that the power of the energies could be retained in a harmless and useful form if they were subjected to *neutralization.* Schubert had compared the soul to a tree, the upper part representing the conscious cerebral system and the lower the unconscious, nourishing ganglion system. But then he depicted the unconscious root, the ganglion system, as the fountain of lust and murder. Therefore, he had to explain how the substance flowing from this fountain could turn into a beneficent, vitalizing sap. He did this by suggesting that the noxious products of the ganglion system were rendered harmless though a transformation which altered their nature. Their vicious sexual and aggressive properties disappeared, rendered inert in an alteration which resembled the destruction of the noxious qualities of a physical substance when it is counteracted by another in chemical combination. Schubert noted that a destructive acid was neutralized when combined with an alkali and then became innocuous: "like acid which burns but which later loses this characteristic altogether when it is combined with calcium oxide to form plaster of Paris" (1968, 114). However, Schubert warned that in this new state the vicious property was merely masked because the chemical action could be reversed and the acid could instantly reappear in its original form. He likened this reversal to the galley slave's prompt return to lascivious, murderous behavior should he be set free (115).

Freud began with a theory endowed with but a single instinct, the sexual, whose energy had to be "sublimated" to be generally useful. Later, when a destructive instinct was added, its energy was "neutralized" by the opposing energy of the sexual instinct. The resultant "neutral" energy was available for non-sexual, non-aggressive employment by the ego. However, neutralization was not accomplished once and for all. Just as the acid of Schubert's metaphor reappeared when the chemical action was reversed, so could neutralization be undone in which case, the sexual and aggressive properties of the instincts energies reemerged.

The theoretical predicaments from which Schubert and Freud were forced to extricate themselves by fanciful means were produced by the model. An easy escape from the predicament is offered by a change of model. If it is not assumed at the outset that the energy-supplying foundation of the mind is also the fount of evil, the problem does not arise.

The id and the ganglion system shared another important characteristic: their contents were ordinarily unconscious, but these contents could make their way into consciousness in dreams. Ordinarily, the conscious surface personality remained blissfully unaware of the terrible urges imprisoned in the basement but occasionally a dream could open a crack in the floor and allow it to catch a glimpse of the subterranean turmoil.

For Schubert, dreams could have many meanings; they could, among other things, keep us advised about the states of our soul, admonish us and remind us of our higher goals. At times, however, they filtered up out of that dungeon where the "shameful part" of the soul, with its insatiable cravings for lechery and murder, was kept in chains; then they reminded us of the ultimately corrupt nature of our being. These dreams were not opaque; their significance did not have to be revealed through interpretation. A glance at the "shadow side" of the self in a dream was all that was necessary because our lower nature, "the seat of our inclinations and desires" appeared there without a mask. It "often shows itself in its real nature" in dreams and "many people learn to know themselves from a different and worse side than that which they show in waking . . . the apparently gentle becoming angry in the dream, even cruel." He himself was disturbed when the dark, unknown part of his personality revealed itself in this way: "I become frightened when I catch sight of this shadow side of myself in a dream" (1968, 118).

Freud had a different opinion; he did not believe that dreamers regularly recognized their own "shadow sides" in dreams; they did not shudder at the sight of their evil wishes because these did not appear in their true guise. Dreams were "masked criminals," according to Freud (*S.E.,* XIX: 132).They were "wolves in sheeps' clothing" (*S.E.,* IV: 183). A censoring agency which played a critical role in the formation of dreams transformed the repugnant wish, endowing it with a deceptive facade, before permitting it to enter dream consciousness. Analysis, based on the dreamer's associations and on interpretation of elements regarded as sexual symbols, could bring the sexual and aggressive wishes to light. Schubert, assuming that dreams were transparent, could find lechery and murder only in those in which these vices put in an actual appearance. Because of his interpretative method, Freud was under the impression that, with a few exceptions, such desires could be located at the foundation of every dream.

The Romantic philosophers, and their admirers and followers in other walks of life, were gripped by fascination with realms beyond ordinary experience. As Schelling put it, they hoped that speculation taking "the freest, most daring flight," risking everything, following truth to its ultimate height, might win the "whole truth, in all of its grandeur" (Beckers, 14–15, 1875) They were convinced that they already had evidence that pure reason had taken them to a reality, proof that the fascinating domain to which their minds had led them, actually existed. Magnetism, they were convinced, had provided this proof.

Schelling had introduced hypnosis into philosophy, not to be used in the exploration of unconscious facets of mind, but to demonstrate the actuality of the sphere the philosophers supposed they had discovered. He believed that the deeply hypnotized subject, the "clairvoyant," was no longer entirely in this world. Hegel, his great rival, shared the conviction: "in the visible liberation of mind in those magnetic phenomena from the limitations of space and time and from all finite associations, there is something akin to philosophy, something which, as brute fact, defies the skepticism of the abstractive intellect and so necessitates the advance from ordinary psychology to the comprehension afforded by speculative philosophy for which alone animal magnetism is not an incomprehensible miracle." For Hegel, the escape from space and time was a "brute fact" (Hegel, 1971, 7).

NOTES

1. This confusion can be found in the theory of a Romantic physician, C.G.Carus, who is often introduced as providing evidence for the Romantic era's supposed contribution to the theory of the personal unconscious. Typically, the opening lines of Carus's book *Psyche* are quoted: "The key to the knowledge of the nature of the soul's conscious life lies in the realm of the unconscious. . . . If it were an absolute impossibility to find the unconscious in the conscious, then man should despair of ever getting a knowledge of his soul, that is of himself. But if this impossibility is only apparent, then the first task of a science of the soul is to state how the spirit of Man is able to descend into these depths" (1926, 1) But what did Carus mean by "unconscious?" Continuing to read, one finds that "the unconscious" oversees the development of the embryo in the womb, that it is concerned with the future and the past, but pays no attention to the present, that it never needs rest, never sleeps, never gets sick. It is impersonal; the unconscious of the individual is a portion of the general unconscious of the human race. What Carus offers is a hybrid theory which is primarily metaphysical but which incorporates fragments of the Leibniz-Wolffian concept of the personal unconscious.

2. Nature is "she," because the German word for "nature" is feminine.

3. Distinct from either of these was the "philosophy of nature" which can be regarded simply as the philosophy of science of the time. It consisted of a number of premises that guided research with considerable success. The assumption of *the unity of the sciences* has been credited with facilitating the discovery of the relation between electricity and magnetism, the fascination with *analogies* led to the recognition of similarities between species of plants and animals that had seemed far apart; the concern with *origins* led to the search for and examination of fossils, paving the way for Darwin.

4. Bertrand Russell (1921, 37–38) was not intimidated by the Freudian unconscious. He said of it that it "becomes a sort of underground prisoner, living in a dungeon, breaking in at long intervals on our daylight respectability with dark groans and maledictions and strange atavistic lusts. The ordinary reader, almost inevitably, thinks of this underground person as another consciousness, prevented by what Freud calls the 'censor' from making his voice heard in company, except on rare and dreadful occasions when he shouts so loud that everyone hears him and there is a scandal. Most of us like the idea that we could be desperately wicked if only we let ourselves go. For this reason, the Freudian 'unconscious' has been a consolation to many quiet and well-behaved persons."

Chapter Ten

Schopenhauer: Ego and Id

When close correspondences were found between a number of central psychoanalytic concepts and important philosophical ideas, there were some who deplored the unnecessary duplication of labor that had been occasioned by Freud's ignorance of earlier thought; not aware that he had predecessors, he had been forced to make his way alone, struggling to attain insights which had already been attained.

Among those who expressed regrets of this kind was Thomas Mann, the celebrated German novelist who, having first studied Schopenhauer, was astonished later when he found what seemed to him to be the same ideas in the work of Freud. He marveled that this isolated laborer, unaware of Schopenhauer's formulations, had nevertheless arrived at a theory which so closely resembled that of the immensely popular philosopher. In 1931, speaking as a great admirer of Freud's, Mann declared:

> Actually we know that Sigmund Freud, that mighty spirit in whose honor we are gathered together, founder of psychoanalysis as a general method of research and as a therapeutic technique, trod the steep path alone and independently, as physician and natural scientist, without knowing that reinforcement and encouragement lay to his hand in literature. He did not know Nietzsche . . . he did not know Novalis . . . he did not know Kierkegaard . . and, finally, he did not know Schopenhauer. . . . By his unaided effort, without knowledge of any previous intuitive achievement, he had methodically to follow out the line of his own researches. . . . And we think of him as solitary—the attitude is inseparable from our earliest picture of the man (Mann, 1947, 412).

Freud's achievements were his own, Mann believed, yet those versed in the ideas of the philosopher would find much in Freud's work that looked familiar: "But Freud's description of the id and the ego—is it not to a hair

Schopenhauer's description of the Will and the Intellect, a translation of the latter's metaphysics into psychology? So he who had been initiated into the metaphysics of Schopenhauer . . . he must needs have been filled with a sense of recognition and familiarity when first . . . he entered the realms of psychoanalysis and looked about him" (Mann, 1947, 416–417).

The close parallels between Freud's and Schopenhauer's basic principles have often been pointed out since. Not long after Mann expressed his opinion, a similar assessment appeared in a psychoanalytic journal; this scholar remarked that Freud's "general philosophy" appeared to be a "faithful reproduction" of that of Schopenhauer (Bischer, 1939, 91). Marcel Zentner, author of the definitive treatise on Freud's debt to Schopenhauer, a work that supersedes all others, has commented on the "astonishing precision with which Freud reproduced Freud's theory" (Zentner, 1995, 177).

THE UNCONSCIOUS WILL

The *World as Will and Representation* was published in 1819, during the Romantic era and the concept of the will as cosmic power was purely Romantic. On the other hand, as soon as Schopenhauer's focus shifted from metaphysics to psychology, the will turned into an unconscious mental force. Schopenhauer's detailed examination of the effect of unconscious motives and emotions on cognition suggest that the Leibniz-Wolffian dedication to psychological realities lived on in him. He may have been acquainted with the publications of J.G.E. Maas in which the power of unconscious motives to sustain or erase memories and to direct the movement of associations were stressed.

As a metaphysical power, the will was active in both the inanimate and animate realms. It was the force which formed the crystal, which turned the magnet to the north pole, which acted in repulsion, attraction and gravitation. In plants, it was the vegetative energy; in animals and humans it was the life force, the organism's urge to survive and thrive, to grow and expand. The will constituted "the inner, true and indestructible nature of man; yet in itself it is without consciousness" (1966, Vol. 2, 201). What we experience are its manifestations: "striving, wishing, shunning, hoping, fearing, loving, hating, in short all that directly constitutes our own weal and woe, desire and disinclination" (1966, Vol. 2, 202).

More than any other thinker in the nineteenth century, Schopenhauer was credited, in that century, with having called attention to the unconscious instinctual roots of cognition, emotion and behavior.

In Schopenhauer's dark vision, all living things were driven ceaselessly by the insatiable will. The satisfaction of every desire was always only momentary; after the briefest respite, hunger and longing began again; the desperate struggle was renewed and misery was the common lot. The idea of "progress" in life or society was nonsense; wisdom consisted of recognizing that human existence was pointless. The cognitive apparatus, however sophisticated, was driven by an insatiable, unconscious life force manifested by yearnings and cravings of all kinds; by dread and terror, by ambition and greed and, last but not least, by sexual lust.

Schopenhauer couched his melancholy assessment of life in magnificent prose which was completely unlike the dry and dusty style of the typical philosophical work of the time. He never belonged to the academic establishment which he mercilessly ridiculed. Wundt, a prominent member of this establishment, deplored his "capricious judgments" and "gusts of temper," but noted ruefully that Schopenhauer was "perhaps the most brilliant, certainly the clearest and most entertaining of our philosophical writers, and he has made it easy for the reader to master his whole system" (Wundt, 1877, 44).

Once Schopenhauer's philosophy caught the popular imagination, it had a tremendous impact. As the "climate of opinion" in the first half of the twentieth century was attributed to Freud, so, in the last half of the nineteenth century, was it ascribed to Schopenhauer. Historians have been united in this assessment: "as soon as Schopenhauer's historical influence began really to be felt, that is, after the middle of the century . . . his metaphysics of the Will seemed almost to have become the articulation of the cultural atmosphere of the age" (Schnaedelbach, 1984, 60). "From the 1850s until the end of the century there were few educated Germans who in their younger years had not been deeply moved by Schopenhauer"; his philosophy exercised a "powerful fascination" (Holborn, 1969, 121). The situation was no different in Freud's Austria. In Vienna, in the 1880s and 1890s, "to have read Schopenhauer was considered necessary for everyone who aspired to the name of a cultured person. It has been said that the society women of those days had a volume of Schopenhauer at hand, to peruse while the maid did their hair" (Allers, 1941, 164).

Schopenhauer's metaphysics of the will impressed Mann as being the original of which Freud's psychology seemed to be a "translation." Some of the important similarities between the theories of Schopenhauer and Freud were due simply to the fact that both were based upon the classical reason-versus-the-passions model; a higher rational part of the mind controlled, or attempted to control, a lower, instinctual part, Schopenhauer supposed that the perennial struggle was between the intellect and the will; for Freud, it was between the ego against the id. Distinctive of both theories was an absolute dichotomy: thinking was restricted to intellect and ego; will and id were purely instinctual. Moreover, both will and id were unconscious.

Schopenhauer maintained that "Unconsciousness is the original and natural condition of all things, and therefore is also the basis from which, in particular species of being, consciousness appears as their highest efflorescence; and for this reason, even then unconsciousness still always predominates" (1966, Vol. 2, 142).

Freud acknowledged that Schopenhauer's "unconscious will is equivalent to the mental instincts of psychoanalysis" (*S.E.,* XIV: 143). Neither will nor id could take account of the environment and neither could do anything but wish. Freud referred to the Id's "blind efforts for the satisfaction of its instincts" (*S.E.,* XXII 75). Schopenhauer's will was a "blind, irresistible urge" (1966, Vol. 1, 275). Schopenhauer discarded the eighteenth-century notion that knowledge precedes desire, that it *must* precede desire because a thing must be recognized as desirable before it is desired. Not so, according to Schopenhauer: desire leads the way, appetite comes first. Human beings, after all, are related to the animals, and these, even the lowliest to whom we can ascribe no intellect, are driven by appetites. We share this "endless striving" to satisfy our needs (1966, Vol. 1, 164).

Schopenhauer assumed that pain, produced by need, antedated pleasure: "*willing* springs from lack, from deficiency, and thus from suffering." Each deficiency stirs a wish for satisfaction but "for one wish that is fulfilled there remain at least ten that are denied" moreover, "the wish fulfilled at once makes way for a new one" (1966, Vol. 1, 196).

The driving will constituted "the inner, true and indestructible nature of man" (1966, Vol. II, 201). "Willing does not need to be learnt like knowing, but succeeds perfectly at once. The new-born child moves violently, screams and cries; it wills most vehemently although it does not yet know what it wills. For the medium of motives, the intellect, is still quite undeveloped. The will is in the dark concerning the external world in which its objects lie; and it rages like a prisoner against the walls and bars of its dungeon" (Vol. II, 234–235).

THE EGO AND THE ID

The will escapes from this darkness when the intellect is gradually developed to serve it. The will "kindles a light for itself," that is to say, it brings forth consciousness (1966, Vol. I, 150). Knowledge is simply "a means for preserving the individual and the species, just like any organ on the body. Therefore, destined originally to serve the will for the achievement of its aims, knowledge remains almost throughout entirely subordinate to its service" (1966, Vol. 1, 152). "Consciousness is a mere accident of our being," a "function of the brain," an organ which "serves the purpose of [the organism's] self-preservation by regulating its relations with the external world" (1966, Vol. II, 201). Consequently, "in all animal beings, the will is the primary and substantial thing; the intellect, on the other hand, is something secondary and additional, in fact, a mere tool in the service of the will" (Vol., II, 205).

Freud's id similarly kindled a light for itself when it brought forth the conscious ego, creating a servant which took on "the task of representing the external world to the id." The ego thereafter protected the id which would be destroyed if "in its blind efforts for the satisfaction of its instincts it disregarded that supreme external power" (*S.E.,* XXII, 75).

Freud maintained that before the ego was formed, the excitation of wishes was regulated automatically by feelings of pleasure and unpleasure. Thereafter, however, as the capacity to think evolved, the excitation could be diverted; it could take a "roundabout path" (*Umweg*) to achieve satisfaction by voluntary movement. (*S.E.,* V, 599). Schopenhauer similarly explained that the will, acting by itself, automatically responded to stimuli: "the stimulus provokes *immediate* reaction." After the development of the intellect, however, the stimulus could travel on a roundabout path (*Umweg*) through the brain, to give rise to an act of volition and to voluntary, rather than automatic, reaction (1897, 238 and 239).

Both the intellect and the ego, in spite of their important functions, remained dependent upon will and id. According to Freud, "nothing but a wish can set our mental apparatus at work" (*S.E.,* V: 567). The strength of the ego was therefore really only the borrowed strength of the id and the ego's freedom to act was accordingly circumscribed. Schopenhauer asserted that the intellect, having no power of its own, was a "mere slave and bondman of the will" (1966, Vol. II, 212).

Both the analyst and the philosopher turned to the metaphor of horse and rider to make this point. According to Freud, the ego, in its relation to the id is "like a man on horseback, who has to hold in check the superior strength of the horse; with this difference, that the rider tries to do so with his own strength while the ego uses borrowed forces. The analogy may be carried a little further. Often a rider, if he is not to be parted from his horse, is obliged to guide it where it wants to go" (*S.E.,* XIX: 25). Schopenhauer remarked "what bridle and bit are to an unmanageable horse, the intellect is to the will in man; it must be led by this bridle by means of instruction, exhortation, training, and so on." In the "height of anger, in intoxication, in despair, the will has taken the bit between its teeth; it has bolted, and follows its original nature" (1966, Vol. II, 213).

The conscious mind, as depicted by Freud and Schopenhauer, was an entity which did not know what was happening behind its back. They pictured it as a dupe of unconscious forces, unaware that it was not master in its own house. Freud declared: "What is in your mind does not coincide with what you are conscious of; whether something is going on in your mind and whether you hear of it, are two different things." In every case "the news that reaches your consciousness is incomplete and often not to be relied on. Often enough, too, it happens that you get news of events only when they are over and when you can no longer do anything to change them (*S.E.,* XVII, 143).

Schopenhauer agreed that the intellect "does not penetrate into the secret workshop of the will's decisions" (1966, Vol. II, 210). "The intellect remains so much excluded from the real resolutions and secret decisions of its own will that sometimes it can only get to know them, like those of a stranger, by spying out and taking unawares; and it must surprise the will in the act of expressing itself, in order merely to discover its real intentions" (Vol. II, 209). Schopenhauer adds:

> We often do not know what we desire or fear. For years we can have a desire without admitting it to ourselves or even letting it come to clear consciousness, because the intellect is not to know anything about it, since the good opinion we have of ourselves would inevitably suffer thereby. But if the wish is fulfilled, we get to know from our joy, not without a feeling of shame, that this is what we desired; for example, the death of a near relation whose heir we are. Sometimes we do not know what we really fear, because we lack the courage to bring it to clear consciousness. In fact, we are often entirely mistaken as to the real motive from which we do or omit to do something, till finally some accident discloses the secret to us, and we know that our real motive was not what we thought of it as being, but some other that we were unwilling to admit to ourselves, because it was by no means in keeping with our good opinion of ourselves. For example, as we imagine we omit to do something for purely moral reasons; yet we learn subsequently that we were deterred merely by fear, since we do it as soon as all danger is removed (1966, Vol. II, 209–210).

The will controlled perception and imagination: we can register only what it permits us to register; we fantasy what it demands that we fantasy: "the will, when its servant, the *intellect*, is unable to produce the thing desired, compels this servant at any rate to picture this thing to it, and generally to undertake the role of comforter . . . as a nurse does a child, with fairy-tales, and to deck these out so that they obtain an appearance of verisimilitude. Here the intellect is bound to do violence to its own nature, which is aimed at truth . . . merely in order to pacify, soothe, and send to sleep for a while the restless and unmanageable will (1966, Vol. II, 216).

The will's tendency to avoid painful insights could be dangerous. Sometimes a person, having considered what seemed to be all of the possible outcomes in a matter of importance, will have missed the most disadvantageous: "while their *intellect* imagined that it surveyed the possibilities completely, the worst of all remained quite invisible to it, because the *will*, so to speak, kept this covered with its hand; in other words, the will so mastered the intellect that it was quite incapable of glancing at the worst case of all" (1966, Vol., II, 217).

The will dominated not only thought but also memory; as the will had developed the intellect to serve its purposes, just so had it brought forth memory. Thought and memory were both tools of the will, self-and-species preservative instruments. Memories were produced and organized by the will: "memory in general requires the foundation of a will as a point of contact, or rather, as a thread on which the recollections range themselves, and which holds them firmly together, or that the will is, so to speak, the ground on which the individual recollections stick, and without which they could not be fixed." Thus will was both creator and preserver of memory (1966, Vol. II, 222).

The will's power to govern the thought process extended not only to the general flow of thought but descended to the sequence of individual associations: "But in the last instance, or in the secret of our inner being, what puts into activity the association of ideas itself, whose laws have been explained above, is the *will*. This drives its servant, the intellect, according to its powers to link one idea on to another, to recall the similar and the simultaneous, and to recognize grounds and consequents. For it is in the interest of the will that we should generally think, so that we may be in the best possible situation for all the cases that arise." Therefore the principle "which governs the association of ideas and keeps it active is ultimately the law of motivation. For that which rules the sensorium [brain] and determines it to follow analogy or another association of ideas in this or that direction, is the will of the thinking subject" (1966, Vol. II, 136).

The intellect was not altogether powerless; the relationship between intellect and will was not entirely one-sided. Ideas and fantasies acted upon the will; if we picture danger, we become anxious; if we picture a wish as coming true, we may quicken with joy; if we remember an insult, we become angry. Here, "the intellect strikes up the tune, and the will must dance to it." Shopenhauer says:

> Yet with all this, the primacy of the will becomes clear again when this will, that becomes, as we have shown, the sport of the intellect as soon as it allows the intellect to control it, once makes its supremacy felt in the last resort. This it does by prohibiting the intellect from having certain representations, by absolutely preventing certain trains of thought from arising, because it knows, or in other words experiences from the self-same intellect, that they would arouse in it any one of the emotions previously described. It then curbs and restrains the intellect, and forces it to turn to other things. However difficult this often is, it is bound to succeed the moment the will is in earnest about it; for the resistance then comes not from the intellect, which always remains indifferent, but from the will itself; and the will has an inclination in one respect for a representation it abhors in another. Thus the representation is in itself interesting to the will, just because it excites it. At the same time, however, abstract knowledge tells the will that this representation will cause it a shock of painful and unworthy emotion to no purpose. The will then decides in accordance with this last knowledge, and forces the intellect to obey (1966, Vol. II, 208).

REPRESSION

Freud agreed that Schopenhauer's concept of repression coincided "completely" with his own but he insisted that he had not read Schopenhauer and that he had been unaware of the philosopher's teaching on repression until his disciple, Otto Rank, bought it to his attention in 1910 (*S.E.,* XIV: 15). Rank had pointed out the following passage from *The World as Will and Representation* (neurosis and psychosis had not been sharply differentiated when this was written):

> The description of the origin of madness given in the text will become easier to understand, if we remember how reluctantly we think of things that powerfully prejudice our interests, wound our pride, or interfere with our wishes; with what difficulty we decide to lay such things before our own intellect for accurate and serious investigation; how easily, on the other hand, we unconsciously break away or sneak off from them again; how, on the contrary, pleasant affairs come into our minds entirely of their own accord, and, if driven away, always creep on us once more, so that we dwell on them for hours. In this resistance on the part of the will to allow what is contrary to it to come under the examination of the intellect is to be found the place where madness can break in on the mind. Every new adverse event must be assimilated by the intellect, in other words, must receive a place in the system of truths connected with our will and its interests, whatever it may have to displace that is more satisfactory. As soon as this is done, it pains us much less; but this operation itself is often very painful, and in most cases takes place only slowly and with reluctance. But soundness of mind can continue only in so far as this operation has been correctly carried out each time. On the other hand, if, in a particular case, the resistance and opposition of the will to the assimilation of some knowledge reaches such a degree that the operation is not clearly carried through; accordingly, if certain events or circumstances are wholly suppressed for the intellect, because the will cannot bear the sight of them; and then, if the resultant gaps are arbitrarily filled up for the sake of the necessary connexion; we then have madness. For the intellect has given up its nature to please the will; the person then imagines what does not exist. But the resultant madness then becomes the Lethe of unbearable sufferings; it was the last resource of worried and tormented nature, i.e. of the will (1966, Vol. II, 400).

Zentner compares this passage with Freud's explanation for the onset of psychosis. In 1894, Freud wrote one is therefore "justified in saying that the ego has fended off the incompatible idea through a flight into psychosis. . . . The ego breaks away from the incompatible idea; but the latter is inseparably connected with a piece of reality, so that, in so far as the ego achieves this result, it, too, has detached itself wholly or in part from reality. In my opinion this latter event is the condition under which the subject's ideas receive the vividness of hallucinations; and thus when the defence has been successfully carried out he finds himself in a state of hallucinatory confusion" (*S.E.,* III: 59–60).

In 1914, in the *History of the Psychoanalytic Movement,* Freud asserted: "The theory of repression quite certainly came to me independently of any other source; I know of no outside impression which might have suggested it to me, and for a long time I imagined it to be entirely original, until Otto Rank showed us a passage in Schopenhauer's *The World as Will and Representation* in which the philosopher seeks to give an explanation of insanity. What he says there about the struggle against accepting a distressing piece of reality coincides with my concept of repression so completely that once again I owe the chance of making a discovery to my not being well-read" (*S.E.,* XIV, 15). He also said that he was prepared "gladly—to forgo all claims to priority in the many instances in which laborious psychoanalytic investigation can merely confirm the truths which the philosopher recognized by intuition" (*S.E.,* XIV: 15–16).

However, Freud seems quickly to have forgotten that he had been glad to renounce "all claims to priority" for a year later, in his paper entitled "Repression," which is regarded as one of his major theoretical writings, he said of it that "it is a concept which could not have been formulated before the time of psycho-analytic studies. It is not easy in theory to deduce the possibility of such a thing as repression" (*S.E.,* XIV, 146). Ten years later, in his *Autobiographical Study* he made the point again: "I named this process *repression*; it was a novelty, and nothing like it had ever before been recognized in mental life" (*S.E.,* XX: 30).

According to Freud, Schopenhauer "intuited" the concept of repression. But how did he come to do that? The question is not unanswerable; a glance at Schopenhauer's chapter "On Madness," from which Rank took the quotation, makes manifest that this concept was suggested by clinical experience in the first place. Schopenhauer's description of insanity plainly reflects the theories of mental illness as they appeared in the medical literature of the time. Moreover, Schopenhauer also stressed that he had observed psychotic patients at first hand; his conclusions were based, not only upon the opinions of medical authorities, but also on personal encounters.

That Schopenhauer had therapeutic contact with mentally ill patients has been confirmed by the astonishing research of Zentner who has unearthed the original hospital intake records. The Napoleonic war was at its height when, between 1811 and 1815, these disturbed men were admitted at La Charité, a Berlin hospital.

Schopenhauer became acquainted with several patients; a closer relationship is documented with two of them, both assigned to the "melancholia" division. His description of the pair suggests that at a later date they would probably have been diagnosed as "manic-depressive." Schopenhauer described them as lucid.

A friend with whom Schopenhauer shared his hospital experiences recalled his deep sympathy for these psychotic individuals. Evidence that a therapeutic relationship was established seems to be indicated by the contents of surviving poems and essays they entrusted to him. Zentner believes that traces of Schopenhauer's discussions with these men can be found in his writings on madness. In his opinion, there can be no doubt that Schopenhauer developed his theory of insanity on the basis of his observations of psychiatric patients. It seems, therefore, that he did not have to rely on the "intuition" which Freud was willing to grant him. It appears moreover that Schopenhauer may have had more clinical experience with seriously disturbed patients than did Freud, who disliked and avoided such cases.

In conclusion, having picked out so many resemblances between the theories of Schopenhauer and Freud, let us remember differences responsible for a gulf between them: Schopenhauer's unconscious was not restricted to the repressed and the repressed was not regarded as a receptacle for the morally reprehensible. For Freud, the unconscious was identified with the repressed and the repressed was the repository for "the evil in the constitution of human beings" (*S.E.,* XV: 146).

Chapter Eleven

Hartmann: The Best Seller

The publisher sent the book out into the world with unprecedented fanfare and was rewarded with a blockbusting best seller. The first edition of *Philosophy of the Unconscious*, which appeared in 1868, was quickly sold out and the reputation of its author, twenty-seven-year-old Eduard von Hartmann, was established overnight. Due at least in part to aggressive promotion efforts, the number of reviews was unprecedented. Journalists took up the book and argued for and against its subject—"The Unconscious." It spawned a literature; it was translated into French and English and the excitement spread. Soon it was attacked and big guns were turned against it; these kept interest at a boil.

The book remained influential throughout the whole last third of the century as edition followed edition but its heyday was in the 1870s when "The Unconscious" was widely debated. Looking back at this decade, the French philosopher Alfred Fouillée recalled that "the unconscious was fashionable: people wanted to see it everywhere" (409). Wundt, the experimental psychologist, remarked that "since the invention of printing no philosophical work of the size has ever had such a success in Germany as the *Philosophie des Unbewussten*" (Wundt, 505).

Eduard von Hartmann was a military officer whose career had been brought to an end by a knee injury. Looking for a new vocation, he had discovered philosophy. Bypassing the universities by reading on his own, he had come upon Leibniz and was captivated by the concept of the unconscious. However, this philosophical notion remained speculative and theoretical, Hartmann believed. He decided to remedy the situation by collecting scientific evidence which would support the concept. He would collect phenomena "to render probable the existence of unconscious ideas and unconscious will from the evidence of the particular cases, and through their combination to raise this probability to a degree bordering on certainty" (1893, 2). To achieve this aim, Hartmann ranged far and wide through the sciences of his time, mustering evidence from the latest research to demonstrate the reality of ideas and acts of which we are unconscious. It was this fusion of speculation and science which captivated readers who, Hartmann averred, were "parched" for philosophy after the long materialist drought of the 1850s and 1860s (1893, x and xv).

Romantic convictions, forced underground, but never entirely extinguished, were revived in a new, acceptable form, as supposedly scientific hypotheses, buttressed on all sides by corroborations which seemed to be of the most respectable kind. Wundt remarked that, at present, "the exact sciences play so great a part that everybody desires to be on a good footing with them. . . . What then could be more opportune than a philosophy that professed to reconcile speculation and natural science?" (Wundt, 505–506) *Philosophy of the Unconscious* was attractive because the fascinating old hypothesis of Leibniz, Wolff and Schopenhauer seemed to have been fortified by massive amounts of hard, scientific proof. Moreover, it was easy to read. Hartmann had not aimed his argument at the academic philosophers in the universities but had written it for the general public and the public welcomed it warmly. It achieved a great social success. Once it had become fashionable, party-goers could not expect to hold their own in the general chatter without at least having dipped into the book. Hartmann was not entirely happy with this state of affairs. He complained that some readers merely turned over a chapter or two and then, their "metaphysical need" satisfied, believed they could "chime in with a good conscience when the topic of conversation is *Philosophy of the Unconscious*" (1893,Vol. I, xxi).

When Hartmann compared consciousness to an oft-ploughed hill and invited readers to forget about the surface and join him in an exploration of the depths, the treasure he ultimately expected to find was the answer to the riddle of the universe. He would begin by demonstrating the existence of "unconscious ideas and unconscious will." Then, having laid bare the fundamental principle of the psychological unconscious, he would show that it could be extended beyond physical and psychical domains to aid in the solution of metaphysical problems. Thereafter, chapter after chapter would show how the world crystallized around this principle until it embraced the cosmos and then stood revealed as "that which has formed the core of all great philosophies, the substance of Spinoza, the Absolute Ego of Fichte, Schelling's Absolute Subject-Object, the Absolute Idea of Plato and Hegel, Schopenhauer's Will and et cetera" (1893, 4). Contemporary scholars quickly picked up that, beneath its scientific decor, *Philosophy of the Unconscious* was a refurbished *Naturphilosophie* and their response was accordingly surly. The ensuing bombardment of the book boosted sales.

Closely following Schopenhauer, Hartmann explained that "an unconscious will exists in us is attested by personal experience." We can catch glimpses of our own unconscious motivations by discovering their effects. Very often we "do not know what it is we really will, nay, [we] even often imagine we are willing the contrary, until by the pain and pleasure resulting from the decision we are instructed concerning our true will . . . we often naively think that we are willing what appears to us good and laudable, e.g., that a sick relation, whose heir we are to be, may not die, or that in a collision between the common weal and our individual weal the former is preferred, or that an engagement formerly entered into may be kept, or that our rational conviction and not our inclination and passion may gain the day. This belief may be so strong that afterwards, if the decision falls out contrary to our supposed will, and yet instead of grief we feel an unbounded joy, we cannot get over astonishment at ourselves, because, now suddenly aware of disillusion, we learn that we unconsciously have willed the contrary of what we had imagined" (1893, 252–253).

Ordinarily, when a conscious willing is satisfied, we experience pleasure, when it is frustrated, unpleasure. Consequently, when we feel either pleasure or unpleasure without being aware of having willed anything, then the willing was unconscious (1893, 251).

Since a number of conscious and unconscious desires could simultaneously cooperate or conflict, what was willed and acted upon was the product of all of them. "The most different kinds of desires cross one another in the greatest number at every moment, and by the very same event some are gratified, others not gratified; accordingly, there is neither *pure* nor *simple* pleasure and displeasure, i.e., there is no pleasure which does not contain a pain, and no pain with which a pleasure is not bound up, but there is also no pleasure which is not compounded of the simultaneous satisfaction of the most different desires" (1893, 254).

The "importance of unconscious ideas for the whole emotional life . . . cannot be rated too highly" (1893, 258). When feelings arise from unconscious ideas, their strength is due to that very unconsciousness of the source: "the power of these feelings appears to us so much the greater the less the independence of the cerebral consciousness" (256). We become more fully conscious of feelings when the unconscious thoughts that give rise to them are translated into conscious thoughts. Once this translation has taken place, the feelings can be expressed and shared with others. He writes, "Only so far as the feelings can be translated into thoughts, only so far are they communicable," and "only so far as feelings are capable of being translated into thoughts can they to be rendered into words." However, the unconscious thoughts that underlie an emotion can never be raised to consciousness completely, something mysterious will always remain: "Let any one take for test whatever feeling he pleases, and seek to grasp it with perfectly clear consciousness in its whole extent. It is in vain; for unless satisfied with the most superficial explanation, he will constantly stumble on an irresolvable remainder, which mocks at every endeavour to illuminate it with the magnifying glass of consciousness" (258).

Feelings are therefore often unrecognized and misunderstood. How often "we fail to understand ourselves; how enigmatical often are our own feelings, especially when they occur for the first time; how liable are we to the greatest self-delusions with regard to them. We are often mastered by a feeling which has already struck firm roots in our inmost being without our suspecting it, and suddenly, on some occasion or other, there fall, as it were, scales from our eyes." As an example, Hartmann suggested that a young woman might unconsciously be completely possessed by a first love which she could with good conscience deny. Some incident could then bring the feeling completely into consciousness; in a moment she could recognize a love that had long existed. This is true of all feelings: "the process in virtue of which we become self-conscious once for all, is the translation of the unconscious ideas which determined feeling into conscious ideas, i.e., thoughts and words" (1893, 259).

Hartmann insisted that the Unconscious was amoral—a concept taken from Schopenhauer that would be developed, although in a different sense, by Freud. There was no moral instinct, Herbart explained, but he accepted "instincts of compassion, gratitude, revenge, selfishness, sensuality, et cetera." He adds, "Nature, so far as it is *unconscious, does not know* the distinction of moral and immoral." However, morality is itself natural: "consciousness being ultimately also only an unconscious product of Nature, the moral also is not an antithesis of the natural, but only a higher stage of it, to which the natural has risen through its own energy and the instrumentality of consciousness" (1893, 266–268).

The Unconscious was the source of all works of genius, according to Hartmann. The dilettante and the competent professional artist who depend upon consciousness alone can create merely technically adequate work. He cautions:

> There is wanting the divine frenzy, the vivifying breath of the Unconscious, which appears to consciousness as higher, inexplicable suggestion, which it is forced to apprehend as fact without ever being able to unravel its law. Conscious combination may, in course of time, be acquired by effort of the conscious will, by industry, endurance and practice. The creation of genius is an unwilled, passive conception; it does not come with the most earnest seeking, but quite unexpectedly, as if fallen from heaven, on journeys, in the theatre, in conversation, everywhere where it is least expected, and always suddenly and instantaneously. Conscious combination works out laboriously the smallest details, and gradually constructs a whole with painful hesitation and head-splitting, with frequent rejecting and resuming of the single parts. The concep-

> tion of genius receives the whole from one mold, as gift of the gods, unearned by toil (1893, 278).

Not only sublime artistic productions, but humor also, clever witticisms and lowly puns, are products of the Unconscious. Whenever we need the "right idea" at the "right time," we must call upon the Unconscious:

> That it is just the *right* idea which appears, for that the Unconscious alone can make provision. . . . A suitable and yet simple example is wit. . . . Every witticism is, according to the common expression, a *flash.* The understanding may perhaps make use of aids to facilitate the flash; practice, especially in the case of puns, can impress the material more vividly on the memory, and altogether strengthen the verbal memory; talent may endow particular persons with an ever-sparkling wit,—in spite of all that, every single witticism remains a gift from above; and even those who think they are privileged in this respect, and have wit completely in their power, must have the experience that just when they most wish to compel it, their talent denies them its services, and that nothing but worn-out absurdities or witticisms learnt by rote will emerge from their brain (1893, 286).

All thought originates in the Unconscious; all thought results from a cooperation between the Unconscious and consciousness. Hartmann illustrated this principle with simple cases of recall because every attempt to remember something requires the aid of the Unconscious which alone has access to the store of memories. The Unconscious may not always come up with precisely the memory which consciousness has requested. In that case, "if an unsuitable idea crops up, consciousness immediately perceives it to be inappropriate and rejects it" (1893, 301). The Unconscious then will keep trying; consciousness may continue to reject, but it should be noted that all of these rejected memories will be associated with the memory being sought: "all of these rejected ideas are by no means absolutely fortuitous in respect of the particular object, but always tend to this goal, although they may not hit the nail upon the head" (302). The reason for this is that all of the memories which arise at such times do so under the compulsion of the same purpose, the recall of a specific memory.

Following Schopenhauer, Hartmann generalized this principle: all association of thoughts is purposeful; associations always arise at the behest of motives. This is the principle supporting the practice of free association that Freud insisted later he had not learned from Hartmann.

Hartmann suggested that "the laws of the association of ideas or sequence of thought contain three essential elements: (1) the evoking idea, (2) the idea evoked and (3) the special interest leading to the calling up of the idea." He put this very strongly: the first two *never* occur without participation of the third; there is *always* a "special motive" connecting ideas and if this seems to be missing, then it is because it is unconscious (1893, 283–284).

Elimination of the "special motive" would be "justified only if there are conditions in human life in which man is free not only from every conscious purpose, but also from the sway or cooperation of every unconscious interest, every passing mood. This is, however, a condition hardly ever occurring, for even if one in appearance completely abandons his train of thought to accident, or if one abandons oneself entirely to the involuntary dreams of fancy, yet always other leading interests, dominant feelings and moods prevail at one time rather than at another, and these will always exert an influence on the association of ideas" (1893, 283–284).

Hartmann believed that the Unconscious was also deeply implicated in the progress of conscious deliberate thought. When the motive was conscious, the Unconscious assisted by making the appropriate mental contents available to consciousness. Consciousness then picked and chose among the alternatives offered to it. Hartmann illustrated this premise with examples taken from the most abstract kind of thinking, the mathematical. In mathematics we can distinguish between two methods of proof, the intuitive and the discursive or deductive. The intuitive is a form of proof in which the solution is given immediately. We see at a glance that the angles of an equilateral triangle are equal. This conclusion is offered to consciousness by the Unconscious "without hesitation and reflection . . . instantaneously" (1893, 313). The discursive or deductive, on the other hand, proceeds step by step; each step is conscious but each step is produced by the Unconscious. The problem-solving process then consists of a number of conscious events interspersed with unconscious productive activity. Hartmann imagined that a "higher mind" might be able to dispense with the deductive method altogether; such a mind would grasp even difficult problems intuitively. Talented mathematicians in fact are able to make intuitive leaps and to skip steps in the deductive process: "all of this allows us to conclude that the discursive or deductive method is only the lame walking on stilts of conscious logic, whilst rational intuition is the Pegasus flight of the Unconscious, which carries in a moment from earth to heaven. The whole of mathematics appears from this point of view as the tools and implements of our poor mind, which, obliged laboriously to pile stone on stone, yet can never touch the heavens with its hand, although it build beyond the clouds. A mind standing in closer connection with the Unconscious, then, would instantaneously grasp the solution of every profound problem intuitively, and yet with logical necessity, as we do in the simplest geometrical problems" (1893, 316).

Like Schopenhauer, Hartmann believed that "unconscious rumination" accomplished much of our thinking for us. We come across an idea which is new and perhaps upsetting. We put it aside and then an "unconscious mental process of digestion and assimilation" goes to work on it. Perhaps months later, "we find to our very great astonishment that we have undergone a mental regeneration on the point, that the old opinions which we had taken for actual conviction up to that moment have been entirely renounced, and that new ones have already become quietly lodged there" (1893, 322).

Our most basic beliefs are products of unconscious statistical inferences. If we were not convinced of certain fundamental propositions, we could not function. For instance, we would be quite helpless if we did not trust that the earth would continue to support our next step. Propositions like this are based upon unconscious inferences. Without our knowing anything about it, inductive logic has been employed and the probabilities concerned have been calculated: "for when I have often seen rain or storms occur, along with such and such signs in the sky, I form the general rule, with a degree of probability of real validity dependent on the number of observations, without knowing anything about Mill's inductive methods of Agreement, Difference, Residues, or Concomitant variations" (1893, 312). Observations of this kind about the personal unconscious were designed by Hartmann to prepare the way for the Unconscious as world-creating and regulating principle.

In some of Hartmann's attempts to clarify phenomena which were considered unfathomable in his time, we see him prematurely trying to answer questions which would only become soluble a century or so later. What Hartmann called "the reparative power of nature" was such a question. Biologists had studied the regeneration of which some of the lower animals were capable. Hartmann described the results of some of these studies, noting that these creatures did not merely replace parts of their bodies if they lost them: in some cases "the animal may be cut into pieces and yet each single piece develops into a perfect example of its kind." How could this happen? It could only be explained, Hartmann averred, if we assumed that in each individual piece there must exist some kind of map or pattern, a copy of the design which could be followed in the reconstruction. This reconstruction was a marvelously skillful operation which could not be attributed to a self-arrangement by unintelligent matter; the assumption of a "material mechanism" was a "sheer impossibility." Therefore, the only remaining hypothesis was that the map was a *mental* pattern and, since it was unlikely that this was conscious, it had to be *unconscious:* "every fragment of the animal must have the unconscious image of the type according to which it accomplishes this regeneration." We know now that Hartmann was right when he assumed that each part of the animal must contain a plan but we have accepted what he called a "sheer impossibility," namely, that it is composed of matter, having put DNA in the place of the "unconscious mental picture" (1893, 144).

Hartmann's scientific and philosophical contemporaries were as ignorant of future developments as he was but they severely criticized him for his irresponsible hypothesizing. They charged that whenever scientists admitted "we don't know what causes this phenomenon," Hartmann, with pseudo-wisdom, insisted: "the cause is the Unconscious."

THE INFALLIBLE UNCONSCIOUS

Hartmann was also assailed for lending what many of his readers were bound to assume was scientific support to some of the most absurd beliefs of animal magnetism. In his treatment of instinct, for instance, he slid from descriptions of the wonderful and quite mysterious abilities of animals to a defense of human clairvoyance. Hartmann began by distinguishing performances due to conscious effort with those accomplished instinctively, that is, unconsciously. Whatever is learned consciously requires intelligence, application and time. Animals are much like ourselves in this regard when they learn consciously. They learn through being taught and improve with practice. Instinct, however, "has this peculiarity, that it never delays and hesitates, but instantaneously operates, if the motive for its operation consciously occurs. The rapidity of result in instinctive action is met with alike in the lowest and in the highest animals." The Emperor moth, for instance, spins a cocoon and constructs for itself a double arch of bristles meeting at their apices, very easy to open from within, but which will resist efforts to penetrate into it from the outside (1893, 91–92). This complicated behavior is unlearned and the caterpillar does this perfectly on the very first attempt. Hartmann took from many examples of this kind the principle that the Unconscious does not make mistakes, that is, that it is infallible: "all instinctive actions give the impression of *absolute certainty* and *self-assurance*, and there never occurs in them, as in conscious resolution, any *delay, doubt* or *hesitation*, never any genuine *error* . . . this feature of absolute accuracy is so characteristic, that it may pass for the only clear defining mark of action from instinct when compared with action from conscious reflection." This conclusion suggested to him that "a principle altogether different from that which underlies conscious action must be at the bottom of instinct and that can only be found in the determination of the will by a process lying in the Unconscious" (98).

Was Freud swayed by Hartmann? Some of his remarks about the assurance of unconsciously motivated actions have a Hartmannian ring. Of movements which seem "clumsy" but which in a highly skillful manner achieve an unconscious aim, Freud stated that "they prove to be governed by an intention and achieve their aim with a certainty which cannot in general be credited to our conscious voluntary movements. Moreover they have both features—their violence and their unerring aim—in common with the motor manifestations of the hysterical neurosis, and partly, too, with the motor performances of somnambulism. This fact indicates that both in these cases and in the movements under consideration the same unknown modification of the innervatory process is present" (*S.E.,* VI: 168). The unconscious skill which Freud had in mind was exemplified in his account of a man who lost keys which were later found lying between a book and a pamphlet: "They were so cleverly placed that no one would have suspected they were there.

He found himself afterwards unable to replace them so that they were equally invisible. The unconscious dexterity with which an object is mislaid on account of hidden but powerful motives is very reminiscent of 'somnambulistic certainty'"—the certainty attributed to sleepwalkers (*S.E.,* VI: 142).

Having established the great skill of the Unconscious, Hartmann went on to attribute to it clairvoyance, that is, the knowledge of future events or an understanding of present events not acquired through experience. As an example of an animal behaving as though it knew what lay ahead, Hartmann mentioned the Stag-beetle. The larvae of these beetles dig cavities for themselves when they are about to pass into the chrysalis state. The female digs a hole as large as she is; the male, however, digs a hole twice as large because he will grow enormous horns, thereby doubling in size. The larvae can hardly be said to "foresee" this and yet the future event determines the present action. The knowledge of the future must therefore have been effective unconsciously. As regards comprehension of a current event that has not been learned through experience, the way in which ferrets and buzzards deal with poisonous adders should be considered. These animals attack non-poisonous snakes without more ado; however, even if they have never before seen an adder, they take hold of it with the greatest care and attempt to crush its head to avoid being bitten. They know, therefore, without having learned it, that the adder is dangerous. This then is another example of unconscious precognition (1893, 96).

Hartmann found "unconscious clairvoyance" throughout the animal kingdom, describing dozens of instances. Most animals know their enemies before they have had any experience; pigeons scatter if a bird of prey approaches, horses fear lions and the saddle horses on the bridle path which ran alongside the lion houses at the Berlin zoo tended to become nervous and restless when they caught the scent of these wholly unknown enemies (1893, 99). Animals know which foods they can eat, males and females always recognize each other even when their forms are different, swallows and storks find their way home, traveling hundreds of miles over strange lands: "the clairvoyance of the Unconscious has enabled them to divine the right path" (101).

However, presentiments of death also occurred and these were fulfilled far more often than not and could therefore not be explained away as being due to imagination. The presentiment of death was common among animals, even those who could not comprehend death. When death approached they crept away and hid in remote, lonely places: "we must only assume that the unconscious clairvoyance, although essentially alike in man and animal, evokes presentiments of different distinctness." That is, the cat creeps away propelled by an unconscious feeling; the human consciously senses the impending end. People have presentiments not only of their own death but also of that of loved ones. Narratives attesting to this "are found among all peoples and in all times, and in part undoubtedly contain genuine matter of fact" (1893, 107–108). The closely allied faculty of "second sight" has enabled people to foresee future or distant events, not only of deaths but of battles and conflagrations. Often such anticipations occur in dreams, although there they may appear in symbolic form: "frequently the presentiments in which the clairvoyance of the Unconscious is revealed to consciousness are dark, incomprehensible and symbolical, because they are obliged to take a sensible form in the brain, whilst the unconscious idea cannot partake of the form of sensibility wherefore it is so easy to regard what, in mental moods, dreams, or the images of sick persons, is accidental as significant.

FREUD'S RELATIONSHIP TO HARTMANN

Had Freud read Hartmann? Naturally, the question was raised. The problem with attempting to link a given concept in the Freudian corpus with a particular idea in *Philosophy of the Unconscious* is that Hartmann worked almost entirely with traditional conceptions. Therefore, although the most important psychoanalytic concepts, and many less significant notions, are to be found in Hartmann's work, conveniently packaged, one cannot know whether Freud actually quarried Hartmann or whether he and Hartmann simply drew from the same sources. Moreover, during Freud's formative years, and beyond, the Hartmannian philosophy was everywhere and Freud could have absorbed his ideas from secondary sources. Nevertheless, Freud was specifically challenged on one point—the originality of his assumption about the role of purposive ideas in free association. The principle in question was used by Freud to justify the practice.

People who are asked to free associate are told to stop thinking purposefully, to suppress their critical faculty, let their minds drift and report the thoughts that occur to them. The train of thoughts that results from this deliberate abandonment of purpose might be expected to be random and senseless. However, in *The Interpretation of Dreams*, Freud insisted that this was not the case because what has been excluded in this process is merely the *conscious* purpose: "it is demonstrably untrue that we are being carried along a purposeless stream of ideas when, in the process of interpreting a dream, we abandon reflection and allow involuntary ideas to emerge. It can be shown that all that we can ever get rid of are purposive ideas that are *known* to us; as soon as we have done this, *unknown*—or, as we inaccurately say, 'unconscious'—purposive ideas take charge and thereafter determine the course of the involuntary ideas. No influence that we can bring to bear upon our mental processes can ever enable us to think without purposive ideas" (*S.E.*, V: 528).

Freud's biographer assumed that this concept was original. "The network of associated ideas described in the Association Psychology of the nineteenth century, with its categories of contiguity, causality, etc. took on a very different appearance when Freud introduced the conception of purposive ideas" in the unconscious" (Jones 1, 378). Here Jones was ignoring the fact that just this priority had been questioned and that, in 1914, Freud had responded to the question in a footnote added to *The Interpretation of Dreams*. There, Freud had conceded that Hartmann had "made a clear statement of the law in accordance with which the association of ideas is governed by unconscious purposive ideas." However, he insisted that "*it was not until later* that my attention was drawn to the fact that Eduard von Hartmann takes the same view on this important matter of psychology" (emphasis added). That is to say, he denied that he had taken the idea from Hartmann.

Historian Donald Capps, who believed that Freud "was in fact deeply influenced by Hartmann," pointed out that there was "clear evidence that Freud read at least portions of the *Philosophy of the Unconscious* before he wrote *The Interpretation of Dreams*" (1970, 164–165). The "clear evidence" consisted of Freud's having mentioned Hartmann's book in *The Interpretation of Dreams*. He had referred to Hartmann there in connection with the latter's dream theory. Capps pointed out that Freud had quoted from the tenth edition of the *Philosophy of the Unconscious* which was published in 1890. "We may therefore assume that Freud's reading of the book occurred between 1890 and 1900, the decade in which he `discovered' the basic tenets of psychoanalysis." Capps concluded "certainly it was not out of character for Freud to disavow from time to time the influence of other individuals on his theoretical formulations."

The assumption that free association was guided by purposive ideas was not as rare as this argument about priorities might suggest. Without attempting a survey, we have come across the concept in the works of Maass, Jakob and Schopenhauer. Moreover, in the latter part of the nineteenth century, we find issues popularized by Schopenhauer and Hartmann being taken seriously by influential academicians.

The promotion of the concept of the Unconscious was Hartmann's life task. In later years, he had reservations about some youthful excesses in the book, attributable to his age at the time of writing. Nevertheless, in the preface to a later edition, he described *Philosophy of the Unconscious* as the "program of my life" (1893, xxix).

And yet he and his book were soon forgotten. No episode illustrates Ellenberger's judgment that the Freudian legend blotted out the past and that Freud was credited with the achievements of his predecessors better than the eclipse of Hartmann. This eclipse, however, was not instantaneous. As late as 1921, the English historian, George Sidney Brett, believed that Hartmann's influence would last. Hartmann, he maintained "powerfully influenced the development of nineteenth century thought. Whatever Hartmann said always came back to the one and only essential conclusion—the Unconscious must be accepted. And it has been accepted. Some writers almost apologize for using the term 'rational.' The old habit of putting 'clear ideas' in the foreground is almost obsolete. We are told that men live by impulses; that actions express the efforts of a vital energy which moves darkly on the wings of heredity through the generations of men; that we do not act from conscious reasons, but rather construct reasons to explain what has been done in and through us. The soberest psychology of the twentieth century is leavened by these ideas. In the analysis of conduct, normal or abnormal, the idea that consciousness does not really act, but rather serves to recognize and appropriate the actions of an unconscious force, is everywhere to be met" (Brett, 1921, 200–201).

This assessment of Hartmann must surely have been one of the last of its kind. In the 1930s, according to Auden, it was Freud who constituted "a whole climate of opinion." The psychoanalytic tide had washed away not only Hartmann, but all of the patrons of the concept of the unconscious before him and with them, a very large chunk of Western intellectual history.

Chapter Twelve

The Ghost in the Freudian Mansion

During the whole of the twentieth century, the spirit of Johann Friedrich Herbart hovered over the psychoanalytic couch, shaping the treatment of every patient who ever occupied it. The near-identity of some pivotal features of Herbart's theory with psychoanalytic formulations establishes that Freud's hypotheses were closely related to the concepts of this philosopher. However, Freud never mentioned Herbart.

Freud insisted that he knew nothing of philosophy; he had read the books of no philosophers. Indeed, he had gone out of his way to avoid them in order to keep his mind free of extraneous ideas; he wanted to focus purely on his own observations and the inferences that could be drawn from them.

However, as Freud's fame spread, after about 1905, as more and more people came across his ideas, it was only a matter of time before surprising parallels between them and some well-known philosophical concepts were noticed. Asked about these similarities, Freud stone-walled; he recognized the similarities, he said; he was actually pleased to recognize them, but they were accidental. Then, in 1932, a German scholar, Maria Dorer, published an important study comparing Freud's theories with those of several philosophers, stressing particularly the psychology of Herbart. She declared that the resemblances between Freud's and Herbart's theories could not possibly be fortuitous, if for no other reason than that Freud made use of this predecessor's unique theoretical vocabulary–for instance, "resistance," "repression," "ego" and a "psychic mechanism" in which a "quota of affect" or "sum of excitation" possessed the characteristics of a "quantity" which increased and diminished. (*S.E.,* III: 60, and Dorer, 1932, 19–20).

Dorer was entirely respectful of psychoanalysis; she disparaged neither the theory nor its author. But she pointed out that analysts were claiming that it had been born in a vacuum; one of them had maintained only recently that it was “a theory . . . entirely independent of history.” All she wanted to do, she explained, was to put psychoanalysis “into its historical context, that is to say, to demonstrate the psychological and the related philosophical foundations upon which psychoanalysis was essentially based” (1932, 1–2).

But Dorer was puzzled; she trusted Freud’s assertion that he was totally ignorant of philosophy, noting that he had made remarks: “I have held fast to the habit of always studying things themselves before looking for information about them in books” (*S.E.,* XIV: 19) and “even when I have moved away from observation, I have carefully avoided any contact with philosophy proper” (*S.E.,* XX: 59, and Dorer, 1932, 60). Pondering what intermediary might have passed Herbartian ideas on to Freud, she ruled out Franz Brentano, a well-known philosopher who was at the University of Vienna when Freud attended it because she knew of no link between Freud and Brentano (1932, 177).

Since then, it has been learned that Freud not only had not “avoided any contact” with philosophy but had actually studied it at the University of Vienna, that he had contemplated obtaining a degree in the subject and that his professor had been none other than the Brentano whom Dorer had ruled out.[1]

Moreover, it has been established that Freud studied Herbartian psychology when he was the equivalent of a “senior” in high school, that is, a student in the last year at the “Gymnasium” (a combined middle-high school). Here, as at all similar educational institutions in Austria, a course in Herbartian psychology was mandatory.[2] Moreover, it was not true that Freud had carefully shunned the studies of his predecessors in order to keep his mind free for his own investigations. On the contrary, determined to acquire the necessary background in the field, he had immersed himself in their works and had complained to his friend Fliess more than once that he found the self-imposed task onerous. It was going to take “years,” he grumbled, to get through “all the psychology” which he was going to have to read (Freud, 1985, 277). On another occasion, reporting that “I am continually occupied with psychology,” Freud was pleased with what he found and remarked that “the oldest ideas are really the most useful ones, as I am finding out belatedly” (1985, 172).

When Freudian scholars conceded that he had been acquainted with Herbartian psychology, they typically minimized its influence. A leading theoretician, Heinz Hartmann, asserted that “while Freud certainly wrote, in the beginning, in the psychological language of Herbart, it does not appear that his psychology had great stimulating power for Freud, who gave the concepts new meanings or discarded them altogether; even more important, it does not seem that Herbart’s concepts were helpful in a specific way for the solution of any of the concrete problems with which Freud was confronted” (Hartmann, 1964, 272–273).

Other Freudian scholars agreed: "the earlier theories of the unconscious of Herbart" had apparently had "little direct effect on the development of Freud's concept of the unconscious, although Freud was probably familiar with a few of them from his youth and was very likely influenced by them in a general way" (Shakow and Rapaport, 1964, 7–8).

What are we to make of this confrontation? According to the psychoanalysts, Herbartian theory had little effect on Freudian conceptions; Dorer believed, on the other hand, that she had come upon the ultimate foundation of psychoanalysis. The opposition may be overcome if we distinguish between the design, or pattern, of Freud's theory, and its content, or subject matter. Its design was undoubtedly Herbartian; its content, on the other hand, was not. An architectural design can serve to guide the construction of very different kinds of houses; they will all have the same floor plan, the same location of windows, doors and fireplaces and so forth, but they may serve very different purposes and look very different.

Dorer was interested in the design; in this respect the theories of Herbart and Freud are remarkably similar. The psychoanalysts were focusing on the subject matter of the theory and here the dissimilarity between the theories was great indeed. Herbart's theory was cognitive; it aimed to account for the thought processes of the normal mind. Freud's hypotheses were centered on psychopathology with emphasis on the instincts in the formation of neurotic symptoms.

Herbart's theory dealt with a range of phenomena, including the moment-to-moment appearance of ideas in consciousness. In that situation, "inhibited" or "repressed" ideas were those which would interfere with attention or with the ongoing flow of thought.[3] The ideas occupying a person's mind at work in the office, for instance, would not allow memories of the festivities of the night before to enter the mind. But the theory was also applicable to the long-range development and preservation of beliefs and attitudes and beyond that, to the formation and protection of character structure. In this case, whole chunks of mental contents could be banished for years, even forever. In theory, the model could also accommodate the repression of immoral or antisocial thoughts, but because the model was designed to be purely cognitive, Herbart paid no attention to the moral dimension.[4]

This dimension was crucial for Freud. What had to be kept out of the conscious mind was the immoral or shameful. The decent, civilized forces of the mind were engaged in an everlasting effort to prevent the coming-to-consciousness of crude sexual and aggressive wishes derived from the primitive instincts.

Yet, once the distinction between the design and the content of a theory has been made clear, a question remains: is it really possible to express a set of psychological hypotheses in the language of a borrowed cognitive theory without the hypotheses being colored by the theory? If clinical conceptions are poured into the mold of an extraneous model, are they not likely to take on the shape of the model? We will find that Freud approached his first hysterical patients equipped with Herbartian presuppositions; he made his observations wearing Herbartian spectacles; his thoughts about neurosis were shaped by the theoretical pattern that had been impressed on his mind in his youth. Thus patterned, psychoanalysis took on the form by which it was recognized throughout the twentieth century.

An intellectual force in nineteenth-century Germany and Austria, Herbart was considered to have had a greater impact on the psychology of these countries than any other thinker during that era. William James, writing about Germany in 1890, commented that "Herbart and his followers . . . until recently may be said to have reigned almost supreme in their native country" (James, 1950, Vol. 1, 603). If anything, the Herbartian hold on Austrian psychology was even more complete.

The unparalleled authority which Herbartian theory enjoyed, an authority which was waning at the end of the century, was due to the peculiar semi-official status conferred upon it in the Austrian empire. This special standing, which explained the teaching of Herbart in the Gymnasium, had been granted because, unlike other major philosophies of the time, that of Herbart did not pose a threat to the doctrine of the Catholic church.

In the nineteenth century, this institution was besieged by anticlerical forces throughout much of Europe as increasingly secularized societies demanded the complete separation of church and state. In the defense of its ancient prerogatives and of its traditional doctrines, the church sought to prevent the spread of teachings which seemed to menace them. Therefore it was hostile to Kant who had demolished the time-honored rational arguments for the existence of God; his *Critique of Pure Reason* was put on the *Index of Forbidden Books*. Kant's successors, Fichte, Schelling and Hegel, did not fare much better for they were regarded as promoters of pantheism (Johnston, 1972, 281–286).

The direction which Herbart took, on the other hand, did not put him onto a collision course with the church. His philosophy did not clash with the scholastic Aristotelianism of St. Thomas Aquinas, the premier Catholic philosopher. Therefore, although he was a Protestant, Herbart's thought was given a cordial welcome in Austria, and, because of the close church-state relationship, achieved a higher status there than it did anywhere else. And so it came about that Freud studied Herbart in the Gymnasium and there acquired some of the fundamentals which would be resurrected later as cornerstones for his own theory.

NEWTONIAN AMBITIONS

In 1895, in his ambitious, albeit never-published *Project for a Scientific Psychology*, Freud announced that the neurophysiological theory which he was creating would be mechanical—mechanical, that is, in the sense of "Newtonian mechanics," the science of matter in motion:

"The intention is to furnish a psychology that shall be a natural science: that is, to represent psychical processes as quantitatively determinate states of specifiable material particles, thus making those processes perspicuous and free from contradiction. . . . What distinguishes activity from rest is to be regarded as . . . subject to the general laws of motion" (*S.E.,* I: 295).

What an odd intention, one might think. Particles? Laws of motion? Why would a neurologist, who had taken an interest in the psychology of hysteria and who had already suggested more than one clinical hypothesis to explain its symptoms, take a turn toward physics in his examination of cerebral processes?

Freud was following an old dream. Ever since Newton astonished the world with a theory which explained the motion of the heavenly bodies, the flow of the tides and the falling of apples by means of a handful of universal laws, physics had reigned as the queen of the sciences, the perfect science which every other ought to emulate. This ideal was most difficult to apply in psychology; a number of attempts had been made, but none was ever so grand, as intricate and as thorough as that of Herbart. Almost surely Herbart produced the most elaborate mechanical model of the mind that the world has ever seen. This theory was taught, without all of the details, but with all due respect, at Freud's gymnasium. Freud apparently learned this lesson early: a clinical theory was all very well, but if it was to achieve eminence as a natural science, a theory had to be mechanical.

Herbart had been much impressed by the Leibnizian psychology which he had encountered as a student but reported that he had been amazed "that such exquisite preliminary studies nevertheless failed to produce any competent psychology" (1858 244). Herbart did not intend to dismiss the psychological reflection of his predecessors; what he did mean was that none of them had attempted to construct what he deemed really necessary: a scientific theory, one which would do for psychology what Newton's simple and elegant formulation had done for physics. Herbart believed that, in order to achieve scientific validity, a model of the mind would have to be, like Newton's, mechanical, that is, it would have to account for psychological phenomena by reference to mental analogues of "matter in motion" and to mathematically expressed universal laws.

The Newtonian world was a great machine, every part of which was related to every other, every motion of which was determined by inexorable laws. Herbart did not represent himself as the "Newton of psychology" and yet his ambitions were manifestly Newtonian. His mental universe was also a machine; the world without was matched by a world within. Every mental element interacted with every other; mental forces were governed by immutable and universal laws of mental motion which were mathematically defined.

To begin with, Herbart needed a mental analog for "matter" but here the decision cannot have been difficult. The British philosophers Locke and Hume had already adopted an atomism of the mind, treating ideas as though they were discrete particles governed mechanically by the laws of association. They had even suggested that these particle-like ideas might be subject to forces similar to those of physics, such as attraction and repulsion, but had taken the concept no further (Lowry, 1971, 67–72). Herbart, however, took the notion seriously and, in his model of the mind, handled ideas like particles and subjected them to the forces of attraction and repulsion.

Herbart also required motion, mental motion—but is there motion in the mind? Yes, Herbart decided, for do not our thoughts "come" and "go"? In fact, he pointed out, thoughts are constantly traveling into and out of consciousness: "Our thoughts become dark, vanish, then return" (1858, 319). He adds later: "The darkening of thoughts, when it runs successively through various degrees, so much resembles motion . . . that it will not appear strange that the theory of the laws of darkening and its opposite, clarification, that is, the reappearance of thoughts in consciousness, is, on the whole, structured like the theory of the laws of motion of bodies" (1858, 325).

Using ideas and their movements as analogues of matter and motion, Herbart created the theory which he expounded both in his *Textbook for Psychology* of 1816 and his much more comprehensive two-volume *Psychology as Science* of 1824. Herbart called his system the "psychic mechanism"; it was also generally known as the idea-mechanism, or "mechanism of ideas" (*Vorstellungsmechanik*) and it was the direct progenitor of Freud's "psychic apparatus."

Herbart's attempt to formulate a law of motion for the mind faced an apparent obstacle: the conscious activities of the mind seemed to be too erratic to be captured by a law. Natural laws were based upon regularities in nature; without regularities, there could be no laws, and without laws, no science.

The great natural scientists of the sixteenth and seventeenth centuries, Copernicus, Kepler, Galileo and Newton had been able to discover laws because they could depend upon the constancy of physical phenomena. This constancy, although not perfect, was yet reliable enough to permit scientists to discover order behind appearances. Without the existence of such order in nature, no laws could be established. When Galileo rolled balls down an incline to investigate their acceleration, he could be sure that they would speed up at the same rate from one trial to the next. Unfortunately, just this feature seemed to be lacking in the psychological field. Thoughts could not be counted on to flow in an unvarying fashion; inevitably there were discontinuities. The stream unpredictably shifted and could take a contrary course from one moment to the next. Since ideas could at any moment pop up apparently out of nowhere, thinking simply did not manifest the constancy which was requisite for the discovery of important general laws. The mind lacked the order which was to be found in the physical universe.

Herbart, equipped with the major Leibnizian postulate, was not deterred by this apparent difficulty. Order in the mind could be discerned, he explained, if it was supposed that the appearance of thoughts in consciousness was a consequence of underlying *unconscious* thought processes. The hypothesis that otherwise inexplicable turns of thought had unconscious causes enabled him to provide a theoretical explanation for discontinuity. If conscious and unconscious thought processes were considered to be intimately interrelated in a single system, then discontinuities simply disappeared.

Herbart pointed out that natural scientists also had been confronted with anomalies. Although events in the world they explored occurred with great regularity, important exceptions had puzzled them for centuries. The heavenly bodies generally moved reliably across the sky from east to west but upon occasion a few of them apparently reversed direction and traveled backwards for a while. Because of this inexplicable behavior they were called the "wanderers." Once Copernicus had explained the true order of the solar system, it was understood that this motion was not irregular at all. The "wanderers" were planets which, like the earth, traveled around the sun and what seemed to be their retrograde motion was an illusion produced by the paths of the orbits. Herbart declared that the supposed vagaries of consciousness were as misleading as those of the heavenly bodies: "the course of our thoughts so often seems to proceed by fits and starts and appears to be altogether irregular" but "this appearance deceives, like the apparent wandering of the planets." If one takes events outside of consciousness into consideration, then it becomes clear that "the lawfulness in the human mind is altogether equal to that of the starry skies" (1850, 20). The assumption that conscious and unconscious thought processes together constituted a unified system would make possible revelation of the hidden laws which governed the mind and this in turn would permit the development of a psychology equaling a natural science.

This consequential hypothesis which accounted for the seemingly capricious leaps of thought and the apparently erratic disjunctions in its flow by postulating unconscious causation is now assumed to have been Freud's. In one of his more dazzling acts of appropriation, Freud laid claim to it himself: "Our assumption of the unconscious is *necessary* . . . because the data of consciousness have a very large number of gaps in them . . . all these conscious acts remain disconnected and unintelligible if we insist upon claiming that every mental act that occurs in us must also necessarily be experienced by us through consciousness; on the other hand, they fall into a demonstrable connection if we interpolate between them the unconscious acts which we have inferred" (*S.E.*, XIV: 166–167). Not satisfied with the take-over of this major concept, the fundamental premise of Herbart's theory, Freud insisted that "philosophy" had had no such notion. As he did on other occasions, Freud coupled his exposition of an idea he had acquired from philosophy with a contemptuous reference to philosophy's supposed denial of this idea. Because of this denial, he asserted, philosophy could never have produced a science: its "psychology of consciousness never went beyond the broken sequences which were obviously dependent on something else, the other view, [the psychoanalytic], which held that the psychical is unconscious in itself, enabled psychology to take its place as a natural science like any other" (*S.E.*, XXIII: 158). However, Freud had merely followed Herbart and Herbart's theory had been solidly grounded in the psychology of Leibniz which, for two centuries, had accepted the premise that "the psychical is unconscious in itself."

THE HERBARTIAN TOPOGRAPHY

Freud's first major theory was known as the "topographic"—the name bestowed upon it not by Freud himself but by his followers because it divided the mind up into "regions" distinguished by states of consciousness: conscious, preconscious and unconscious. Unconscious contents were forcibly kept out of awareness by repression; the preconscious were unconscious also but could easily change their state; a simple shift of attention could bring them to consciousness. These regions could be pictured as layered, with the unconscious at the bottom, the preconscious just above it and the conscious on top. A censoring barrier was situated between the unconscious and the preconscious. Herbart classified contents in much the same way.

The critical distinction between these states or systems, for both Herbart and Freud, was not between conscious and preconscious but between them and the unconscious. The censoring threshold, in the theories of both, isolated the unconscious. An unconscious idea that crossed the threshold in an upward direction did not become conscious, it became preconsious. In this state, it could either capture attention or remain unnoticed.

That states of consciousness lend themselves to this tripartite division was not a rare idea; it was, for instance, clearly described in the *Encyclopedia Britannica*. In the "*Psychology*" article of the ninth or 1878 edition, "subconscious" stood for what is now called "unconscious," as the context makes clear. We read there that the "widely understood" assumption of "three grades of consciousness" seems "justified." These are "(1) a centre or focus of consciousness within (2) a wider field, any part of which may at once become the focus." and (3) sub consciousness: "Presentations [ideas] in sub-consciousness have not the power to divert attention, nor can we voluntarily concentrate attention upon them. Before either can happen, the subconscious presentations must cross the threshold of consciousness, and so cease to be subconscious; and this, of course, is far from being always possible" (Ward, 1895, 47).

Freud, however, believed that he had been the first to notice that ideas could occur in the three states which he felicitously renamed and wondered how this had happened: it would be "difficult to explain concisely how it came about that psychoanalysis made a further distinction in the unconscious, and separated it into a preconscious and an unconscious proper" (*S.E.*, XX: 32). However, the explanation is not so difficult if we bear in mind, as Freud did not, that he had a Herbartian education. In this case, as in others, he had apparently remembered a concept but had forgotten its source.

For the sake of convenience, when referring to these three states, I will use Freud's well-known, helpful terminology, rather than the long-forgotten, cumbersome language of the Herbartians.

HERBART'S THEORY

Herbart's picture of the mind at a given moment was that of a structure having a conical shape, that of a tepee, for instance, broad at the base and rising to a peak. In the very small space at the peak was consciousness which could attend to only a very few ideas at a time. However, consciousness was the old "internal sense," the metaphorical inner "eye" which could "see" many, albeit not all, of the ideas which filled the area below it. Although its capacity, like that of the eye, was small at a given moment in that it could focus on only a few items at a time, like the eye, it could shift rapidly over the whole field available to it. It "possessed an extremely small pupil but the highest degree of mobility" (1850, 91).

The space below consciousness was filled with ideas, ranging in an unbroken Leibnizian continuum, from the most conscious, those actually occupying consciousness, at the top, to the most unconscious, at the bottom. Ideas were said to move "up" toward consciousness," or "down" toward the unconscious. In Herbart's idiom, they "rose" and "sank." The space was partitioned horizontally, divided into upper and lower areas by a barrier to which Herbart gave the name: "threshold of consciousness."[5] Ideas below the threshold were unconscious, beyond the range of the inner eye; those above the threshold were preconscious, they could become conscious by a turning of attention.

HERBARTIAN *DYNAMICS*

Herbart created a dynamic model of the mind when he proposed that ideas were continually at war with one another, all being rivals for the attainment of consciousness. Every idea below consciousness attempted to rise and enter it; this entailed its pushing opposing ideas down to lower levels of consciousness, forcing them, ultimately, below the threshold. The struggle was endless as the ideas driven below the threshold by this "repression" (*Verdrängung*) or "inhibition" (*Hemmung*) ceaselessly attempted to return to consciousness and those above it, engaging in "resistance" (*Widerstand*), prevented this return by exerting a constant counter-force (1850, 15–21).

Ideas attempting to rise above the threshold faced an obstacle in the form of a discriminating process which determined their suitability for consciousness. If, following Freud's example of the "censor," we personify the process, then we have a border guard or customs inspector who, after appraising ideas decides whether or not they will be able to mingle peacefully with those already inhabiting consciousness and who rejects troublemakers, forcing them to remain below the threshold. This official, like Freud's censor, can subject ideas to alterations which will allow them to pass muster; in their new form, no longer unsuitable, they can be assimilated with those above the threshold.

Ideas coming from the outer world through the senses—perceptions—were subjected to the same process. They also were initially unconscious and had to undergo scrutiny before either being admitted to consciousness, subjected to modifications which made them acceptable, or repression. The antecedents of modern hypotheses about "subliminal perception" as well as the concept of "perceptual defense" (the repression of unacceptable percepts), can be located in Herbart's theory.

In an assessment of the "positive findings of psychoanalysis" which Freud wrote in 1915, the theoretical assumptions, terminology aside, are closely related to those of Herbart. Herbart's three states of consciousness have become features of Freud's three "regions" of the mind and have been worked into "systems." The unconscious reappears in the "system Ucs," preconscious and conscious are lumped as they were in Herbart's classification and treated as defining aspects of the "system Cs." Freud used the expression "psychical act" instead of Herbart's "idea."

Freud explained that "in general a psychical act goes through two phases as regards its state, between which is interposed a kind of testing (censorship). In the first phase the psychical act is unconscious and belongs to the system Ucs; if, on testing, it is rejected by the censorship, it is not allowed to pass into the second phase; it is then said to be 'repressed' and must remain unconscious. If, however, it passes this testing, it enters the second phase and thenceforth belongs to the second system, which we will call the system *Cs*.

But the fact that it belongs to that system does not yet unequivocally determine its relation to consciousness. It is not yet conscious, but it is certainly *capable of becoming conscious* . . . that is, it can now, given certain conditions, become an object of consiousness without any special resistance. In consideration of this capacity for becoming conscious we also call the system *Cs.* the 'preconsious.' . . . By accepting the existence of these two (or three) psychical systems, psycho-analysis has departed a step further from the descriptive 'psychology of consciousness' and has raised new problems and acquired a new content" (*S.E.*, XIV: 173).

The close match here is between structural elements of the theories of Herbart and Freud, but not of their contents. It is important to keep in mind that, for Herbart, what was repressed were ideas incompatible with consciousness for any reason. Anything momentarily at odds with the thoughts which occupied attention just then could be repressed, although repression could also be long-lasting. Freud's concept was much narrower; for him the repressed consisted of the forbidden instinctual, the sexual desires and hostile impulses which originated in early childhood and later wishes associated with them.

However, when he began to plan the theoretical framework which would contain these contents, Freud's thinking veered in a Herbartian direction. The design which had been stamped on his mind in school emerged and, asserting itself, directed his speculations into the channels of the familiar pattern.

NOTES

1. According to historical researcher William W. Hemecker, (1991, 135–140) philosophy courses taught by Brentano at the University of Vienna, attended by Freud between 1874 and 1876, were "*Ancient and Modern Logic*," "*The Philosophy of Aristotle*" and, in three consecutive semesters, three seminars on "*Selected Philosophical Writings*."

2. Jones (1953, 374) reported that the textbook Freud had used had been the first edition of Gustav Adolf Lindner's *Lehrbuch der empirischen Psychologie nach genetischer Methode* (*Textbook of Empirical Psychology by Genetic Method*), published in 1858. Thereafter, all writers, this one included, relied on Jones' testimony when they referred to Freud's textbook. However, Hemecker, examining records and consulting officials in Austria, has established that the edition actually mandated for the year 1872–1873, when Freud took the psychology course, was the third, dated 1872. The book was titled *Lehrbuch der empirischen Psycholgie als inductiver Wissenschaft (Textbook of Empirical Psychology as Inductive Science*), Vienna, Gerold. 1872.

3. Herbart generally used the word "inhibited," interchanging it, upon occasion, with "repressed." In either case, the term referred to an idea's keeping another out of consciousness. In his earliest writings, Freud made use of "inhibition" in this sense but soon replaced it with "repression" (*S.E.*, I: 121, 122, 125, 126, 127, 138, 153, and 324). Later, he turned to it only rarely, employing it, for instance, in his very Herbartian description of the dynamic point of view for the fourteenth edition of the *Encyclopaedia Britannica:* "psychoanalysis derives all mental processes (apart from the reception of external stimuli) from the interplay of forces which assist or inhibit one another, combine with one another, enter into compromises with one another, etc." (*S.E.*, XX: 265). In this book "repression" will generally be used as the term which is more familiar today.

4. Emotions, and therefore also motives, played a secondary role in Herbart's theory because he was trying to explain cognition and he believed that emotions rose out of and were dependent upon cognition. In this his assumptions were those prevalent in the eighteenth century. It was then supposed that knowledge precedes desire because in order to want something one must first know about it; a thing is perceived; it is then judged to be desirable and only thereafter is it desired. The philosopher Arthur Schopenhauer, writing at almost the same time as Herbart, set this hypothesis on its head. He insisted that we can want something without knowing what we want: instinctual appetite precedes cognition.

5. The expression "threshold of consciousness" was coined by Herbart: "We are accustomed to speak of the 'entrance of representations [ideas] into consciousness. Therefore I will refer to that boundary which a thought seems to cross when it passes from a totally inhibited state to a degree of actual representation as the threshold *of consciousness*. *Calculation of the threshold* is an abbreviated expression for the calculation of those conditions in which a representation can only just maintain an infinitely small degree of actual representation, below which it will stand exactly on that boundary. We speak of the 'rising and sinking' of representations; therefore I will refer to a representation as being *below the threshold* when it lacks the strength to fulfil these conditions. The state in which it then exists is always one of complete inhibition; nevertheless, it can be *more* or *less deep below the threshold*, depending upon the amount of strength which it lacks, and with which it would have to be provided in order to reach the threshold. Similarly, a representation will be referred to as being *above the threshold* when it has attained a certain degree of actual representation" (1858, 341).

Chapter Thirteen

The Psychic Mechanism

Herbart's psychic mechanism, designed to do for the mind what Newton's system had done for the universe, was an all-encompassing system; every idea belonged to it, just as every star was included in the cosmic order. No event was fortuitous; the strangest, most vagrant idea was as strictly determined as that of a wandering comet. Motion in this system was due to the action of forces which constantly raised some toward consciousness even as it forced others away from it. The mental universe was orderly but the order was the result of the balance of conflicting forces. Conflict was endless because opposition of ideas was perpetual. "Man is an aggregate of contradictions," Herbart maintained (1850, 11), and Freud, after him, declared that "mental life is the arena and battle-ground for mutually opposing purposes or, to put it non-dynamically, that it consists of contradictions and pairs of contraries"[1] (*S.E.*, XV: 76–77).

The psychoanalytic dictionary of Laplanche and Pontalis, commenting on "the originality of Freud's position," notes that "attention has often been drawn to the fact that psychoanalysis replaces a conception of the unconscious described as static with one which is dynamic." In Freudian writings "dynamic" was employed "to characterize the unconscious, in so far as a permanent pressure is maintained there which necessitates a contrary force—operating on an equally permanent basis—to stop it from reaching consciousness" (1973, 126).

Herbart's unconscious was dynamic in just this way. The theories of Herbart and Freud are exactly alike in describing the unconscious as exerting a "permanent pressure" to reach consciousness, a pressure counteracted only by an "equally permanent" opposing force. They differed in their hypotheses about the antagonists involved: for Freud, instinctual sexual and aggressive urges were checked by moral principles; for Herbart, ideas inconsistent with those in consciousness were opposed by a process which protected mental organization and functioning.[2]

The primary force in Herbart's mechanism consisted of the innate "striving" of ideas to attain the state of consciousness. The model's ultimate power source was the natural, ineradicable tendency of ideas to move up toward consciousness. Every repressed idea strove perpetually to rise toward the desired goal. Herbart himself pointed out that this hypothesis had no precedent; physics seemed to have no such notion and its like could not be found in the Leibniz-Wolffian tradition either. This school had assumed that ideas rendered unconscious by more powerful ideas lost none of their strength and continued to exist; when the impediment which obscured them gave way, they naturally reappeared. The standard metaphor had been that of starlight obliterated by sunshine; no one, however, had imagined that the hidden starlight would *exert pressure* to return to visibility. But Herbart supplied unconscious ideas with just such a "striving" (*Streben*). He endowed them with an innate and inextinguishable tendency to seek consciousness, to move out of mental darkness into the light.

This natural force might be compared, in a reversed sense, with gravity. Just as a material object would fall if it were not supported, so would an idea return to consciousness unless prevented. In the spatial model, this disposition was responsible for the upward motion of ideas. Left to itself an idea always moved up toward consciousness; it stopped only if it met an impediment in the form of a more powerful opposing idea; it moved away from consciousness only if it was pushed. Under no circumstance did an idea ever lose this tendency to rise. No matter how deeply into the unconscious it was driven, no matter how long it was kept there, at the first opportunity to do so, the idea would resume its climb. Only a constant downward counter-pressure could prevent its return. The equilibrium achieved in this manner by myriad forces and counter-forces was responsible for the never-entirely-stable order of the mental universe.

In Freud's version of the mental mechanism, we find the same hypothesis of an intrinsic force driving what was unconscious into consciousness. The unconscious, Freud claimed, had a natural "upward drive"; it desired "nothing better than to press forward across its settled frontiers into the ego and so to consciousness" (*S.E.,* XXIII: 179). His use of quotation marks around the phrase "upward drive" probably signified his recognition that it was borrowed from another source. Herbart and Freud differed, however, as to the nature of this drive. Herbart assumed that the forces of the mind arose within the mind it self; he ascribed the upward drive to ideas as an innate disposition. Freud located the power source of the mind outside of the mind, in the instincts which originated in the body. For him the upward drive was due to the instinctual urge to achieve satisfaction.

According to Herbart, the mind needed powers which would enable it to create and maintain order. Herbart proposed that the order-creating forces were "attraction" and "repulsion," which, he declared, played as great a role in the mental as they did in the material universe.

Attraction was the receiving power, responsible for the intake and subsequent synthesis of ideas. Repulsion was the rejecting force which kept unsuitable or useless ideas out of consciousness and subjected them to repression. Repression was as important as intake and assimilation in this theory; it was necessarily involved in every cognition: perceiving, remembering, thinking logically, fantasizing—all required the elimination of incongruences. The simplest recognition of an object demanded the cooperation of two "acts,"—a "taking in" and a "pushing out." The judgment, "This object is an x," asserts not only that the object is an x, it also rules out everything that is *not* an x. Noticing the object, keeping it in mind, thinking about it, requires a continuous shutting out of other ideas. In addition, the formation of stable beliefs and principles relies as much upon the exclusion of some concepts as upon the welcome extended to others. Creating and safeguarding strength of mind and, beyond that, the establishment of a stable character, depends upon the contrasting but cooperating abilities to accept and to reject.

Herbart compared the mind to a system made up of innumerable metal springs which were compressed against each other, each spring exerting a force kept in place only by a counterforce. Remove one of the springs and the other would immediately snap back to its original position. Just so would a repressed idea return to consciousness if the repressing idea were taken away. The multitude of forces in this system were in equilibrium only until an additional spring joined the assembly. A readjustment of force involving all of the springs in the system then took place and a certain amount of time passed before a new equilibrium was attained. Herbart explained that the mind responded to every incoming idea in this way; disturbance of equilibrium occurred constantly. Ceaseless adjustments had to be made to accommodate the myriad perceptions from the external world and the countless thoughts which originated within.

This adjustment preserved the organization of the mind as the dynamics of the system forced each new idea to settle somewhere along the continuum of consciousness ranging from total darkness to the ultimate clarity of full attention. Mental equilibrium was only an ideal state; its achievement was a goal which was never finally reached and organization was never complete. Herbart's psychic mechanism was a device which continually sought, but never found, ultimate balance and order.

The concept of equilibrium, or "principle of constancy," was an essential feature of Freud's theory also. However, here the theories of Herbart and Freud part company: for Herbart, the achievement of equilibrium was an internal affair; it was brought about by the ideas themselves. Freud, however, envisaged the mind as powered by an outside source; the instincts regularly supplied it with a flow of energy. Equilibrium was attained by discharging this energy in action (*S.E.*, I: 146 and 153–4, and III: 64–65).

Herbartian dynamics demanded that ideas have "strengths" or "intensities." But could "strength" be attributed to an idea? What property did it have that could be quantified? How could it be weighed or measured? Herbart came to a decision which would have far-reaching consequences later in the century when the experimental psychology was born: he concluded that in the absence of *absolute quantities*, psychology could make use of *relative quantities*. He thought that this proposal had empirical support because, he pointed out, "everyone knows" that some of our beliefs, for instance, are stronger than others. In fact, there were "an endless number of quantitative determinants of the mind. Our ideas are stronger, weaker, clearer, darker, their coming and going is quicker or slower, their quantity in any given moment is greater or smaller, our receptivity for sensations, our sensitivity for feelings and affects, vacillates incessantly between a more and a less" (Herbart, 1822, 7). This principle survived in Freud's "economic point of view" in which Herbart's "quantities" became "amounts of excitation."[3] This view, Freud explained, "endeavours to follow out the vicissitudes of amounts of excitation and to arrive at least at some relative estimate of their magnitude" (*S.E.*, XIV: 181).

In the combat which took place between ideas, relative quantity was what counted; the victory of an idea, or of a unified group of ideas, depended upon two things: their relative strengths and the degrees of their opposition. Herbart supplied a mathematical formula for the resolution of this clash of forces; he calculated exactly, although hypothetically, the conditions which would allow an idea to ascend to consciousness or doom it to repression in the unconscious.

Herbart used attraction and repulsion to explain the formation of mental structures such as beliefs, attitudes and intentions. The force of attraction brought about the fusion of similar ideas; assimilation resulted in the production of compounds; a compound with sufficient "aggregate force" had an advantage in the competition for consciousness. A compound could become strong enough to come to the rescue of ideas too weak to rise by themselves: the sinking of feeble ideas is "interrupted by the more powerful masses which drive away what is opposed to them, even though by itself it would rise, and halt and fuse with the homogeneous what, by itself, would sink" (1850, 33).

Thus, ideas could extend "help" to each other. An idea struggling to rise out of the unconscious state could succeed if it received adequate support from similar ideas, whether they were located above or below the threshold. Where the strength of one was not enough, the compounded upward striving of a number could prevail. Reciprocally, ideas at a higher level of consciousness helped those below to rise by attraction. This was true in special measure of ideas reaching the mind from the outside; Herbart believed than an incoming perception enjoyed a temporary advantage and exerted a strong upward pull on related ideas, including those in a state of repression. Freud could therefore assume that he was facilitating the rise of a repressed idea when he broached a subject with a patient, advising him or her that a particular wish was lurking beneath the threshold. The upward-pulling attractive force of the idea conveyed by the analyst would reinforce the upward-pushing force of the repressed idea. Critics would see in this practice not support for a repressed idea's urge to rise but the planting of an idea, a suggestion.

The same attraction which brought single ideas together was in effect between compounds as well. As a result, the compounds themselves united and formed an overall organization, a "dominant mass of ideas" also known as the self: "the ego" (*das Ich*). Psychologists at the end of the century customarily used these expressions to designate the synthesizing, regulative agency of the mind. Freud himself sometimes employed the term "dominant mass of ideas" in the sense of "ego" (*S.E.*, II: 116).

REPRESSION

In an examination of Herbart's concept of repression, the difference between the contents of his theory and Freud's must be kept in mind. There is no Oedipus complex in Herbart, no incest, no murder. His unconscious is not Freud's hellish seething cauldron although there is room in it for morally reprehensible ideas. Some casual remarks suggest that Herbart took the repression of evil impulses by conscience for granted but he gave this particular conflict no special treatment (1858, 83). Herbart's model was designed to account for such things as the appearance of a certain idea in consciousness at a given moment as well as the gradual long-term development of personality and the ultimate organization of the mind. What might be said to be repressed, for instance, was the exciting memory of last night's festivities, driven below the threshhold by obligations at the office but returning to consciousness when the working day was over. On the other hand, mental contents might be repressed for years, perhaps forever (1858, 340).

MENTAL "STATICS" AND "DYNAMICS"

Repression could be effective or ineffective, according to both Freud and Herbart. A successfully repressed mental content was incapable of disturbing the conscious mind; the unsuccessfully repressed continued to impinge upon it. Repression was envisaged as occurring in degrees; the higher the degree of repression, the "deeper" it could be said to be. In Freud's model, repression was the result of a conflict between a moral force and an unacceptable wish; a successfully repressed wish was imprisoned so far beneath the threshold of consciousness that it was rendered harmless. No matter how powerful it might be in itself, no matter how indefatigable its tendency to rise, superior counter-forces paralyzed it. The troublesome wishes were those whose repression was relatively weak; these could break through the threshold into consciousness in the form of neurotic symptoms, their nature usually disguised. This scheme clearly resembled Herbart's but the Herbartian design was more complex; to begin with it featured not one, but two thresholds.

Herbart's unconscious consisted of two layers, one stratum beneath the other. The upper threshold separated consciousness from that portion of the unconscious whose elements, only weakly repressed, were still active and troublesome. Beneath the lower threshold, all motion ceased; elements at this depth were immobilized and rendered harmless by the repressive pressure. Inspired still by physics, Herbart called this portion of this theory the "dynamics" and "statics" of the mind. His concept was an elaboration of Leibniz's idea that mental forces could be compared to those of mechanics; mechanics, however, is divided into two branches—dynamics and statics—and Herbart took the next step. He reasoned that, just as physical dynamics deals with forces whose action produces motion in bodies, just so, metaphorically, do mental forces account for the "motion," the activities, of ideas. And as physical statics treats of forces which hold bodies in equilibrium, so do mental forces explain their "motionlessness," or inactivity. An idea in motion is unrepressed, or according to some later terminology, "unbound." A totally repressed idea is motionless, or "bound." Introducing dynamics and statics into a theory of the mind was perfectly acceptable, Herbart maintained, since these sciences were to be found wherever a system of forces existed.[4]

Below the first, or dynamic, threshold, repression was incomplete; equilibrium had not been achieved. The repelling force was strong enough to drive these ideas into the unconscious but it lacked the power to render them ineffective. Since the fight was not over, the repressed ideas could be pictured as continuing to struggle, stubbornly thrusting up against the repressing threshold and thereby constantly impacting on the conscious mind. These were the ideas which were responsible for those gaps in the train of ideas, those strange twistings and turnings of thought which seemed to occur without reason. Of an idea in this condition, Herbart asserted that "it is not to be considered as ineffective, rather it continues to work against the ideas in consciousness with all of its strength. It brings about a state of consciousness, although it is not represented in consciousness" (1850, 19). It also had a powerful effect on emotional states and could create obscure feelings of discomfort. An unconscious idea pressing against consciousness could afflict a person with "objectless feelings of anxiety" (1850, 19). When Freud remarked about this odd state of apparently unmotivated anxiety, he assumed that what was below the threshold must be sexual: "Anxiety appears without the subject knowing what he is afraid of. We must suppose that there was present in the Ucs [unconscious] some love-impulse demanding to be transposed into the system pcs [preconsious]" (*S.E.*, XIV: 182).

Beneath Herbart's second, or static threshold, repression was complete; counter pressures were strong enough to immobilize the ideas driven to this depth; here, they could no longer disturb the peace of the mind. Herbart explained that when opposing forces are equally strong, there is turmoil in the mind; however, "if one of these forces is related to the others in such a manner that it drives them to the static threshold, then a harmonious relationship exists" (1850, 30).

An immobilized idea had not lost its striving to return to consciousness but just as in the physical world a body is rendered motionless in static equilibrium, just so was an idea below the static threshold incapacitated by forces acting upon it: "although it continued with all of its might," the effort of such a deeply buried idea was "as ineffective, notwithstanding its continuous struggle, as if it were not present at all." (Herbart, 1850, 18). One might be tempted to regard such ideas as "dead" and contrast them with the "living," Herbart suggested. This would be wrong, however, because although in this condition "they are unable to accomplish anything by means of their own striving to rise" they are "surely anything but dead" (1850, 33). Given any relaxation of the opposing force, an idea would automatically begin to rise: "as soon as the impediment gives way, the idea will come forward again through its own striving" (1850, 16). Freud, remarking on the need for constant, uninterrupted counter-pressure, used the same life-versus-death comparison to describe the state of an idea subjected to such a force: "The process of repression is not to be regarded as an event which takes place *once*, the results of which are permanent, as when some living thing has been killed and from that time onward is dead; repression demands a persistent expenditure of force, and if this were to cease the success of the repression would be jeopardized, so that a fresh act of repression would be necessary. We may suppose that the repressed exercises a continuous pressure in the direction of the conscious, so that this pressure must be balanced by an unceasing counter-pressure" (*S.E.*, XIV: 151).

Although Freud did not postulate dynamic and static thresholds, he did distinguish between successful and unsuccessful repression; neurotic symptoms and dreams were caused by unacceptable wishes which were not being sufficiently contained. Repression in these cases was too weak, according to Freud; the dam which was supposed to hold back the trouble-making wish was leaking and one of the goals of psychoanalytic treatment was to repair and strengthen the faulty barrier. The repression had to be "constructed afresh out of more solid material;" "new dams" had to be built "of quite a different degree of firmness from the earlier ones; we may be confident that they will not give way so easily before a rising flood of instinctual strength" (*S.E.,* XXIII: 277). In Herbart's terminology, Freud's disruptive unconscious wishes which created symptoms and dreams were merely below the dynamic threshold; those behind the strong dam were beneath the static threshold and therefore incapacitated.

Herbart's theory of repression had another unprecedented feature which, picked up by Freud, played a crucial role in his theory. As a philosopher, Herbart was well aware of the old objection to the contradiction in the expression "unconscious idea" when an idea has been defined as something which is conscious. An idea, Locke had asserted, was that which the "mind is applied about whilst [consciously] thinking" (Vol. I, 121). What then could an "unconscious" idea be? Herbart got around this logical embarrassment by proposing that an idea had two aspects: its "quality" or content, and its "quantity," its strength or intensity. The quality was always conscious or preconscious. When an idea was pushed below the threshold, its quality disappeared, becoming latent. Its quantity, however, survived, and was in no way diminished. It turned into a "striving," a packet of energy which ceaselessly exerted upward pressure in an attempt to return to consciousness. At the moment in which it succeeded in breaking through the barrier, its quality reappeared. This assumption solved the philosophical problem; the logical contradiction vanished because the unconscious idea, as such, did not exist. What existed were conscious ideas and unconscious strivings which became conscious ideas as soon as they crossed the threshold. In common parlance, a striving could still be referred to as an "unconscious idea" but this was merely a convenient manner of speaking.

Herbart's ingenious solution to the philosophical problem entailed a serious departure from the traditional Leibniz-Wolffian conception. According to the tradition, the ideas in the continuum from the most unconscious to the most conscious were all of a kind; they did not differ except in their degrees of clarity. In Herbart's system, this uniformity was lost. The continuum still existed, but above the threshold ideas were manifested by qualities, below it, quality was lost and the idea turned into a mere striving. This formulation had a very peculiar consequence which Herbart was willing to accept: the unconscious idea became unalterable. Once an idea was repressed, it could not be changed. For how does an idea change? Only by contact with another idea or ideas. But an idea which has been stripped of quality, which has been reduced to a mere energetic striving, is not capable of such contact; it no longer belongs to the realm of associated ideas which are interrelated and which interact. Below the threshold, ideas "cannot enter into association with others because they have completely turned into a striving against certain others and are therefore isolated" (Herbart, 1850, 21).

Using the Herbartian pattern, Freud, in his *Project for a Scientific Psychology*, arrived at the same conclusion. Adopting the "quantity-quality" terminology as well as the concept, Freud assumed that a distinction could be made between the content of an idea and its "excitation" (*S.E.,* I: 295 and 310). The quantity of power which constituted the "striving" in Herbart's model became Freud's "sum of excitation" and an idea "repressed from consciousness" was "excluded," or "cut off" from psychical association. (S.E., II: 116).[5] For Freud, therefore, as for Herbart, repressed ideas could not be influenced by other ideas, conscious or unconscious. Since the unconscious system of the topographic theory consisted of unconscious ideas, it followed that the unconscious itself could not be altered. It remained unchangeable throughout life, lacking the ability to learn, adapt or grow. Herbart formulated his hypothesis about the loss of quality of ideas below the threshold, with its unavoidable sequel that unconscious ideas became impervious to change, purely for theoretical reasons; the notion was in no way empirical. Its adoption by Freud severely maimed his concept of the unconscious.

Freud's incorporation of the principles of Herbart's psychic mechanism in his own psychic apparatus had critical consequences for his psychology and, since psychoanalysis was the dominant depth theory for decades, it determined general attitudes toward the hypotheses of unconscious cognition and unconsciously motivated behavior for generations.

NOTES

1. In the description of the Herbartian theory which follows, I have necessarily had to be brief and have had to highlight those features which have an immediate bearing on the most important, most central, of Freud's hypotheses. A comprehensive presentation of the two complex theories with an exhaustive comparison of their features would require a lengthy monograph.
2. Motives played a secondary role in Herbart's psychic mechanism because he was trying to explain cognition and he assumed that motives rose out of and were dependent upon the interaction of ideas. In this his assumption was that prevalent in the eighteenth century. It was then believed that knowledge precedes desire because in order to want something one must first know about it: a thing is perceived; it is then judged to be desirable and only thereafter is it desired. The philosopher Arthur Schopenhauer, writing at almost the same time as Herbart, set this hypothesis on its head. He insisted that we can want something without knowing what we want: instinctual appetite precedes cognition.
3. "In mental functions something is to be distinguished, a quota of affect or sum of excitation—which possesses all the characteristics of a quantity . . . which is capable of increase, diminution, displacement and discharge" (*S.E.*, III: 60).
4. The usage of the terms "mechanical" and "dynamic" has varied. "Mechanical" today is generally used to refer to the combination of the sciences of dynamics and statics. Herbart, however, used "mechanics" in place of "dynamics." The translation in this book replaces Herbart's obsolete use with the modern one: his "mechanics" becomes "dynamics." Herbart definition "Statics" refered to objects which were motionless because forces upon them were in equilibrium while dynamics had to do with objects out of equilibrium and therefore moving.
5. See also *S.E.*, I: 295 and 310.

Chapter Fourteen

The Herbartian Legacy

The psychoanalytic defenders of Freud's absolute originality denied that he was in any way seriously indebted to psychological or philosophical forebears. To maintain this position, they had to insist on the irrelevancy of Herbartian theory. Forced to concede that Freud had been on familiar terms with this theory, they asserted that Herbart's concepts nevertheless had not been really "helpful"; they had apparently had "little direct effect on the development of Freud's concept of the unconscious" (Shakow et al., 1964, 7). Moreover, "while Freud certainly wrote, in the beginning, in the psychological language of Herbart, it does not appear that his psychology had great stimulating power for Freud" (Hartmann, 1868, 273).

Devout followers such as these often felt free to minimize his recognizable borrowings from other thinkers because they believed that his great achievement was unparalleled and lay elsewhere. Whatever contribution another may have made to psychological theory supposedly paled when compared to Freud's astonishing revelations about the unconscious, the treasures he had brought up and given to the world after his courageous self-analysis. This exploration had taken him into a swamp of unholy desires, the existence of which the likes of Herbart, with his cool, cognitive apparatus, could never have suspected.

And yet, it will be seen that Herbart's influence was effective even here, in the formulation of Freud's most distinctive clinical speculations. Paramount among these, a scheme which Freud himself regarded as one of his major contributions to psychology, was the Oedipus complex. Situated at the core of clinical theory, the complex played a fundamental part in the development of the personality and a major role in the explanation of psychopathology. It was concerned with central Freudian clinical concepts: the sexuality of childhood with its incestuous and murderous desires and the dire consequences of these desires for the neurotic adult.

No hypothesis seems to be more characteristic, more purely "Freudian," than this one. Nevertheless, examination reveals a Herbartian matrix. The matrix includes the general premises about the unconscious, the conflict of forces, repression, and so forth but it also extends to particulars, to the crucial theoretical details upon which the supposed pathogenicity of infantile sexual desires depends. It will be seen that when Freud poured his clinical concepts into the Herbartian mold, the mold inevitably shaped the concepts.

Herbart was not the only contributor to the Oedipus complex. Important components had received attention before Freud. The idea of infantile sexuality was not new; the preference of opposite sex parents and children for each other and the rivalry which could exist between same sex parents and offspring was not unheard of. However, the particular constellation in which these ideas appeared in the Oedipus complex was Freud's own creation. Freud had supposedly discovered that the little boy, sexually desiring his mother, hated his father as a rival and wanted him out of the way. In consequence, he feared that his father would castrate him. These wishes and worries of the toddler did not die away in time; on the contrary, they were repressed and, once repressed, they lasted forever. In the grown up neurotic, repression was incomplete and the forbidden wishes of the child for incest and murder escaped to make their way into dreams and symptoms. Castration anxiety, surviving intact, could then be expressed in any number of irrational ways. Any male authority, for instance, could unconsciously come to represent the castration-threatening father, and so cause what seemed to be unmotivated tension

These were ideas at which Freud had seemingly arrived all by himself. One might well ask where Herbart's influence was to be found in such idiosyncratic constructions? Nevertheless, they had Herbartian underpinnings.

THE HERBARTIAN NATURE OF THE FREUDIAN WISH

When he framed the Oedipus complex, Freud speculated in the light of presuppositions which he apparently took for granted; at least, he seems never to have questioned them. Three of these were responsible for the coming-to-be of the uniquely Freudian species of repressed desire, the indispensable component of psychoanalytic theory. Freud took from Herbart the principles that what was repressed was: l) immortal, 2) indefatigable and 3) immutable and applied them to wishes. These features of the Herbartian repressed idea were attributed to the Freudian repressed wish and psychoanalytic theories of neuroses and dreams were shaped accordingly. Bequeathed to generations of psychoanalysts, Herbartian premises were given clinical application although they had not been derived from a study of human nature. Postulates of Herbart's highly abstract, physics-inspired model, they served as foundation of theory and therapy for the better part of a century.

THE IMMORTAL WISH

The Herbartian idea was an ineffaceable acquisition of the mind; once formed, it survived (1858, 455). This hypothesis did not originate with Herbart; it was traditional. The concept had a long history and had been quite popular. The premise was that nothing was ever really forgotten; anything which had ever made an impression on the mind was permanently stored somewhere. The mind, like a video camera which was always turned on, recorded every last detail of every experience and the tape was then filed away in a repository from which it could always be retrieved, at least in principle. Supposed empirical evidence for the belief consisted of intriguing anecdotes about how an event long consigned to oblivion had been suddenly recalled in all of its original immediacy, as vividly "as though it had happened yesterday." One suggestion that had been made in its support was that all of these stored memories would be required when the soul appeared in the celestial court on the Day of Judgment.

Freud was taught in school that memories could not really be lost; temporary lapses and long-term amnesia alike were not due to the destruction of memories but only to their repression by forces which were superior in strength. They survived and could always return if and when inimical forces were removed or sufficiently weakened. According to his textbook, "forgetting (amnesia) is the opposite of remembering. It consists in the inability to reproduce [recall] an idea one once had. This inability, however, is only relative and temporary." One can never say "that an idea has been forgotten absolutely, just as one can never say that a gold ring that has been tossed into the sea is absolutely lost; even though retrieving the ring, or the idea, may be difficult, it cannot be said to be impossible." The forgetting was due only to the weakness of an idea relative to the greater strength and number of "antithetical ideas"; the idea could be remembered "if one succeeds in disposing of these antitheses in some way" (Lindner, 1872, 64).

But how could one dispose of these antitheses? How could one bring to the surface of the mind an idea which was being held down by a superior force? The textbook explained that, upon occasion, superior forces gave way on their own. Repressed ideas could then rise to consciousness unimpeded. This was what happened in dreams: "in sleep, when the antitheses of waking life are removed, such 'forgotten ideas' often emerge with astonishing clarity" (64). The emergence of repressed ideas in dreams, which Freud later described as his own discovery, was not a daring new idea in 1872. Textbooks are not given to the presentation of rare and revolutionary hypotheses; in this instance, a familiar belief was being reported.

Freud turned this "immortality" of an idea into a psychoanalytic rule, applying it to wishes: "Indeed it is a prominent feature of unconscious processes that they are indestructible. In the unconscious nothing can be brought to an end, nothing is past or forgotten" (*S.E.,* V: 577). Repression did not destroy an idea: "We have learnt from psychoanalysis that the essence of the process of repression lies, not in putting an end to, in annihilating the idea which represents an instinct, but in preventing it from becoming conscious" (*S.E.,* XIV: 166).

This idea had a life-long hold on Freud. Close to the end of his career, he was still comparing unconscious wishes with artifacts and could have been echoing the schoolbook metaphor of the lost gold ring when he wrote that only in "rare circumstances as those of Pompeii or of the tomb of Tut'ankhamun"—do archaeological objects endure like repressed desires: "All of the essentials are preserved; even things that seem completely forgotten are present somehow and somewhere, and have merely been buried and made inaccessible to the subject. Indeed, it may, as we know, be doubted whether any psychical structure can really be the victim of total destruction. It depends only upon analytic technique whether we shall succeed in bringing what is concealed completely to light" (*S.E.,* XXIII: 260).

THE EVER-ACTIVE WISH

The idea that was forced beneath the surface was not merely immortal, it was also endowed with an inextinguishable tendency to return to consciousness. Herbart had audaciously attributed this disposition, a sort of reverse-gravity, to ideas because he needed an upward-driving force for his psychic mechanism. The mechanism was permanently activated due to the continuous "striving" for consciousness of ideas. Not merely would an idea last forever but it would also never give up its quest to reach consciousness.

Freud adopted this premise also: "unconscious wishes always remain active"; (*S.E.,* V: 577) "wishful impulses derived from infancy" could "neither be destroyed nor inhibited" (SE 5, 604). Because the repressed was not "dead," its tendency to return was inextinguishable and because of this immortality and indefatigability of the repressed idea, repression could never cease; a constant counter-pressure was needed to keep it at bay.

THE IMMUTABLE WISH

Freud's attribution of the features of the Herbartian idea to his repressed wish, rendered the wish not only immortal, not only everlastingly active, but also unchangeable. According to Herbart, when an idea was repressed, its content, that is, its "quality" disappeared but its "quantity," or energy, survived below the threshold as an energetic striving. Since an idea can only be changed by association with other ideas, it follows that a repressed idea, stripped of content and reduced to a mere striving, is not subject to any alteration. Freud, emulating Herbart, made the same quality-quantity distinction and accepted the immutability of the unconscious wish.

SOME CONSEQUENCES

When Freud adopted the three Herbartian premises, the repressed wish of his theory turned into a peculiar entity. For one thing, the nature of conscious and unconscious wishes differed in important respects. When a conscious wish was forced below the threshhold, it underwent a radical transformation. The desires of the Oedipus complex, for instance, the toddler's wish for sexual gratification with one parent and his or her desire for the elimination of the other became *imperishable*, *inexhaustible* and *immutable*. Each of these wishes was "immortal," each retained its "upward urge," its effort to force its way to consciousness" (*S.E.,* XXIII: 95) and each was impervious to change. Freud vividly pictured the ever-living, ever-striving wishes imprisoned in the unconscious: "These wishes in our unconscious, ever on the alert, and, so to say, immortal, remind one of the legendary Titans, weighed down since primaeval ages by the massive bulk of the mountains which were once hurled upon them by the victorious gods and which are still shaken from time to time by the convulsion of their limbs." They share the "character of indestructibility with all other mental acts which are truly unconscious. . . . If I may use a simile, they are only capable of annihilation in the same sense as the ghosts in the underworld of the Odyssey—ghosts which awoke to new life as soon as they tasted blood" (*S.E.,* V: 553).

The Herbartian attributes of Freud's unconscious wish are hardly insignificant; they are hooks on which much of psychoanalytic theory hangs. To remain with the Oedipus complex, this hypothesis depends entirely on the three Herbartian postulates. Without these, Freud could not have attributed enduring pathogenicity to the Oedipal wishes. For suppose that these wishes were not imperishable; suppose that, except for our not being aware of them, they were exactly like ordinary, conscious wishes. Then we could expect that, in time, they would fade away and be truly forgotten. How many longings of early youth have disappeared in just this fashion? Even if we were to grant that the small child had powerful incestuous and murderous wishes, we could expect that, in time, they would simply vanish.

What would happen if, for the sake of theoretical argument, we were to allow that repressed wishes were imperishable but assumed that they did not possess an everlasting striving to achieve satisfaction? The perpetual energetic efforts would presumably gradually die out. If an Oedipal wish were like ordinary childhood wishes in this respect, it would become inactive, like a battery which loses its charge. It might then be said to still exist in memory, but it would have been rendered harmless.

Going further yet, we might suppose that Oedipal wishes were both immortal and supplied with inexhaustible energy but that they could be altered. Consciously, we modify our mental states all of the time. The most powerful grudge may be mitigated as we grow older and wiser. Our appraisal of the original circumstances may change; perhaps we come to understand that we share some of the blame; perhaps the wrongdoer expresses remorse and seeks to make amends; perhaps we simply become more forgiving. Ultimately the rancor and the desire for revenge may be dispelled.

According to Freudian theory, if the grudge is unconscious, we can do none of these things; resentment will continue to fester forever at its original strength. Conscious experiences can have no impact on the unconscious wish. If it were not so, if unconscious wishes were subject to the same modification as those which are conscious, their permanent pathogenicity could not be assumed. If Oedipal desires, the sexual craving of the toddler for the parent, the murderous hatred for the other parent, could be forgotten, or weaken, or change, the Freudian theory of neurosis would have had to take a different form.

THE HERBARTIAN INHERITANCE

The consequences of the Herbartian features of the unconscious wish were enormous, not only for psychoanalytic theory but also for psychoanalytic practice. Of necessity, mental excavation became the supreme requirement of therapy. Because of the nature of the unconscious wish, the only way to help the neurotic patient escape the suffering it caused was to bring it to the surface. Only by making what was unconscious conscious could the wish be deprived of its fearful power. Non-analytic therapies could only be palliative, unable to deal with the cause. The cause was hidden, buried like a tumor, and only the analyst, surgeon of the mind, could locate and remove the growth.

Freud explained this to his patient Dr. Ernst Lanzer, the famous "Rat Man": the "discovery of the unknown content" of the mind had a therapeutic effect because of "the fact that everything conscious was subject to a process of wearing away, while what was unconscious was relatively unchangeable."

Illustrating his remarks, he called the patient's attention to the antiquities which he had collected and which stood about the room, adding that "They were, in fact . . . only objects found in a tomb, and their burial had been their preservation: the destruction of Pompeii was only beginning now that it had been dug up" (*S.E.*, X: 176).

The conceptualization of the repressed wish as an archaeological artifact also had serious consequences for Freud's therapeutic procedure as well as for his theory. Although other factors were also probably at play, Freud's underestimation of the dangers of suggestion was encouraged by this image of the wish. By the 1890s most physicians, particularly those who had treated hysterics and other neurotics, had learned a significant lesson. Important colleagues, leaders in the field, had been badly burned by their experiences with the uncanny phenomenon of unconscious suggestion. An important theory of hysteria put forth by Freud's teacher, the famed French neurologist Jean-Martin Charcot, had collapsed when it was shown that investigators had unwittingly cued subjects and the reverberations of the disaster had been international. Thereafter, many physicians were hypersensitive to the risks entailed by suggestion. Freud, however, may well have been emboldened to take a cavalier approach to the problem by the image of the repressed wish as a lost artifact; the wish could only be altered after it was dug up. Before that, it was impervious to influences of any kind. Therefore, so far as suggestion was concerned, the psychoanalyst could act like a surgeon who suspects the existence of a tumor. No matter what the surgeon says to the patient, he will not encourage the growth of a tumor if there is none, nor will an extant tumor grow larger or smaller or turn into something else as a result of the doctor's explanations. In any case, Freud had no compunctions about his long preparatory conversations with the patient, predicting the kind of discoveries that would be made, informing the Rat Man, for instance, that "the evil self was the unconscious," and that uncovering the reason for his feelings of guilt would be therapeutic (*S.E.*, X: 177). He ignored the many charges that the findings of psychoanalysis were contaminated by suggestion and that the cures he claimed were due to his treatment could also have resulted from suggestion alone.

The same assumption which allowed Freud to ignore the peril of suggestion may also have had an impact on his view of the physician-patient relationship. According to a very old tradition, the patient's positive personal relationship with the doctor was an important healing factor in treatment. Freud's contemporaries who practiced hypnosis had inherited this understanding from the physician-hypnotists of earlier times but Freud's belief that he was dealing with wishes as unalterable as buried artifacts may have allowed him to ignore the tradition. The doctor-patient relationship could have no effect on the wish; only the disinterring of the wish could bring relief. Therefore Freud could recommend "emotional coldness" to the analyst, advising followers to model themselves on the surgeon "who puts aside all his feelings, even his human sympathy, and concentrates his mental forces on the single aim of performing the operation as skillfully as possible." This was not cruelty on Freud's part; given his theory, it could seem to him that "human sympathy" might interfere with effective treatment. Of course, on other occasions, Freud expressed himself quite differently and he famously disregarded his own advice. Nevertheless, many of his followers took it seriously for a very long time (*S.E.,* XXII: 115).

Moreover, the concept that a repressing force was constantly active in the patient unavoidably introduced an adversarial element into the treatment. On the basis of the theory, the analyst had to assume that, although the patient might appear to be cooperative and forthcoming, yet this helpful attitude would not extend to the real analytic work. As soon as one of the analyst's exploratory feelers threatened to subvert the repression, the patient would unconsciously resist. Patient and analyst had different aims: the patient unconsciously wanted to keep something hidden; the analyst sought to ferret out just this secret. In this respect, they had to be chronically at odds.

Because Freud turned Herbart's principles into axioms, psychoanalysts became archaeologists of the mind. The classical analyst "knew" when a neurotic patient walked in, that this person was suffering from the repression of inadmissible wishes which could be eliminated only by the undoing of the repression. If, after a passage of time, treatment seemed to be ineffective, then this was because a reprehensible desire still remained to be flushed out.

The concept of the inadmissible wish, together with its specification as infantile, incestuous and murderous, came from Freud. But the premise that relief could be provided only by excavation of the repressed wish was due to Freud's adoption of the principles of Herbart's psychic mechanism. It was because the repressed wish could never be forgotten, assuaged or changed, that it was permanently pathogenic. Without the Herbartian features, an infantile wish, however reprehensible, would not have caused a neurosis of the Freudian type and would not have had to be disinterred. The Herbartian features were what made psychoanalysis *necessary.*

REPRESSION

Freud's modeling of his theory of neurosis on Herbart's general theory of cognition had as consequence an enormous overemphasis on repression as cause of mental pathology at the expense of alternate explanations which would have merited attention. As though transfixed by the Herbartian concept of ever-warring forces which could be impressively likened to the forces of physics, Freud attributed all neurotic symptoms to an underlying conflict of mental forces, to a struggle between the moral standards imposed by civilization and the immoral urges emanating from the instincts. Because, like Herbart, he sought universal laws, he could not regard repression as merely one of a number of possible determinants of symptoms but generalized it as the fundamental cause of neurosis. The theory of repression became for him "the cornerstone on which the whole structure of psychoanalysis rests" (S.E., XIV: 16) He thus rode roughshod over other hypotheses available at the time and consigned them, for a while, to near-oblivion.

Among these, the oldest, established since ancient times, was trauma theory, the theory that mental disturbances were due to something having happened or having been done to the person. The mind supposedly gave way because it had been harmed; it cracked under the burden of overwhelmingly painful experiences it had been forced to undergo. In the early part of the nineteenth century, many physicians still held to the ancient belief that deep psychological wounds could cause mental illness. The question doctors asked the patient was: "what happened to you?" And later, when insanity was attributed to brain disease or to a postulated brain defect or malfunction, physicians continued to agree that psychological trauma, if it did not cause the malady could at least precipitate it. Freud himself began with a trauma theory; he believed that the cause of neurosis was sexual abuse of the child. He soon abandoned it however, replacing it with the hypothesis of repression. Thereafter the question was no longer "what happened to you?" It was "what do you (unconsciously) want? What forbidden desire do you harbor?"

For decades then, trauma practically disappeared as a major determinant of symptoms in psychoanalytic accounts of the genesis of neurosis. Apologists for Freud point out that he never *denied* the importance of trauma and found a place for it in his later theory but in fact this place always remained subsidiary. In none of Freud's case histories, for instance, did psychological trauma inflicted on the patient by confused or neurotic parents play a significant etiological role.

UNIVERSAL LAWS

Freud's perennial quest, his search for "laws" of human nature, may also have been encouraged in good part to his early Herbartian indoctrination. As Herbart, in pursuit of the Newtonian ideal, had tried to establish universal laws for a scientific psychology, so did Freud seek such laws for a scientific psychoanalysis. Newton had proclaimed laws that were universal, laws which admitted no exception; the principles of mechanics were not in effect only occasionally. Just so, did Freud maintain that *all* children, not only some, went through the Oedipal phase, breeding ground of all neurosis. He was forever seeking universal explanations, single causes to which he might attribute a multiplicity of heterogeneous phenomena.

The alacrity with which Freud generalized was one of his major failings, a failing which shaped the future of his movement and ultimately proved to be detrimental to his cause. For what could followers do if they came across what seemed to them to be exceptions to the Freudian rules? The rules were inelastic; therefore, if a psychoanalytic practitioner found cases of neuroses in which castration anxiety or penis envy did not seem to be determining factors, he or she had nowhere to go with the observation. Whoever seriously doubted the universality of the general law had either to stifle these doubts or leave the movement. Rival theories which came into existence after splits of this kind tended to adopt generalities themselves, thus inviting further splitting. The establishment of a variety of psychoanalytic schools thus became inevitable.

References

Alexander, Franz G. and Sheldon T. Selesnick. *The History of Psychiatry.* New York and Toronto: The New American Library, 1966.

Allers, Rudolf. *The Successful Error: A Critical Study of Freudian Psycho-Analysis,* London: Sheed & Ward, 1941.

Allport, Gordon. Quoted in Henryk Misiak and Virginia Staudt Sexton. *History of Psychology: An Overview.* New York: Grune & Stratton, 1966.

Altschule, Mark. *Roots of Modern Psychiatry.* New York: Grune & Stratton, 1957.

Aquinas, Thomas. *Basic Writings of Saint Thomas Aquinas.* Edited by Anton C. Pegis. In two volumes, New York: Random House, 1945.

Aristotle, *The Complete Works of Aristotle*, edited by Jonathan Barnes. Bollingen Series LXXI.2. Princeton University Press. 2 Vols. 1984.

Aristotle. "On Memory," *The Complete Works of Aristotle,* edited by Jonathan Barnes. 2 vols. Princeton N.J.: Princeton University Press. Bollingen Series LXXI.2, 1984.

Aristotle. "Sense and Sensibilia." *The Complete Works of Aristotle*, edited by Jonathan Barnes, in two volumes. Princeton University Press. Bollingen Series LXXI.2, 1984.

Auden, W. H. "In Memory of Sigmund Freud," in *Collected Shorter Poems,* 1927–1957, New York: Random House, 1934.

Augustine. *Confessions.* Translated by R. S. Pine-Coffin. New York: Penguin Books, 1986.

Augustine, *Concerning the City of God against the Pagans.* Translated by Henry Bettenson. New York: Viking Penguin Inc., 1987.

Beck, Lewis White. *Early German Philosophy: Kant and His Predecessors*. Bristol, England: Thoemmes Press, 1996.

Beckers, Hubert. *Schelling's Geistesentwicklung in Ihrem Inneren Zusammenhang.* Munich: Verlag der K. B. Akademie, 1875.

Beiser, Frederick. *The Fate of Reason, German Philosophy from Kant to Fichte.* Cambridge and London: Harvard University Press, 1987.

Bischer, W. Schopenhauer and Freud: A Comparison. *Psychoanalytic Quarterly*, Vol. 8, 1939, 88–97.

Bouveresse, Jacques. *Wittgenstein Reads Freud: The Myth of the Unconscious.* Princeton, N.J.: Princeton University Press, 1995.

Boyle, Robert. "An Essay of the Intestine Motions of the Particles of Quiescent Solids. Where the Absolute Rest of Bodies Is called in Question.*" The Works of Robert Boyle.* Volume 6. Publications of 1668–71. London: Pickering & Chatto, 1999.

Bréhier, Emile. *The History of Philosophy, Volume VI: The Nineteenth Century: Period of Systems, 1800–1850*, University of Chicago, 1973.

Brenner, Charles. *An Elementary Textbook of Psychoanalysis*. New York: International Universities Press, 1955.

Brenner, Charles. *The Mind in Conflict*. New York: International Universities Press, 1982.

Brett, George Sidney, *Modern Psychology,* in Volume III of the trilogy *A History of Psychology,* New York: The Macmillan Company, 1921.

Brown, Peter. *Augustine of Hippo.* Berkeley and Los Angeles: University of California Press, 1967.

Capps, Donald, "Hartmann's Relationship to Freud: a Reappraisal," *Journal of the History of the Behavioral Sciences*, 6, 1970, 162–175.

Carlson, A. J. *The Psychology of the Leibnizian Monad,* Rock Island, Ill.: Lutheran Augustana Book Concern, 1899.

Copleston, Frederick. *A History of Philosophy, Vol. 7, Part I: Fichte to Hegel.* Garden City, New York: Image Books, a Division of Doubleday & Company, Inc., 1965.

Delumeau, Jean. *Sin and Fear: The Emergence of a Western Guilt Culture 13th–18th Centuries.* New York: St. Martin's Press, 1990.

Descartes, René. *The Passions of the Soul.* In *The Philosophical Works of Descartes.* Elizabeth S. Haldane and G.R.T. Ross. Cambridge University Press, Volume 1, 1973, 329–427.

Descartes. "Letter to Chanut, June 6, 1647." In *Descartes: His Moral Philosophy and Psychology.* John H. Blom, translator and editor. Hassocks, Sussex, Great Britain: The Harvester Press Limited, 1978.

Dessoir, Max. *Geschichte der Neueren Deutschen Psychologie*, two volumes, Berlin: Verlag von Carl Duncker, 1902.

Dewey, John, *Leibniz's New Essays Concerning the Human Understanding.* Chicago: S. C. Griggs & Company, 1888.

Dorer, Maria. *Historische Grundlagen der Psychoanalyse*. Leipzig: Verlag von Felix Meiner. 1932.

Drobisch, Moritz Wilhelm. *Psychologie Empirische nach naturwissenschaftlicher Methode.* (1842). *Zweite Auflage (2nd edition).* Hamburg und Leipzig: Verlag von Leopold Voss, 1898.

DuPrel, Carl, "Wie sich die Medizin mit fremden Federn schmückt," *Sphinx: Monatschrift für due geschichtliche und experimentale Begründung der übersinnlichen Weltanschauung auf monistischer Grundlage,* published by Hübbe-Schleiden, IV Jahrgang, Achter Band, 1889, Expedition der Sphinx in Gera (Reuss).

Ellenberger, Henri F. *The Discovery of the Unconscious*. New York: Basic Books, 1970.

Erdelyi, Matthew Hugh. *Psychoanalysis: Freud's Cognitive Psychology*. New York: W. H. Freeman and Company, 1985.

Fouillée, Alfred, *Psychologie des Idées-Forces.* Two volumes. Paris: Félix Alcan, Éditeur, 1893.

Freud: *The Complete Letters of Sigmund Freud to Wilhelm Fliess: 1887–1904.* Translated and edited by Jeffrey Moussaieff Masson. Cambridge: The Belknap Press of Harvard University Press, 1985.

Freud, Sigmund. *The Standard Edition of the Complete Psychological Works of Sigmund Freud,* James Strachey, ed., New York: W.W. Norton & Company, 1976.

Freud, Sigmund. *The Complete Letters of Sigmund Freud to Wilhelm Fliess 1887–1904*. Translated by Jeffrey Masson. The Belknap Press: Cambridge, Massaschusetts, and London, England, 1985.

Grau, Kurt Joachim. *Die Entwicklung des Bewusstseinsbegriffes im XVII und XVIII Jahrhundert: Abhandlungen zur Philosophie und ihrer Geschichte*. Series editor: *Benno* Erdmann. Halle A.S.: Verlag von Max Niemeyer, 1916.

Griesinger, Wilhelm. *Mental Pathology and Therapeutics.* New York: Hafner Publishing Company, 1965.

Hartmann, Eduard von. *Philosophy of the Unconscious,* London: Kegan Paul, Trench, Trübner, & Co. Ltd, 1893. (Original German publication, 1868).

Hartmann, Heinz. "The Ego Concept in Freud's Work." In *Essays on Ego Psychology: Theory* Selected Problems in Psychoanalytic. New York: International Universities Press, 1964. 272–273.

Hegel, Georg Wilhelm. *Philosophy of Mind. Part Three of the Encyclopaedia of the Philsophical Sciences (*1830) Translated byWilliam Wallace. Oxford Clarendon Press.1971.

Hemecker, Wilhelm W. *Vor Freud: Philosophiegeschichtliche Voraussetzungen der Psychoanalyse.* Philosophia Resources Library. Munich: Philosophia Verlag, 1991.

Herbart, Johann Friedrich. *Lehrbuch zur Psychologie,* in *Johann Friedrich Herbart's Schriften zur Psychologie*. Editor: G. Hartenstein, Leipzig: Verlag von Leopold Voss, 1850.

Herbart, Johann Friedrich. "Psychologische Untersuchung über die Stärke einer gegebenen Vorstellung, als function ihrer Dauer betrachtet," 1812; pp. 29–71; on p. 36; and "Über die Möglichkeit und Nothwendigkeit, Mathematik auf Psychologie anzuwenden," 1822; (129–172, on pages 154–155); both *in Schriften zur Psychologie,* dritter Theil, in *Sämmtliche Werke,* Vol. VII, G. Hartenstein (ed.); Leipzig: Verlag von Leopold Voss, 1851.

Herbart, Johann Friedrich. *Psychologie als Wissenschaft, neu gegründet auf Erfahrung, Metaphysik und Mathematik* in *Johann Friedrich Herbart's Schriften zur Psychologie*, Editor: G. Hartenstein. Leipzig: Verlag von Leopold Voss, 1858.

Herbart, Johann Friedrich. "*Üeber die Möglichkeit und Notwendigkeit, Mathematik auf Psychologie anzuwenden,*" (1822) *in Schriften zur Psychologie, Sämmtliche Werke,* VII, p. 138, G. Hartenstein, Leipzig: Verlag von Leopold Voss, 1851 (129 – 172).

Hoeffding, Harald, *A History of Modern Philosophy*, 2 vols. Dover Publications, 1955.

Holborn, Hajo. *A History of Modern Germany.* Taylor & Francis, 1969.

Holborn, Hajo. *A History of Modern Germany: 1840–1945.* Princeton University Press, 1969.

Holmes, Oliver Wendell. "Mechanism in Thought and Morals,*" Pages from an Old Volume of Life: a Collection of Essays, 1857–1881,* Boston and New York: Houghton, Mifflin and Company; 1892.

Humphrey, Nicholas. "Commentary," *Journal of the American Psychoanalytic Association,* Vol. 45, No. 3, 1997, 726–731.

Jakob, Ludwig Heinrich. *Grundriss der Erfahrungs-Seelenlehre*. Halle: Bey Hemmerde und Schwetschke. Zweyte ganz umbearbeitet Auflage, 1795.

James, William. *The Principles of Psychology*, 2 vols. Dover Publications, Inc., 1950.

Janet, Pierre. *L'automatisme Psychologique. Bibliothèque de Philosophie Contemporaine*. Paris: Librairie Félix Alcan. Tenth edition. 1930.

Jodl, Friedrich. *Lehrbuch der Psychologie.* Zweite Auflage. Erster Band. (second edition, Vol. I) Stuttgart und Berlin: J.G. Cotta'sche Buchhandlung Nachfolger. 1903.

Johnston, William M. *The Austrian Mind: An Intellectual and Social History*, 1848–1938; (281-286) Berkeley: University of California Press, 1972.

Jones, Ernest. *The Life and Work of Sigmund Freud. Vol. I. The Formative Years and the Great Discoveries. 1956–1900.* New York: Basic Books 1953.

Jones, Ernest. *The Life and Work of Sigmund Freud. Vol. II. 1901–1919. Years of Maturity*, New York: Basic Books, 1955.

Jones, Ernest. *The Life and Work of Sigmund Freud. Vol. III. 1919–1939. The Last Phase*. New York: Basic Books, 1957.

Kant, Immanuel . *Critique of Pure Reason.*Translated by Norman Kemp Smith. New York: St. Martin's Press, 1965.

Kant, Immanuel, *Metaphysical Foundations of Natural Science, in Philosophy of Material Nature,* Translation by James W. Ellington, Indianapolis: Hackett Publishing Company, 1985.

Jones, Ernest, *The Life and Work of Sigmund Freud. Vol. 1. The Formative Years and the Great Discoveries*. New York: Basic Books, 1953.

Kant, Immanuel. *Anthropology from a Pragmatic Point of View*. Translated by Victor Lyle Dowdell. Carbondale, Ill: Southern Illinois University Press, 1978.

Kant, Immanuel. *Critique of Pure Reason.*

Kihlstrom, John F. *"The Cognitive Unconscious."* Science, vol. 237, 1987.

Klein, D.B. *A History of Scientific Psychology: Its Origins and Philosophical Backgrounds*. New York: Basic Books, 1970.

Kluge, Carl Alexander Ferdinand. *Versuch einer Darstellung des animalischen Magnetismus als Heilmittel,* Berlin: in der Realschulbuchhandlung, 1818.

Koestler, Arthur. Introduction to *The Unconscious before Freud* , Lancelot Law Whyte. 1978.

Laplanche, J. and J.-B. Pontalis, *The Language of Psycho-Analysis*, translated by Donald Nicholson-Smith. New York: W. W. Norton, 1973.

Leibbrand, Werner. *Die speculative Medizin der Romantik.* Hamburg: Claassen Verlag. 1956.

Leibbrand, Werner and Annemarie Wettley. *Der Wahnsinn: Geschichte der Äbendländischen Psychopathologie.* Munich/Freiburg: Verlag Karl Alber, 1961.

Leibniz, G. W. *New Essays on Human Understanding*, Peter Remnant and Jonathan Bennett, eds., Cambridge University Press, 1981.

Leibniz, G.W. "On the Doctrine of Malebranche—A Letter to M. Remond de Montmort, containing Remarks on the Book of Father Tertre against Father Malebranche, 1715." In *Leibniz Selections.* New York: Charles Scribner's Sons, 1951, 552–558.

Leibniz, G.W. "The Monadology." In *Philosophical Papers and Letters*; *A selection.* Translated and edited, with an introduction by Leroy E. Loemker. Chicago: University of Chicago Press, 1956. Vol. 2, 1044–1061.

Leibniz, G. W. "The Principles of Nature and of Grace, Based on Reason." In *Philosophical Papers and Letters; A selection.* Translated and edited, with an introduction, by Leroy E. Loemker. Chicago: University of Chicago Press, 1956. Vol. 2, 1033–1043.

Leibniz, G.W. "A Fragment on Dreams." *Theological Writings Related to the Catholic Demonstrations, 1668–70.* In *Philosophical Papers and Letters.* Translated and edited with an introduction by Leroy E. Loemker.Chicago. University of Chicago Press, 1956, Vol. 1, 175–178.

Leibniz, G. W. *Theodicy: Essays on the Goodness of God, the Freedom of Man and the Origin of Evil.* Edited and with an introduction by Austin Farrer. LaSalle, Ill.: Open Court, 1985.

Leibniz, "Freedom of Man in the Origin of Evil, in *Theodicy.* La Salle, Illinois: Open Court, 1985.

Leibniz G.W. et al. *The Leibniz-Clarke Correspondence.* Edited by H.G. Alexander. Manchester: Manchester University Press, 1956.

Lewes, George Henry. "Consciousness and Unconsciousness," *Mind*, Vol. 2, 156–167, 1877.

Leopold. *Bewusstsein und psychisches Geschehen: die Phänomene des Unterbewusstseins und ihre Rolle in unserem Geistesleben.* Wiesbaden: Verlag von J. F. Bergmann, 1913.

Lindner, Gustav Adolph. *Lehrbuch der empirischen Psychologie als inductiver Wissenschaft. Dritte Auflage.* (Third edition) Wien: (Vienna:) Druck und Verlag von Carl Gerold's Sohn, 1872.

Locke, John. *An Essay Concerning Human Understanding*, Two Volumes; New York, N.Y. Dover Publications, Inc., 1959.

Löwenfeld, Leopold. *Bewusstsein und psychisches Geschehen: die Phaenomene (umlaut ') des Unterbewusstseins und ihre Rolle in unserem Geistesleben,* Wiesbaden: Verlag von J. F. Bergmann, 1913. Leibniz, "Freedom of Man in the Origin of Evil," in *Theodicy.* La Salle, Illinois: Open Court, 1985. *Grenzfragen*

Lowry, Richard. *The Evolution of Psychological Theory: 1650 to the Present.* Chicago: Aldine Publishing Company, 1971.

Maass, Johann Gebhard Ehenreich. *Versuch über die Einbildungskraft*, verbesserte Ausgabe, Halle und Leipzig bei Johann Gottfried Ruff, 1797.

Maass, Johann Gebhard Ehrenreich. *Versuch üeber die Leidenschaften.* Vol. I, 1805; Vol. II, 1807.

Malebranche, Nicolas. *The Search after Truth,* translated and edited by Thomas M. Lennon and Paul J. Olscamp, Cambridge (England): Cambridge University Press, 1997.

Mann, Thomas. "Freud and the Future." *Essays of Three Decades.* N.Y.: Knopf, 1947, 411–428.

McMullin, Ernan. *Newton on Matter and Activity.* Indiana: University of Notre Dame Press, 1978.

Meier, Georg, Friedrich. *Beweis: das keine Materie dencken könne,* Zweyte vermehrte Auflage, Verlegts Carl Hermann Hemmerde, 1751.

Merkel, Franz Rudolf. *Der Naturphilosoph Gotthilf Heinrich Schubert und die Deutsche Romantik.* Munich: C. H. Beck'sche Verlagsbuchhandlung, 1913.

Meynert, Theodor. *Klinische Vorlesungen über Psychiatrie.* Wien: Wilhelm Braumüller, 1890.

Misiak, Henryk, and Virginia Staudt Sexton. *History of Psychology: An Overview*. New York: Grune & Stratton, 1966.

Moritz, Carl Philip (ed.), 8 Vols, *Magazin zur Erfahrungseelenkunde* (1783–1793); Nördlingen: Franz Greno, 1986.

Neu, Jerome, *Emotion, Thought and Therapy*. London and Henley: Routledge & Kegan Paul, 1977.

Newton, Isaac, *Principia [Sir Isaac Newton's Mathematical Principles of Natural Philosophy and his System of the World,* Translation revised and supplied with an historical and explanatory appendix by Florian Cajori, Vol. 1, The Motion of Bodies. University of California Press, Berkely, Los Angeles; London, 1934,

Nietzsche, Friedrich. *Joyful Wisdom*, New York: Ungar, 1987.

Nisbett, Richard E. and Timothy DeCamp Wilson. "Telling More Than We Can Know: Verbal Reports on Mental Processes. " *Psychological Review,* 84.3 (1977): 231–259.

Norris, John. *"Cursory Reflections upon a Book call'd An Essay concerning Human Understanding."* In *Christian Blessedness*. (London, 1690) New York and London: Garland Publishing, Inc., 1978.

Pascal, Blaise. *Pensées* .Penguin Books, 1966.

Pilkington, Roger. *Robert Boyle: Father of Chemistry*. London: John Murray, 1959.

Planck, Max. "Kausalgesetz und Willensfreiheit." In *Vom Wesen der Willensfreiheit und andere Vorträge*. Frankfurt: Fischer Taschenbuch Verlag, 1990.

Platner, Ernst, *Neue Anthropologie für Aerzte und Weltweise*. Leipzig: Bey Siegfried Lebrecht Crusius, 1790.

Plato. *The Collected Dialogues of Plato*. Edited by Edith Hamilton and Huntington Cairns. Princeton, New Jersey: Princeton University Press. Bollingen Series LXXI. 1973.and Huntington Cairn. Princeton,

Plotinus. *The Enneads*. Translated by Stephen Mackenna. London: Penguin Books, 1911.

Rapaport, David and Merton M. Gill. "The Points of View and Assumptions of Metapsychology." *The Collected Papers of David Rapaport,* edited by Merton M. Gill. New York: Basic Books, 1967, 795–811.

Royce, Josiah. *The Spirit of Modern Philosophy*. New York: Dover Publications. 1983.

Russell, Bertrand. *A History of Western Philosophy*, London, George Allen and Unwin, Ltd., 1946.

Russell, Bertrand, *The Analysis of Mind,* London: George Allen & Unwin, 1921, 37–38.

Schelling, F. W. J. *Ideas for a Philosophy of Nature*. Introduction by Robert Stern. Cambridge, New York, New Rochelle, Melbourne, Sydney: Cambridge University Press, 1988.

Schenk, H. G. *The Mind of the European Romantics: an Essay in Cultural History*. London: Constable, 1966.

Schnaedelbach, Herbert. *Philosophy in Germany, 183l-1933,* Cambridge: Cambridge University Press, 1984.

Schnitzler, Arthur. *Der Schleier der Beatrice (The Veil of Beatrice)*. In *Gesammelte Werke von Arthur Schnitzler*. Zweiter Band. *Theaterstücke*. Berlin: S. Fischer Verlag, 1915.

Schopenhauer, Arthur." On the Will in Nature." *On the Fourfold Root of the Principle of Sufficient Reason and On the Will in Nature*. London: George Bell and Sons, 1897.

Schopenhauer, Arthur. *The World as Will and Representation*. Two volumes. Translated by E. F. J. Payne.New York: Dover Publications, 1966.

Schopenhauer, Arthur. *On the Freedom of the Will*. Translated with an introduction by Konstantin Kolenda. Oxford: Basil Blackwell, 1985.

Schubert, Gotthilf Heinrich. *Die Symbolik des Traumes,* with an epilogue by Gerhard Sauder. Facsimile of 1814 edition. Heidelberg: Verlag Lambert Schneider, 1968.

Shakow, David, and David Rapaport. *The Influence of Freud on American Psychology. Psychological Issues*, Vol. IV, No. l, Monograph 13. New York: International Universities Press, 1964.

Sigerist, Henry E., "Psychiatry in Europe at the Middle of the Nineteenth Century." *100 Years of Psychiatry*. American Psychiatric Association. 1944, 29–43.

Solomon, Robert C. *Continental Philosophy Since 1750: the Rise and Fall of the Self*. Oxford: Oxford University Press, 1988.

Spinoza, Benedict de, *The Ethics* in *On the Improvement of the Understanding, The Ethics, Correspondence.* New York: Dover Publications. Original Dover publication*: The Works of Spinoza,* Vol. 2, 1955.

Stewart, Charles. *Dreams and History: The Interpretation of Dreams from Ancient Greece to Modern Psychoanalysis.* Ed. Daniel Pick and Lyndal Roper. New York: Brunner-Routledge, 2004.

Stone, Alan A. "A Brief Note on Kant and Free Association." *International Journal of Psycho-Analysis,* 10, 1983.

Strümpell, Ludwig. *Die Natur und Entstehung der Träume.* Leipzig: Verlag von Veit & Comp., 1874.

Sulzer, Johann Georg, "Erklärung eines psychologischen paradoxen Satzes: Das der Mensch zuweilen nicht nur ohne Antrieb und ohne sichtbare Gründe sondern selbst gegen dringende Antriebe und überzeugende Gründe handelt und urtheilet," (1759) in *Vermischte philosophische Schriften,* Vol. I, Leipzig, 1773; Vol. II, Leipzig, 1781.

Vitz, Paul C. *Sigmund Freud's Christian Unconscious.* New York: Guilford Press, 1988.

Voltaire, "The Ignorant Philosopher," in Voltaire, *Collected Works of Voltaire: The Complete Romances, Including Candide, and The Ignorant Philosopher,* New York: Greystone Press. 1928.

Ward, J. "Psychology," *Encyclopedia Britannica, Vol. XX.* Thomas Spencer Baynes and W. H. DePuy (eds.). Chicago: The Werner Company, 1895.

Watson, J.B. Rayner, Rosalie. "Conditioned Emotional Reactions." *Journal of Experimental Psychology.* Vol.III, No.1, February, 1920.

Watson, J.B. "Behavior and the Concept of Mental Disease." *The Journal of Philosophy, Psychology and Scientific Methods.* Vol. XIII, No.22, October, 1916a.

Watson, J.B. "The Psychology of Wish Fulfilment." *The Scientific Monthly,* Vol. III, November, 1916b.

Watson, J.B. "Does Holt Follow Freud?" *The Journal of Philosophy, Psychology and Scientific Methods.* Vol. XIV, No. 4, February, 1917a.

Watson, J.B. and Morgan, J.B. "Emotional Reactions and Psychological Experimentation." *The American Journal of Psychology.* Vol. XXVIII ,No. 2, April 1917b.

Watson, J.B., and Rayner, Rosalie. "Conditioned Emotional Reactions." *Journal of Experimental Psychololgy.* Vol. III, No. 1. February, 1920.

Whyte, Lancelot Law. *The Unconscious before Freud.* London: Tavistock Publications, 1962.

Windelband, Wilhelm. *A History of Philosophy,* 2 volumes. New York: Harper & Brothers, Publishers, Harper Torchbook, 1958.

Wolf, A. *A History of Science, Technology, and Philosophy in the Eighteenth Century,* London: George Allen & Unwin, Ltd, 2nd ed., 1952.

Wolff, Christian. *Vernünftige Gedancken von Gott, der Welt und der Seele des Menschen, auch allen Dingen Überhaupt,* in *Gesammelte Schriften,* 1 Abt., Deutsche Schriften, Band 2; Hildesheim, Zurich, New York: George Olms Verlag, Herausgegeben von Charles A. Corr, 1982.

Wundt, Wilhelm. *Grundzüege der Physiologischen Psychologie.* Three volumes. Leipzig: Verlag von Wilhelm Engelmann, Sixth edition, 1911.

Wundt, Wilhelm, "Philosophy in Germany," in *Mind,* Vol. II, 1877, 493–518.

Wundt, Wilhelm. *Lectures on Human and Animal Psychology,* translated from the second German edition, London: Swan Sonnenschein; New York: Macmillan & Co., 1894.

Zentner, Marcel. *Die Flucht ins Vergessen: Die Anfänge der Psychoanalyse Freuds bei Schopenhauer.* Darmstadt: Wkissenschaftliche Buchgesellschaft, 1995.

Index

About the Author

Rosemarie Sponner Sand has been a psychoanalyst for twenty-five years. She is a member of the Institute for Psychoanalytic Training and Research and the International Psychoanalytical Association. Her works include *Early Nineteenth Century Anticipation of Freudian Theory*, *Confirmation in the Dora Case*, *Pre-Freudian Discovery of Dream Meaning: the Achievements of Charcot, Janet, and Krafft-Ebing*, *On a Contribution to a Future Scientific Study of Dream Interpretation*, and *Freud and the Western Dream Tradition*. She specializes in antecedents to Freudian theory.

CPSIA information can be obtained at www.ICGtesting.com
Printed in the USA
BVOW08*1626121213

338843BV00003B/5/P

9 781442 231733